100
ONE-NIGHT
READS

100
ONE-NIGHT
READS

A Book Lover's Guide

~

DAVID C. MAJOR

and

JOHN S. MAJOR

Ballantine Books • *New York*

A Ballantine Book
Published by The Ballantine Publishing Group
Copyright © 2001 by David C. Major and John S. Major

www.randomhouse.com/BB/

LIBRARY OF CONGRESS CATALOGING-IN-PUBLICATION DATA
Major, David C., 1938–
100 one-night reads : a book lover's guide / David C. Major and
John S. Major.—1st ed.
p. cm.
ISBN 0-345-43994-5
1. Best books.   2. Books and reading.   I. Title: One hundred
one-night reads.   II. Major, John S.   III. Title.

Z1035.9 .M34   2001
001'.73—dc21   2001016135

Text design by Holly Johnson

Cover design by Min Choi
Cover illustration by Jenny Tylden-Wright

Manufactured in the United States of America

First Edition: June 2001

10 9 8 7 6 5 4 3 2

FOR GRAHAM AND STEVE

Contents

~

Contents

by Category

~

HISTORY, PUBLIC AFFAIRS, AND THE ENVIRONMENT

INTRODUCTION

~

If you have picked up this book in a bookstore, or even more if you have already bought it and brought it home, you have proclaimed yourself to be a reader. You will recognize in the authors of this book kindred spirits who take pleasure in reading and who wish to share that pleasure with you. We hope to enrich your reading life by recommending to you one hundred books that we have read and loved over the years, that we believe you will enjoy greatly as well, and that you can read in a single evening.

In part what we want to share with you is our own good fortune. As children, if we said (as all children sometimes say), "There's nothing to do," our mother would respond, "Of course there is. Get a good book and read it." And because that seemed to be excellent advice, and because we were lucky enough to live in a home where good books were readily available and in a town with a well-stocked public library, we both formed at an early age the lifetime habit of reading. Books have been our friends and companions for decades; we have learned that books expand the world in which one lives, and expand one's mind to match that world.

All too few people have learned how much reading has to offer. We have often heard people say, "I don't have time to read." It is true that modern life seems to consist of exhausting work and family obligations, after which one only wants to rest and relax. But the small amount of leisure available often fails to live up to its promise: It doesn't refresh or restore. Modern leisure does not provide enough to us because it often does not demand enough of us. Much of the entertainment available today—TV programs, movies, and magazines of uninspiring banality— demands nothing at all; one is reduced to the role of a mere spectator. Reading, in contrast, is an *activity*. Though one sits nearly motionless in a comfortable chair, reading challenges and engages one's mind.

A reader is a participant in his or her own recreation and finishes a book with a sense of accomplishment, a feeling of engagement, and an awareness that he or she has been restored and refreshed in a way that spectatorship cannot provide.

Of course, you already know this, or you would not be reading this book.

What we have done in compiling this book is fairly simple. We describe, in these pages, one hundred books that can be read with great enjoyment in the course of a single evening. (Sometimes, admittedly, the evening will last a little beyond your normal bedtime, and, if you prefer, the books can be read over the course of several days instead of in one evening; but many of the books we recommend will be hard to put down once you have started them.) For each of our one hundred one-night reads we have written a concise essay describing the book, telling something about its author, and, most important, explaining what we think is truly special about the book—why it is a book that you will particularly want to read. In these essays we try to give enough of a sense of each book to provide you with a good overall concept of the work and insight into its distinctive qualities. But of course we don't say everything—there are surprises in store for you in each of the books.

These essays are our way of sharing with you our own lives as readers. We hope that you will enjoy them in their own right, and that they will inspire you to read many of the books that we recommend. Because we mean the essays to be, in effect, letters from us to you, we often mention ways in which the books we describe have some personal significance for us—for example, because they represent links to some person or place that has been special in our lives. We are sure that you, too, will find, sometimes quite unexpectedly, similar significance in the books that you read.

The main reason we have devoted this book to one-night reads is that these are books to read for pleasure. We are not proposing that you treat our recommendations as a course of study: The books that we suggest are not yet another attempt to define "the hundred greatest books of all time" or some other version of "the canon." These are, however, all very good books. Some of them are books to read for pure entertainment; others might have a real and lasting influence on how you view yourself and the world around you. All, in our view, far surpass ordinary bestsellers in their capacity to give lasting satisfaction. These are books that have made a difference to us, books that we remember vividly, sometimes many years after first reading them—books to which we have returned to read again with great pleasure. Moreover, these books are worthy of discussion with friends. You might enjoy talking about them, and their meaning to you, at one of the book circles or reading groups that have increased in number in recent years.

As you begin to read each book, here is something to ponder: The difference between a well-educated person and one who is not is about one thousand well-chosen books. (This was pointed out to us by a profoundly well-educated and humane graduate professor at Harvard, and it impressed us deeply.) Twenty books a year for fifty years; and at the end of that time, a sense of having participated in much of what is finest in human culture. We think that people who like books will read at least one every few weeks; so the books listed here, if you read all of them, will last you several years, and they will constitute a worthwhile part of your lifetime reading. We hope that after you read our essays, the excitement of the books that we recommend will stay with you even if you are not able to read them immediately. The name of an author or the title of a book, lodged firmly in your mind, will guide your selections at some later time, when you are in a bookshop, library, or using an online book service.

A few words about the organization and content of the essays are in order. The books that we recommend include both fiction and nonfiction. The contents of the book are arranged alphabetically by author. Just after the alphabetical table of contents, we have included a list of the books grouped by category—fiction, humor, memoirs, and others, with some books listed more than once. Because the question of exactly what to read on a given night depends in part on one's mood, we've tried to make it easy to choose a book that seems right for a particular evening. We hope that even within categories that you know well, we will have listed a few books that will be new to you, or that you've meant to read but have not yet gotten to. We hope, also, that we will be able to tempt you to read within categories that have not been part of your reading life so far. While our two tables of contents list the books alphabetically and by category, we do not intend that you necessarily read the essays in alphabetic or categorical order. We invite you simply to browse at random among them, just as in a library it can often be richly rewarding to wander through the stacks to see what catches the eye and the imagination.

In many cases, after discussing a book we note other works by the same author that we think you will enjoy. In our experience, when we read a book with particular enjoyment we immediately want to read other works by the same author, and we think you will feel this way, too. In addition, from time to time in these essays we take note of ways in which the books we discuss are in some way related; we hope that the cross-references we provide will be helpful to you. If you find them distracting, feel free to ignore them. In any case, a parenthetical reference to page so-and-so does not mean that we think you should turn to that page immediately, but rather that you might wish to do so sometime at your leisure.

For each of the one hundred books we recommend, we give some information about publishers and editions. This information is not intended to be comprehensive. (In any case, an attempt to be comprehensive would be doomed by the realities of modern publishing and bookselling, which ensure that books go out of print or out of stock with distressing speed.) However, we have made every effort to ensure that the information we provide was accurate as of the time this book went to press. Where possible, we give the original hardcover publisher and date, information on one or more readily available paperback editions, and information on any other editions that we find particularly appealing. Many of the books that we recommend have achieved the status of standards or classics, and it is likely that you will be able to find them for sale in one edition or another. Others are more obscure and may be unavailable in most bookstores; but we believe that all of them can be found, sometimes after a bit of pleasurable hunting in libraries or on the shelves of used-book stores. You might also want to consult one of the several excellent online services that have made it quite easy to find out-of-print books nowadays. Our reason for giving original publication information, even when the date may be long ago and the publisher long since out of business, is that we hope some of you might be tempted to find and acquire first editions of books that you particularly love; this is a rewarding way to build a personal library in which you will feel pleasure and pride.

We know from experience that reading more is one of the easiest and most satisfying of all ways to enrich and enlarge one's life. This book is our attempt to share with you some of the joy that we have found in books. We hope that our book will be a useful companion for a long time in your reading life, both through the one hundred books we describe and recommend and the further works to which they lead.

As all readers will appreciate, the task of acknowledging those who have encouraged us, helped us, and given suggestions for good reading over the course of several decades is impossibly large, encompassing many helpful librarians, teachers, and friends; we are grateful to far more people than we can name here. However, we want to acknowledge with thanks our agent, Robert Lescher, and our editor, Joe Blades, exceptional professionals and fine people both. And we owe much to our wives, Patricia Hart and Valerie Steele, and our sons, Graham and Steve, for encouragement and thoughtful advice.

100
ONE-NIGHT
READS

CHINUA ACHEBE
Things Fall Apart

~

A common element of many great books is the plight of people caught up in social and political change. In the case of Chinua Achebe's *Things Fall Apart* the changes are earthshaking. This fine book takes its title from a poem of the Irish poet William Butler Yeats; in the story the phrase refers to the traditional life that did not so much dissolve as fall apart under the impact of British colonialism.

Achebe is a member of the Ibo ethnic group in what is now Nigeria, a former British colony that is the most populous country in Africa. He was born to a family that had adopted Christianity, yet he was able to learn of and understand the older ways that had largely disappeared just decades before his birth. Since the failure of the secession of the Ibo ethnic province of Biafra in 1967–70, Achebe has lived much of the time abroad and is now a college professor in the United States. It is our good fortune that his skills as a writer enabled him to capture the clash of the village world and the impact of European incursions in this fine novel.

Most of *Things Fall Apart* is a depiction of traditional life in Iboland. It is part of Achebe's skill that he involves us so deeply in this life that its destruction later in the novel is felt all the more keenly. The book is concerned with life in the village of Umuofia and the nearby villages that together make up a larger social unit. The principal character, although by no means the only one drawn in some detail, is Okonkwo. In many ways we come to admire Okonkwo, his wise friend Obierika, and their friends and relatives. Okonkwo is a man whose own father was not a success in the village; he was something of a layabout who liked nothing better than to relax by playing his flute, was not a hard worker, and, always in debt, could not provide his son with a good start in life. Okonkwo grew up determined to do better: He early became a great wrestler and warrior, worked hard to establish his farm, and became a considerable man in the village, with a prosperous compound, three wives, and many children.

He and his neighbors live in a highly developed society of norms, rituals, and religious beliefs that help people make sense of their world. Some of these would be familiar anywhere: Men trade proverbs for a time before engaging in serious conversation, because "proverbs are the palm oil with which words are eaten." Others are different but entrancing: There is a sacred silk-cotton tree, in which the spirits of good children are said to dwell as they wait to be born, and young women who desire babies come to sit in the shade of this tree. Others are very difficult: The male tendency in a strictly patriarchal society is to be extremely rough on wives and children, and at one point Okonkwo shoots at one of his wives for a trivial transgression, fortunately missing with his ancient rifle. And there is bitter warfare when other methods of settling disputes do not work. Okonkwo himself has taken heads, and on great occasions such as the funeral of a village celebrity he drinks his palm wine from the skull of his first killing. Achebe describes Umuofia just as it was, with what we would see as both good and bad.

Misfortune befalls Okonkwo when, during a great funeral, his rifle fired in celebration explodes, killing the son of the dead man, the elder Ezeudu. Tradition decrees that for this inadvertent killing Okonkwo and his wives and children must live in exile for seven years in his mother's village; his compound in Umuofia is destroyed. (Perhaps this disaster was earlier prophesied by Ezeudu himself; he had warned Okonkwo against participating in the ritual killing of a boy who had been sent to Umuofia by another village as reparation for a murder.) It is during the time of exile that the colonial incursions of church and government begin in earnest. Okonkwo's inability to comprehend the changes under way and his loss of influence on them stem in part from his detachment from the web of interrelationships in his own village.

The church moves into his mother's village, and among its early converts is Okonkwo's eldest son, of whom he has never approved. Once again Achebe shows us both good and bad: The church is willing to take in the village outcasts and teaches people to read and write in its schools, yet there is gross disrespect of old customs, and many of the British and their locally recruited henchmen can be evil indeed. When Okonkwo finally goes back to Umuofia, thinking to regain and improve his old standing, the new order has moved in too strongly to be rooted out, and Okonkwo is stymied. After a humiliating betrayal by the district commissioner and his lackeys, Okonkwo lashes out one more time and seals his own fate. He has in some ways vindicated himself, but we wonder about the destinies of his wives and children. This is tragedy in the classic sense: Okonkwo, a strong and successful man, has the flaw of being unable to grow out of the habits of mind and action that made him great in the first place, and it is these very habits that bring him to grief within the newly evolving society of his people.

What is special about this penetrating novel is how successfully it integrates new and old with the personal consequences of change. Its straightforward, accessible style embodies a dense overlay of ideas and emotions that draws us into the story and keeps us thinking about its meaning. It is as if, for Americans, a member of the Iroquois Confederacy had captured in beautiful and compelling prose the calamities that ensued with the onset of European settlement.

A graduate of University College, Ibadan, Achebe has been a prolific writer of novels, short stories, and plays; *Things Fall Apart* is his best-known work. Among his other books, we especially like *A Man of the People*.

Chinua Achebe (1930–), *Things Fall Apart* (New York: McDowell, Obolensky, 1958). The Anchor paperback reprint (1994) is readily available.

ERIC AMBLER
A Coffin for Dimitrios

~

The implication of the title is that Dimitrios needs a coffin. Why would that be? Well, because he is dead, of course. But is he really? And if not, whose body is it that was plucked out of the Bosporus by a fisherman and now reclines on a slab in the Istanbul morgue? These questions frame the plot of one of Eric Ambler's cleverest and most satisfying novels. In this story, we find the inoffensive Charles Latimer, ex-lecturer in political economy at a minor British university and current writer of successful drawing-room mystery tales, being drawn unwittingly into the sordid affair of Dimitrios by the mysterious Colonel Haki.

Published in 1939, *A Coffin for Dimitrios* is in some ways closer to the gentlemanly Sherlock Holmes puzzle stories of Sir Arthur Conan Doyle than to the grimly realistic spy novels of Graham Greene and John Le Carré (though both were Ambler fans). Ambler is recognized today as one of the modern masters of the international thriller, a writer who, as one commentator put it, "elevated the genre to literature." In our own time, when thrillers dominate the bestseller lists and many are indistinguishable in their cardboard characters, gratuitous violence, and fascination with weapons technology, it is a pleasure to turn to the works of Eric Ambler for the more traditional novelistic virtues of ingenious plots, attractive and plausible characters, authentic settings, and excellent prose.

But if *A Coffin for Dimitrios* displays some old-fashioned virtues, its plot contains elements that are surprisingly modern. One might think, for example, of drug smuggling as a fairly recent phenomenon. But in the novel, the unsavory and not-quite-dead-yet Dimitrios turns out to have made some of his ill-gotten fortune by smuggling heroin into France in coffins, for which he ingeniously finds more than one use. International procurement of prostitution, assassination for hire, money laundering, espionage, and political subversion—Dimitrios has been a very busy man.

Latimer, the novelist-protagonist of the story, follows the trail of Dimitrios around Eastern Europe and on to Paris, just doing research, he tells himself, for his next book. But instead he is involved ever more deeply in a web of danger and deceit. The crimes of Dimitrios, he learns, are by no means confined to the past, and their consequences can still be quite deadly. Who, Latimer wonders too late, is the mysterious and oddly helpful Mr. Peters, who seems so anxious for Latimer to find Dimitrios? The book ends with Latimer happy to return to writing the decorous mystery novels from which he has learned to make a comfortable living; Balkan intrigue has proven to be rather too much for his taste.

Even this brief summary will convey something of the pleasure in store for the readers of Ambler's work. He was a master of the thriller plot who was able to devise a story complicated enough to hook readers and keep them guessing and create a resolution clever enough to leave readers both surprised and satisfied, while avoiding the contradictions, unlikely coincidences, gaping holes, and obvious red herrings that can sabotage the work of lesser mystery writers. His characters are engaging, with villains who are villainous but not caricatures of villainy. His heroes tend to be likeable embodiments of how the British prefer to see themselves—as quintessential amateurs, perhaps superficially bumbling and ineffectual but plucky, resourceful, and resolute when the going gets tough.

Many of Ambler's best books are set in Eastern Europe, the Balkans, and Turkey, where literally Byzantine political intrigues have been standard fare for very much longer than any of us have been alive. Dedicated movie-goers and video hounds may be familiar with *A Coffin for Dimitrios* under its film title, *The Mask of Dimitrios* (1944); Ambler's 1962 novel *The Light of Day* became the hit crime-caper film *Topkapi* (1964), noted for its stellar cast and its unforgettably tense depiction of a burglary at the sultan's palace in Istanbul.

Born in 1909, Ambler graduated from the University of London and took postgraduate training in engineering. He then worked as a vaudeville performer, songwriter, and advertising copywriter before settling down to his vocation as a novelist. During World War II he served with a British army unit that produced training and propaganda films, and after the war was a screenwriter and producer for the Rank Organisation, one of Britain's major film studios. He produced a steady stream of thriller novels that are like fine old brandy, waiting to be savored and enjoyed. They are ideal books to read for relaxation and pure pleasure; among our other favorites are *Epitaph for a Spy* and *Journey into Fear*.

Eric Ambler (1909–1998), *A Coffin for Dimitrios* (New York: Alfred A. Knopf, 1939). Paperback edition, Carroll and Graf, 1996.

KINGSLEY AMIS
Lucky Jim

~

Kingsley Amis is often regarded as one of the "angry young men" of 1950s Britain, a time when long-standing and complex cultural norms and barriers were seriously out of sync with the aspirations of ordinary British people. Amis' first novel, *Lucky Jim,* reflects this situation. The comic hero, Jim Dixon, is a lecturer in medieval history at a provincial university filled with class bias, limited possibilities, and some extremely wacky people. That Jim comes out all right in the end, after many vicissitudes, is, as the title suggests, something of a bit of luck.

The book takes place during Jim's first (probationary) year at the university. The plot is a long series of very funny mishaps that get Jim ever deeper into trouble, in a situation where he constantly has to worry whether he will be rehired. His route to the teaching of medieval history was a checkered one in the first place; he took it because it was one of the easiest courses at his own college. He doesn't care much for the subject or the work, but on the other hand he has no notion of what he could do as an alternative in England's rigid social and employment structure. So he is panicked about staying.

The characters, in addition to Jim, include Ned Welch, his department chair and arbiter of his fate. Welch is egocentric and forgetful— many academics will feel at home with such a chair—and has a dreadful family, including his wife and two pretentiously arty sons, Bertrand and Michel. (The Welches are collectively known to his underlings as "the Neddies.") In addition there is Jim's hysteric colleague, Margaret Peel; a luscious girlfriend of Bertrand's named Christine Callaghan; her uncle Julius Gore-Urquhart; and assorted fellow lodgers and other matey and not-so-matey types. Only one student is genuinely interested in pursuing Jim's subject under his guidance, but

Michie has the disadvantage in Jim's eyes of having commanded a tank platoon at the Anzio landings during World War II in Italy, whereas Jim (typically) was a Royal Air Force corporal safely and ineffectively stationed in western Scotland.

Jim himself is far from perfect. His response to the world around him tends to be either terribly awkward or simply reactive, although in the end he comes forward to have an effect on his fate. He is highly sensitive to the words and gestures of others, which causes both an inability to react to some situations and overreaction to others. He also has the endearing, to the reader at least, habit of making a weird assortment of faces, some with names (such as "crazy peasant"); unfortunately for Jim, several of these efforts at private self-expression are witnessed by others.

There are humorous elements in the book that you will remember for a long time. Most famous is Jim's lecture on "Merrie England" at a big do at the end of the school year. This is a classic of comic writing, and if you lecture or make other public presentations, you will enjoy this part of the story immensely. You will, however, have to be very careful not to think of this lecture when you are about to stand at a podium; it wouldn't do to burst out laughing in the middle of one of your own presentations. There are other fine things as well, such as Jim's dismal article "The Economic Influence of the Developments in Shipbuilding Techniques, 1450–1485," which he tries desperately to publish anywhere to bolster his academic position. This would-be publication represents all the worst of academic scholarship, and Jim knows it; the article suffers a suitably awful fate.

Amis also treats his readers to what might be the funniest description of a hangover in all of English literature. In fact, to modern eyes, the book depicts an amazing—even shocking—amount of smoking and drinking; the health effects of both were not widely appreciated, and getting roaring drunk was part of the way Jim and his contemporaries dealt with their frustrations. (One gets the sense, too, in reading about Amis and his circle that there actually was a great deal of alcohol-fueled unpleasantness in their lives.)

There is also a good measure of serious matter in this essentially humorous book. The long discussion by Carol Goldsmith, the wife of one of Jim's colleagues, on the false maturity of one's twenties both reflects Amis' views and will resonate with many readers. This level of honesty and insight is part of what made Amis such a good writer and what keeps *Lucky Jim* from being merely parody or farce.

Lucky Jim is screamingly funny, but it also is a book that offers real insight into our lives. It will speak to anyone who has faced unreasonable barriers to justified expectations of growth and progress.

Amis made his career as a writer, but none of his other works have had the popularity of *Lucky Jim*, perhaps because the anger at society became more dominant than the humor, whereas the two elements are finely balanced in this uproarious novel.

Kingsley Amis (1922–1995), *Lucky Jim* (London: Victor Gollancz, 1953; Garden City, N.Y.: Doubleday, 1954). Widely available; we like the Penguin paperback reprint (1993). Amis' son, the writer Martin Amis, has given us a portrait of his father in *Experience: A Memoir* (New York: Talk Miramax Books, 2000).

LOUIS AUCHINCLOSS

The Education of Oscar Fairfax

∼

This is a novel in the form of a memoir, told in the voice of its protagonist. The effect of a life recalled seems so real that one might at first
wonder if the book is actually a disguised autobiography rather than a
work of fiction. But it cannot be so; the novel's protagonist is a full generation older than the author, and Louis Auchincloss cannot personally
have had many of the experiences that he provides for Oscar Fairfax
(though it is quite possible that he draws on the experiences of some of
his older family members and friends). The book is set within the mi-
lieu of the Eastern WASP elite that played a large role in American social, cultural, economic, and political life in the period between the
Civil War and World War II, and of which Auchincloss himself is a
member.

The book's story does not comprise a continuous narrative, but
rather a series of meditations on key periods in the protagonist's life; in
fact, one could regard *The Education of Oscar Fairfax* as a series of
tightly linked short stories rather than a conventional novel. The effect
is to demonstrate, as the book's title suggests, that a person's education
takes place throughout an entire lifetime, and that life never stops providing us with lessons—sometimes hard ones. We follow Oscar Fairfax
from his childhood, when we see him wrestling with a dawning awareness of the expectations placed on him by his family, to his retirement
and old age, when he is led to think seriously about his motives for
meddling (to good effect, he hopes) in other people's lives. As one
episode follows another, we are aware that we are forming in our minds
an increasingly complex and nuanced view of a man whose life is worth
our attention. Oscar Fairfax, by the end of the book, is a person whose
company we have come to enjoy greatly.

Throughout the book we see Fairfax confronting in different ways the issues of privilege and responsibility that are the birthright of members of his class (it is the sense of responsibility as the necessary complement to privilege that makes the members of this class an elite, rather than simply a collection of rich people). His father is a prominent Wall Street lawyer, his maternal grandfather an Episcopalian bishop. From infancy he is clearly destined for a good private school, an education at Yale, and a partnership in his father's firm; what he makes of all that is up to him. A work in progress throughout his life, Oscar Fairfax is a very appealing character. We find him learning an important lesson in tolerance in his dealings with an elderly gay teacher at school, and coping with jealousy as he is forced to sort out his feelings about a Yale classmate more talented than himself. We observe with vicarious pain how he makes an ass of himself in the course of a year in Paris, where he turns out to be far less sophisticated than he thought, and later as he is outmaneuvered in the hardball world of New Deal politics. He grows in wisdom and in grace over the years, kept suitably humble by a loyal but exacting wife and a somewhat difficult son. As we learn of his efforts to foster the careers of various younger protégés, we think how wonderful it would be to have such a mentor.

In all of this we see the hand of the author himself, and the book surely derives some of its feeling of authenticity from taking place among the sorts of people and in the sorts of settings that Louis Auchincloss knows very well. If a scene is set in the exclusive Bar Harbor Swimming and Tennis Club on Mount Desert Island, Maine, we can be sure that the club looks, and its members behave, exactly as described. And so for every scene in the book. We can readily suspect, too, that the novel contains an element of wish fulfillment on the author's part. As the biographer of Edith Wharton, for example, he would surely have loved to attend just such a luncheon at Mrs. Wharton's Paris town house as he provides for Oscar Fairfax in the book.

Louis Auchincloss has had two concurrent careers, as a lawyer and as a writer. To be a partner in a big New York law firm demands enormous dedication and hard work; no less is required to become a best-selling author of more than fifty books. To combine the two careers and achieve distinction in both is very remarkable. Many of his works of fiction are set in the New York business and legal worlds (*The Partners, The Embezzler*); others are similar to *The Education of Oscar Fairfax* in exploring an individual's moral and ethical universe (*Portrait in Brownstone, The Rector of Justin*). Auchincloss is especially admired for his short stories, ideal vehicles for his beautifully controlled prose and his insight into human character. He has written many works of nonfiction as well, most recently a biography of Woodrow Wilson. His memoir of his own early years, *A Writer's Capital,* is a charming book, and it is fascinating to compare the author's upbringing with that of his fictional Oscar Fairfax.

Louis Auchincloss (1917–), *The Education of Oscar Fairfax* (New York: Houghton Mifflin, 1995). Now out of print.

RUSSELL BAKER
Growing Up

~

Russell Baker, the distinguished former columnist of *The New York Times*, was born in the backwater town of Morrisonville, Virginia. His mother, Lucy Elizabeth, was a schoolteacher; his father, Benny, was a stonemason and laborer and a member of the extended Baker clan that dominated the little town.

This deeply affecting memoir of Baker's early years follows the author from Morrisonville, through the death of his father, living for years with an uncle's family in New Jersey, moving to Baltimore, and at last to his mother's remarriage and a home of her own. Many people talk about the effects of the Depression, but this memoir makes clear what it entailed: living with relatives, charity, backbreaking work when it was available, hopes for the future.

Morrisonville in the 1920s had no electricity or other utilities. The lifestyle of the town hadn't changed substantially in a hundred years: The women worked like serfs in the garden and the home, the men (at least those who stayed away from moonshine) did what work they could, and entertainment was limited to church and extended family. One of the Bakers' neighbors, Annie, was born a slave and had been freed by Mr. Lincoln. With medical care spotty and inadequate in the days before penicillin and most vaccines, death was a frequent visitor, arriving at all times and places to take young and old alike. Some of the locals relied on a kind of witchcraft called "powwowing," an attempt to talk away disease and wounds of all kinds. A job on the railroad in Brunswick, Maryland, the nearest real town, was the pinnacle of success. Baker had an uncle there whose house included indoor plumbing, the first that Baker had ever seen. (In Morrisonville, a two-hole privy with a Montgomery Ward catalog was considered the top of the line.)

Grandma Baker disapproved of her daughter-in-law, perhaps because of her learning, perhaps because Baker had been conceived prior to the couple's marriage. In any event, death came soon enough to his father, a diabetic, and for Baker, at five, the world was changed forever. His youngest sister was given up for adoption to his uncle and aunt in Brunswick, and he, his mother, and his sister Doris moved to the house of his Uncle Allen and Aunt Pat in Newark, New Jersey.

It is here that the role of the Depression becomes clear. What was to be a temporary stay while the family got on its feet lasted for years. His mother finally got a job in an A&P laundry for staff uniforms and was able to contribute something to Uncle Allen's household finances and to save for her dreams of the future. Baker suffered the hard knocks of urban life both in Newark and in the gritty suburb of Belleville, to which Uncle Allen and Aunt Pat moved. (The *Belleville News* had the honor of printing Baker's first publication, a schoolboy essay on wheat, largely ghosted by his determined mother.) The role of relatives in hard times was substantial: Anyone with a decent job was expected to help others in the family. In addition to the Bakers, Uncle Allen and Aunt Pat's household included Uncle Charley, who had never worked except for a brief stint on the *Brooklyn Eagle* and, it seems, was not expected to work again. For a time it also included Uncle Hal, a failed businessman with romantic schemes for financial success in the walnut veneer industry. Idiosyncracies abounded: Uncle Hal liked to have a bicarbonate of soda after each meal, followed by a tremendous belch to clean out the poisons. Everyone told stories, many embroidered, and Baker learned early to listen to adults with a skeptical ear, a talent that served him well as a Washington correspondent. The one great success in the family, who apparently had little to do with his down-at-heel relatives, was Edwin James, a cousin of Lucy Elizabeth's, who was the managing editor of and a columnist for the *Times*.

The family moved to Baltimore as part of a harebrained business scheme of Uncle Hal's, which wasted part of the Baker family's small savings. There were more Depression hard knocks for the family, but with the help of Lucy Elizabeth's determination and their relatives, things turned out well. Lucy Elizabeth, who constantly pushed Baker in his studies, had her great success when Baker was accepted at an elite Baltimore high school. He then got to Johns Hopkins on scholarship, enlisted in the Navy Air Corps, and became a pilot, though he missed overseas service (to his mother's intense relief) because the war ended. After college, Baker started on the *Baltimore Sun* at the bottom of the ladder, phoning police news in to rewrite men. Ultimately he rose to become one of these himself, and he met and finally married Mimi, an enterprise that involved an unduly extended courtship. The book chronologically ends at this point, concluding with a later memory of a visit to his mother, bereft of her mental links to the outside world.

Baker says that he wanted to write this book for his own family, realizing how little he knew about his own forebears and wanting to pass on the meaning and circumstances of his own life. What Baker's memoir makes us realize is how close to misery, failure, and illness everyone is, and how things such as a strong mother and a good high school—clichés though they be—make a huge difference in life. We also see how Baker got his ability to be humorous and to judge the great with a level eye. He early learned to see buffoonery, overstatement, and lies for what they were. In his days with the *Times*, Baker's writing was at a uniformly high level, something not easy for a columnist to achieve as part of the weekly grind. What made Baker's work successful was his generally humorous and skeptical attitude, combined with the colorful background of an extended Southern family and, just perhaps, his mother's insistence that he should achieve something in life. We are in his debt for making this memoir available to us, and we may be forgiven for thinking that the picture that he draws of himself, as a generally ineffectual layabout, is just possibly not the whole truth.

Russell Baker (1925–). *Growing Up* (New York: Congden and Weed, 1982). Penguin paperback reprint, 1995.

LOUIS BEGLEY

Wartime Lies

~

This breathtaking novel tells the story of how two fiercely determined and resourceful young people—a boy and his aunt—managed to survive the Holocaust in Poland throughout World War II.

The tale opens in the 1930s in a small Polish city, where the young boy Maciek lives with his family in great comfort and security. Highly assimilated, the family consider themselves Jewish Poles, not so different from their friends and neighbors who are Catholic Poles. (The distinction, soon to come, between "Poles" and "Jews" would make no sense to them.) Maciek's father is a doctor, a member of the local gentry; Maciek's mother died in childbirth, but her younger sister, Aunt Tania, lives with the family. There are many servants, especially Maciek's beloved nanny, Zosia. His grandparents—Tania's delicate, querulous mother and her fierce, irrepressible father—visit often. Maciek's family becomes increasingly aware of the rising tide of Polish anti-Semitism and of the danger of invasion from Hitler's Germany; like many others, they find the implications of these facts impossible to believe and delay trying to find ways to leave the country until it is too late. With the German invasion, the retreating Russians draft Maciek's father as a military doctor and take him away.

As her comfortable world collapses around her, Tania, hitherto regarded even by her mother as willful and spoiled, emerges as a different sort of figure entirely. Vowing to do whatever is necessary to ensure the survival of what remains of her family, she learns quickly to be devious, resourceful, brave, and above all self-disciplined; nothing is going to distract her from her task.

Arrangements are made; her ailing mother must be hidden, her father must make his way to Warsaw to assume a new identity. She and

Maciek will become Catholic Poles, mother and son, with forged papers and forged personalities to match. Tania becomes the mistress of a sympathetic German officer; when he is betrayed, she and Maciek flee to Warsaw, just ahead of the Gestapo. There they stay for a while in reasonable security, but Tania worries constantly that Maciek will not be able to maintain the fabric of lies that cloaks their lives—he is, after all, still a young, sensitive, and impressionable child. Hardship becomes routine; witnessed atrocities are important only as things to be avoided for oneself. Again and again they must flee from danger into the unknown. With discipline, nerve, and luck, through many adventures and hair-raising escapes, Tania and Maciek manage to survive the war but at a cost that will take a long time to reckon.

This vivid story is told entirely from the viewpoint of Maciek and entirely in narrative, with not a single line of dialogue. Framing passages in italics at the beginning and end of the book make clear that the story is told not in the voice of the child that Maciek had been at the time, but as the interior monologue of a much older man who, through a multiplicity of lies in wartime and beyond, has shed Maciek's identity entirely and become someone else. (Our narrator, a cultivated and ironical observer of his own past, makes clear his detachment by comparing his memories to the voyeurism of Dante and Virgil as they tour the circles of Hell in *The Inferno*.) This allows Begley to accomplish the very deft literary trick of maintaining the narrative point of view of Maciek the child while endowing the narrative itself with a maturity and depth that are anything but childish.

Wartime Lies apparently is based to some extent on Begley's own childhood. Born Ludwik Begleiter in Poland, he did in fact survive the war with the aid of papers describing him as Aryan. But Begley has been very reticent about his own past and has expressed the hope that whatever germ of personal experience lies behind his novel will not distract readers from what is essentially a work of fiction.

Louis Begley, like Louis Auchincloss (see p. 13), is a successful New York lawyer who has become famous as a writer. In Begley's case, the legal career preceded the literary one by many years; *Wartime Lies,* published in 1991, was his first novel. Its publication was greeted with a chorus of praise. Begley has published five subsequent novels, all of them dealing with the personal and professional lives of men somewhat like himself—men who are rich and successful, live in New York, summer in the Hamptons, and feel at home in Venice and Rome. Are these, one wonders, somehow incarnations of the man Maciek has become, successful, insecure, ungrounded in any true sense of self?

It would, we think, be a mistake to look for straightforward autobiography in Begley's work. It is rather that in each of his books Begley seems to invent for himself an alternative autobiography that rings true in an uncanny way, as if the author's characters were all metamorphoses of his own psyche. The slight air of detachment and restraint that, along with a suffusion of slightly perverse eroticism, is the hallmark of his writing heightens the impression of psychological truth by seeming to hold something back. Begley's later novels amply confirm the promise of *Wartime Lies*, and he is now widely regarded as one of America's finest living novelists; of his other novels, we recommend especially *About Schmidt*.

Louis Begley (1933–), *Wartime Lies* (New York: Alfred A. Knopf, 1991). The Ballantine paperback reprint (1992) is widely available.

E. F. BENSON
Queen Lucia

~

E. F. Benson was born in Berkshire, England. His father was the head-master of Wellington College (what Americans would call a private school) and later became bishop of Cornwall and finally archbishop of Canterbury. The family was eccentric, well educated, and literate: All of the Benson siblings who grew to adulthood were published authors. Benson himself wrote some one hundred books; his first big hit, *Dodo,* a satirical novel, came when he was still in his twenties. His father's position and his own success made for a comfortable life. Benson, in addition to his literary efforts, worked in the British Foreign Office; he lived his later years in Henry James' former residence in Rye, on the southeast coast of England, and served three terms as mayor of the town.

Benson is best known today for his Lucia and Mapp novels, of which *Queen Lucia* is the first. The Lucia and Mapp stories begin in Riseholme, based on the village of Broadway in the Cotswolds, and move to London and the fictional Tilling (Rye). There are altogether six novels and several short stories. The two principal characters are Emmaline Lucas (Lucia), whom we meet in this first novel, and her rival Miss Elizabeth Mapp, who appears later in the series. You may well find these novels addictive, as have so many readers; one old family friend told us that she reread the entire series every few years.

The central element in *Queen Lucia* is Lucia's overwhelming desire to remain the undisputed social and cultural arbiter of Riseholme, which is to say, to be the unchallenged queen of a very small and insignificant kingdom. The humor in the novels stems from the enormous energy and the comically complex strategies that Lucia, Mapp, and their friends, neighbors, and enemies devote to maintaining their pretensions in the face of every possible challenge, pretensions that matter not at all to any except themselves. Lucia has the advantage of being supported in her endeavors by her husband, who is wealthy and retired, and her friend Georgie Pillson, her faithful aide-de-camp in all things Riseholmian.

Among the things that loyal Riseholmians are expected to believe are that Lucia knows Italian, which of course she does not, aside from the few words and terms of endearment that she drops into every possible sentence; that Riseholme's cultural life is unrivaled, even by London's; and that Lucia is an expert on art, literature, and music (she plays the first movement of Beethoven's *Moonlight Sonata* to conclude Riseholme cultural evenings, but as she can't quite deal with the difficulties of the other two movements, she pretends that she doesn't wish to play them because they are musically inferior).

The plot is driven by the collision of Lucia's ambitions with challenges to them stemming from neighbor Daisy Quantock's manic insistence on new ways of reforming her life (a fraudulent guru and pills to increase one's height among them) and the arrival in town of Olga Bracely, an opera singer who is, in her genuine warmheartedness and lack of guile, everything that Lucia is not quite. In the end, despite social calamity, pretensions are maintained and everything is (temporarily) well for Lucia's reign in Riseholme. Along the way you will be delighted by myriad details of Riseholme life, such as the long prose poems that Lucia's husband writes and has privately printed by a press funded by himself. The names of the first two collections are, suffice to say, *Flotsam* and *Jetsam*. Georgie Pillson makes paintings that he gives as framed gifts to his friends; these have titles, neatly lettered in gilt, such as "Golden Autumn Wonderland" and "Bleak December."

One reason that the Lucia and Mapp novels are so insidiously appealing is that we all have foibles like Lucia and her friends, but for the most part we keep them submerged. What Benson does for us is to create a world in which our human faults are on display in their embarrassing detail and comic essence. Moreover, Benson's skill is to make Lucia and her friends, for all of their pretensions and silliness, ultimately rather likeable. (Perhaps we can say the same about those we care for, and perhaps they can say the same about us.) Benson has a remarkable fluency of style that carries the reader effortlessly through his stories, and we rather like it that he is fully up to skewering the prejudices of his characters along the way. Perhaps the most astonishing thing about *Queen Lucia* is that you will find yourself fully engaged in its world and then be very surprised to learn that at the end you haven't yet even met Miss Mapp. Please be fully prepared for that formidable personage as you move on to other novels in the series.

E[dward] F[rederick] Benson (1867–1940), *Queen Lucia* (New York: George H. Doran, 1920). This and the other Lucia and Mapp volumes are widely available. The Moyer/Bell paperback (1999) of *Queen Lucia* is a comfortable choice. The Harper Perennial editions (1980s) of the Lucia and Mapp novels are now mostly out of stock.

MARY BRINGLE
Hacks at Lunch

~

A resident of New York City, Mary Bringle is the author of seventeen books in her own name and several others under pseudonyms. Modestly successful and not famous, she is an ideal guide to the unglamorous side of the New York literary life. *Hacks at Lunch,* her best-known novel, is a funny, satirical, but also compassionate and moving look at a few hours in the lives of four writers who occupy some of the lower rungs of the literary ladder.

As the book opens, Clare, Sigrid, Joseph, and Douglas, self-described hacks, have assembled for their every-other-Tuesday long lunch at Eugene McCloy's welcoming but nondescript bar on New York's Upper West Side. Theirs is a dwindling company; once the hacks' lunch could muster ten participants or more, but death and defections have taken their toll (one former member, envied and hated, has gone to Hollywood to be a scriptwriter).

The hacks write trashy books bound in lurid paper covers, books that are never reviewed in or even noticed by *The New York Times.* Sigrid and Clare specialize in historical bodice-rippers that feature Scottish lairds or swashbuckling pirates with icy blue eyes, broad chests, and thighs of steel, paired with raven-haired women with heaving bosoms who secretly long to be ravished by these manly rogues. Douglas and Joseph write macho action/adventure books—Joseph's long-running hero is a hard-drinking, hard-fighting American tank captain in North Africa. The hacks do everything they can to laugh at their own predicament, writing forgettable books for little money, living precariously from one royalty check to the next, poking fun at the foibles of the characters they create. But they know, at heart, that although they are really good at what they do, they will never be more than hacks, that dreams of writing "real novels" are to be sneered at (because they are too dangerous to take seriously), that their place in the literary world amounts to almost nothing. Even McCloy's other customers sense this: *"Writers,"* one whispers. "Don't they have anything better to do?"

The lunch on this day starts out in the usual style of friendly banter, but the hacks quickly detect some disturbing undertones. Joseph, deserted by his wife some months before, seems more emotionally fragile than usual. Douglas is visibly twitching, upset about something that the others cannot fathom. Sigrid, younger than her friends, perpetually well groomed and perfect looking, affects a studied detachment and struggles to keep straight the lies from which she constructs the face she presents to the world. Clare, myopic and slightly overweight, tries hard to maintain the group's customary good cheer. The hours roll by, and Gene McCloy wonders why his writers (of whom he is very fond) have not left at their accustomed time. The dynamic of the group is different this time, and no one seems able to bring the lunch to an end.

As the afternoon wears into evening, convivial drinking gives way to drunkenness (variously agitated, belligerent, and lugubrious), and the ties of shared endeavor and camaraderie that have held the hacks' lunch together over the years threaten to unravel altogether. Finally the gathering breaks up, and the hacks, badly shaken, scatter to their homes. But they are a resilient bunch, and we can expect that two weeks hence the hacks will gather for lunch once again.

This is a book that would translate well to the theater. Indeed, the experience of reading it is akin to watching a well-wrought comedy of manners onstage. *Hacks at Lunch* was published in 1985, and some of the details of the setting already seem far in the past: Reagan is in the White House, writers work at typewriters instead of computers, and Joseph's Walkman is an intriguing new machine, much admired by his friends. But despite these reminders of times past, the characters are so vivid, and their conversation so convincing, that the book is not confined to any particular time.

What makes Mary Bringle's novel special is its perspective: that of someone who knows this world as an insider. The book is a comedy but not a parody; every detail seems real. And it succeeds as a comedy because Bringle takes her characters seriously and treats them with dignity. They may be small potatoes as writers, but they are not contemptible. One could say of them what Willy Loman demands for himself in *Death of a Salesman*: "Attention must be paid!"

Mary Bringle (1938–), *Hacks at Lunch* (New York: St. Martin's Press, 1985). Out of print, but not hard to find in used-book stores or through the Internet.

TRUMAN CAPOTE

Breakfast at Tiffany's

~

Breakfast at Tiffany's, Truman Capote's most popular work, is the story of Holiday (Holly) Golightly, a hardscrabble Southern kid whom we meet, transformed, as a classy nineteen-year-old darling of café society in New York City. Holly's parents, we learn, died when their offspring were young, and the children were placed in (perhaps) mean families. Holly and her beloved brother, Fred, ran away and ended up being cared for by Doc Golightly, a widowed horse doctor in the town of Tulip, Texas. Holly married Doc at the age of fourteen, thus coming by her wonderful last name legitimately—that is, if the marriage was legal in the first place, which Holly thinks it wasn't. Holly soon looks for wider horizons, leaves Doc, his kids, and Fred, and moves on to Hollywood. Her admirers and sponsors there provide a sophisticated remake for the country girl, but she doesn't want to push for movie success and instead moves to New York.

It takes some time for the narrator, a young man who is an aspiring writer, to learn about Holly, the somewhat disorganized tenant of the apartment beneath the narrator's own in a brownstone in the East Seventies. Holly tells her story reluctantly, and we are sure of only some of it. The time is during World War II; the only person Holly is genuinely fond of is Fred, in the service and finally killed during the war. (Holly briefly calls the narrator "Fred" also, but he is otherwise unnamed.) Holly exists splendidly by retailing her classiness and the pleasure that others take in being around her; she has scads of admirers to foot the bills for her company in restaurants and nightclubs, but not often, it would seem, for sexual activity, which she is experienced in engaging in or not, as she wishes. The fairy-tale quality of the story is that Holly lives a high-risk existence yet always seems to land on her feet.

Among other events, Doc arrives unexpectedly, having gotten her address from Fred. He tells his story to the narrator and seems to assume that Lulamae (Holly's real name) will return to him and the children, which of course she does not.

Perhaps like Capote himself, Holly is really looking for a place that is right for her. The lovely title of the story captures her quest. Holly likes Tiffany's, the famous jewelry store on Fifth Avenue, where she feels that nothing bad can happen to anyone; she thinks that someday she will want to find a real place like it where she can be at home ("buy some furniture and give the cat a name"). Whether Holly ever finds her real-life Tiffany's is left to the reader to imagine; after many New York adventures chronicled in the book, she disappears for Brazil and (possibly) Africa. Despite the uncertainty, the book has a charming, winsome ending. The 1961 film of *Breakfast at Tiffany's*, directed by Blake Edwards, did an excellent job of translating the novel to the screen, so much so that for many people it is impossible to visualize Holly Golightly except as Audrey Hepburn.

What is so attractive about the book is that it embodies Capote's essentially poetic gift: The story is told beautifully, gracefully, and with restraint, a piquant blend of rural South and elegant New York. We come to feel that were we to meet Holly, we might well be taken in by her charm, although we, like most of her friends, would have our share of exasperation with her. Capote is direct in talking about sexuality (he was ahead of his time in this) in a way that is just right in context. But there is something more about the story. It is not just about Holly; it is also about the narrator and by extension about all of us who might dream of having a perfect introduction to New York. It is this quality that seems to draw us completely into the book. The narrator achieves his first publication during the story (no payment for the piece, of course—the journal is a small review), and he has a suitably tacky first apartment in New York in a decent neighborhood with a good local bar, colorful neighbors, and lots to write about. We feel that the narrator, observing and befriending Holly, could be us.

Truman Capote was born in New Orleans to an unsuccessful salesman and his teenage bride. He was sent early to live with relatives in Monroeville, Louisiana; Harper Lee, the author of *To Kill a Mock-*

ingbird, was a childhood friend. His parents soon divorced, and his mother remarried and moved to New York with her new husband and her son (Truman took the last name of his stepfather); Capote's mother later ended her own life. Capote attended private schools in New York City and public schools in Greenwich, Connecticut, at which point his formal education ended. He took a job as an office boy at *The New Yorker* and began to publish early. Although Capote appeared to be the ultimate Southern Gothic, most of his life was in fact spent in Europe and in New York.

Capote's talent for storytelling and acute observation of people and their situations was both his merit and ultimately his downfall. In his last, unfinished book, *Answered Prayers,* written in the midst of serious personal problems, the gracefulness and beauty are gone and he succeeds in producing only a smutty tell-all about his "friends," a sad ending to a fine career as a writer. Among his books we recommend one of his fine works of reportage, *In Cold Blood* (1966), his "nonfiction novel" of the murder of a farm family in Kansas and its aftermath.

Truman Capote (1924–1984), *Breakfast at Tiffany's* (New York: Random House, 1958). There is a handsome Modern Library edition (1994).

WILLA CATHER
Death Comes for the Archbishop

~

A book of exceptional beauty and aesthetic harmony, this truly wonderful novel tells the story in fictionalized form of Archbishop Lamy, the first Roman Catholic bishop of the Southwest under United States rule.

Willa Cather's fictional version of Father Lamy is Jean Latour, a French priest from the Auvergne, in south-central France. The novel covers a span of some thirty-five years, from his arrival in Santa Fe as an energetic young bishop to his death there as an old and greatly revered archbishop. In the course of the book we learn also of his early years in France with his fellow seminarian and lifelong friend, Father Joseph Vallaint, and their youthful service as missionaries in Ohio. Bishop Latour's story is presented here not as a continuous narrative, but instead in a series of loosely connected episodic chapters that gradually cohere into a rich and multilayered story, rather as if a set of snapshots slowly arranged themselves to form a larger and more complex picture.

Cather, in her exceptional prose, depicts the Southwest and its complex admixture of cultures with great accuracy, and treats her characters with respect. Her mastery of the interrelationships of the United States, its new southwestern territories and their indigenous inhabitants, France, the Vatican, Mexico, and the Spanish settlements is dazzling. The story is set in a political and theological framework that provides enrichment without ever seeming didactic.

This is a powerful work that imaginatively re-creates the past. It's not a history lesson, though the details of the story always ring true. Cather knows, for example, just how Latour travels when he makes the laborious journey from Santa Fe to Baltimore for a religious conference, or what it is like when Latour and a local guide take shelter from a blizzard in a mountain cave. She populates her books with a wonderful range of characters, showing without mawkishness the affection between Latour and Vallaint, and between both of them and their parishioners, such as the Navajo leader Eusabio, and with others such as Kit Carson. It is striking also that Cather, writing in the 1920s, has the elderly archbishop expressing at the end of his life a thoroughly modern satisfaction with the emancipation of black slaves and the return of the Navajos to the native lands from which they had been expelled by a cruelly misguided American government.

One of Cather's great strengths was her ability to paint verbal pictures that both sparkle with beauty and have the resonance of truth. Here she describes how "the declining sun poured its beautifying light over those low, rose-tinted houses and bright gardens" and how ancient adobe walls "had that irregular and intimate quality of things made entirely by the human hand." The towering mesas of Navajo country, she writes, "were inconceivable without their attendant clouds, which were a part of them, as the smoke is part of the censer, or the foam of the wave." Because of such images, this is a book that will stay with you throughout your life, shaping your thinking about the Southwest and enriching your visits there.

Willa Cather was born in Virginia and moved with her family when she was ten years old to the town of Red Cloud in southern Nebraska, a brand-new prairie settlement and commercial center, where her father was an accountant. A visit to Red Cloud is one of the most evocative of literary pilgrimages: The town is much the same as it must have been in Cather's time, and many of the buildings she depicted in her fiction still stand within a few short blocks of each other. It is easy to imagine how this new civilization must have impressed itself upon a young girl's mind and shaped her writer's imagination.

Cather never married, and in the course of a long and successful career she had several intense friendships with other women. Her biographers disagree about whether these friendships were sexually consummated or whether Cather's sexual life was entirely sublimated in her work. Some critics, however, have argued that her (for her times) nontraditional identity as a single woman and author gave her a special sympathy for the characters that she placed in marginalizing circumstances on the expanding frontier, in French Canada, and in the newly American Southwest. This argument seems insightful to us; one of the great strengths of Cather's fiction, and one of the reasons it endures so well, is its sensitivity to nuances of character.

After reading *Death Comes for the Archbishop*, you might wish to reread *My Ántonia*, the story of a bohemian girl on the Nebraska prairie, which perhaps you first read in high school (it was once ubiquitous on school assigned-reading lists). If that was your first contact with *My Ántonia*, you will be pleasantly surprised to find that it is a far better novel than you remember. Another of our favorites is *Shadows on the Rock*, set in the harsh and unforgiving environment of colonial Quebec.

Willa Sibert Cather (1873–1947), *Death Comes for the Archbishop* (New York: Alfred A. Knopf, 1927). A comfortable edition is the Vintage Classics paperback (1990). Cather's complete novels are collected in a two-volume hardcover edition from the Library of America (1987, 1990).

RAYMOND CHANDLER
The Big Sleep

~

Raymond Chandler was born in Chicago but spent most of his early life in England. He attended Dulwich College and fought with Great Britain's Royal Flying Corps during World War I. After the war he returned to America, settled in Los Angeles, and had a successful business career during the 1920s in California's booming oil industry. He was wiped out financially by the 1929 stock market crash and the Great Depression that followed it, and began to write crime stories for pulp magazines to make a living. Persevering in this precarious career, he won acclaim in 1939 with the publication of his first novel, *The Big Sleep*. He wrote six more novels over the course of the next two decades, all featuring his tough-guy detective hero, Philip Marlowe. In 1943, Chandler began to write film scripts as well as novels and stories, and he achieved considerable success in the gritty and often grim films that French critics would later call *cinéma noir*.

Chandler's novels were strongly influenced by the work of his contemporary Dashiell Hammett (p. 92), to the extent that Hammett and Chandler are sometimes described as founders of a "California school" of hard-boiled detective fiction. (A notable feature of Chandler's novels, especially, is that they convey very effectively the atmosphere of corruption that was characteristic of Los Angeles politics and the city's police department and criminal justice system for much of the twentieth century.) Philip Marlowe is a tough character whose attitudes and personal code are very much in the mold of Hammett's Sam Spade, though Marlowe is, generally speaking, a classier sort of detective than Spade and deals with a richer, more polished clientele. Like all heroes of the genre, Marlowe is essentially a lone wolf who lives by his own private moral code. He is interested in justice more than in material success, and will sometimes (as in this novel) pursue a case further than his client has asked in order to satisfy his own sense of what is right.

In *The Big Sleep,* Marlowe is hired by aging, infirm General Sternwood to look into attempts by parties unknown to extort money from him in what amounts to blackmail. The general's daughters are both involved in unwise activities. Vivian, the beautiful elder daughter, is a compulsive gambler, which has given her some unsavory associates; these include her recently disappeared husband, Regan, an ex-bootlegger and Irish Republican Army veteran. The younger daughter, Carmen, is a seriously disturbed personality whose problems include substance abuse, promiscuity, and a total lack of moral sense. One element of Carmen's difficulties is that she has been photographed naked by Geiger, a distributor of illegal pornography. (Given the ubiquity of porn nowadays, it seems rather quaint that part of the plot of this novel turns on a conspiracy to distribute dirty pictures. How times change!) Geiger's business, in turn, is involved with that of Eddie Mars, a promoter of gambling and other illegal activities, who is someone with whom Vivian has been involved.

Of course, all of these people are immersed in murky dealings that involve one another, and other parties as well, in unexpected and labyrinthine ways. Marlowe's job is to disentangle as much of this as possible while remaining true to himself and while shielding his client, the noble and admirable General Sternwood, from learning too much about the unsavory activities of his daughters (though he guesses a great deal anyway). Romantic sparks fly between Marlowe and Vivian Sternwood, but the circumstances under which they meet make it impossible for a relationship to develop. At the end of the book, Marlowe is as he was at the beginning, a loner and an idealist.

This is a very entertaining read, even if not every element of the plot holds together as tightly as one might like, and even though it is no longer possible to summon up the expected amount of outrage over Geiger's illegal activities. Marlowe is a wonderful character, and Chandler's spare, tough language is exactly appropriate for the genre. It is fun for the dedicated crime-novel reader to observe, too, how later practitioners have learned from this early master of the form. The 1946 film of *The Big Sleep*, starring the immortal team of Humphrey Bogart and Lauren Bacall, is a true classic (William Faulkner worked on the excellent screenplay).

Raymond Chandler (1888–1959), *The Big Sleep* (New York: Alfred A. Knopf, 1939). Vintage Crime paperback reprint, 1992.

BRUCE CHATWIN
In Patagonia

~

As a child, Bruce Chatwin was fascinated by a fragment of animal hide sent to England from Patagonia by Charley Milward, his grandmother's cousin and a boyhood hero to Chatwin. Milward, the captain of a merchant ship, wound up in Patagonia after a shipwreck. The hide, Chatwin's mother outlandishly assured him, was a piece of skin from a brontosaurus. As we later learn, it was in fact the preserved skin of an extinct giant ground sloth found in a cave by Milward (in other words, thousands rather than tens of millions of years old; most of the specimens were sent to the British Museum).

While Chatwin situates *In Patagonia* within the frame of his childhood fascination with objects and stories, the book is much more than a simple reminiscence—it is a beautifully crafted blend of history, travel, family, and self. The book is divided into ninety-seven short sections, each a vignette of Patagonian land or people, a historical sketch, or in a few cases a story from the unpublished writings of Charley Milward. Because of Chatwin's skill as a writer, all of these cohere remarkably well.

Patagonia is a special place. It is the area of southern Argentina and Chile between the Andes and the Atlantic, a vast, lightly settled region of semiarid plateaus, mountains, and ocean shores. It has an end-of-the-world quality—as one Argentine friend told us, Patagonia, like Argentina itself, isn't on the way to anywhere else. The degree of its isolation can perhaps best be seen when we consider that Argentina, which occupies most of Patagonia, has a land area nearly equal to India's, but only 4 percent of that country's population—and in Argentina, most of the population is in Buenos Aires and other cities in the north of the country.

Patagonia is a place of immigrants primarily from European countries, including notably the British, who have a long history of commerce and farming in Argentina. The descendants of the indigenous
peoples have been largely marginalized. Patagonia also has a place in
the history of science—it is one of the areas visited by Charles Darwin
as he developed his theory of evolution.

One of us read this book immediately after it was published, having just completed a book of our own about resource management in
the area at the northernmost border of Patagonia. We found the book to
be evocative both of our own experience and of the stories that we
heard about the region. Chatwin can be something of a fabulist, but
the book rings true in many of its essential insights, presenting Patagonia as real-life magic realism.

Chatwin's pilgrimage to Patagonia began in the Southern Hemisphere spring (fall in the Northern Hemisphere). His visit started in
Buenos Aires in 1974, with Christmas decorations already in the shops.
Chatwin then visited both towns and remote country areas in Patagonia, walking long distances when required, accepting rides from the occasional trucker or sheep farmer, asking questions, and talking with
people who knew his relations or who simply had stories to tell. His
gifts for observation and meaningful conversation served him well here.
He was a real traveler, willing to take risks when required, as in some of
his lonely hikes, and his descriptions of the Patagonian landscape and
its flora and fauna are excellent.

The fascinating people you will meet in this book are of many
origins: the Welsh sheep farmers of the area back of Port Madryn; the
English; the Germans, some the descendants of nineteenth-century
emigrants and others of more recent and less palatable (from the standpoint of those who arrived earlier) origin; the Italians; and the Indians.
To an astonishing degree, these people appear to live in what are almost time capsules. For example, among those Chatwin encounters
are descendants of South African Boers, who refuse to speak to an
Englishman.

What gives the book its extraordinary richness and depth is the
way Chatwin weaves his adventures and conversations into his reading
of memoirs and books about Patagonia from earlier times. We learn

something about Darwin, about the uprising led by the Spanish anarchist Antonio Soto, and about Butch Cassidy, the famous American outlaw on the lam in Patagonia. Chatwin's historical touch is deft. For example, he takes the time to examine the original manuscripts of Thomas Bridge's dictionary of the Yaghan language in the British Museum and tells us how it feels to touch and read these as he reports on his visit to Bridge's house and his granddaughter in the town of Harberton. A fine element of the work is that Chatwin was in many cases able to find people who knew those about whom he writes, and to talk with them (*interview* is too intrusive a word in the context of this excellent work). From Milward's daughter, a resident of Lima, he obtains information and manuscripts from which some of Charley Milward's gripping stories included in this volume—especially that of his shipwreck on Desolation Island—are taken.

Chatwin visits Charley Milward's sheep station at Valle Huemeules and sits in Charley's church pew at St. James' in Punta Arenas. And, in the end, Chatwin succeeds in getting to the cave, much the worse for wear by humans since Milward's finds, and extracting another piece of sloth skin to replace the one thrown out by his mother upon his grandmother's death. This completion of a quest is done with a gentle touch and gives the reader a feeling of satisfaction rather than of artifice. Patagonia is, indeed, a separate world, because of both its landscape and its history, and Chatwin's achievement is to capture the region in both of these ways.

Chatwin was an exceptionally fine writer, and this is his best work, a highly unusual volume. An individual of troubled personality, a man of great personal beauty and charm who tended to impose unreasonably on his friends, Chatwin was a compulsive wanderer who died early from what he insisted was a mysterious fungal disease but is generally thought to have been AIDS. Of his other works we recommend particularly *The Songlines*, a fictionalized account of his travels in the Australian outback.

Bruce Chatwin (1940–1989), *In Patagonia* (New York: Summit Books, 1977). Available in a Penguin paperback (1988).

WALTER VAN TILBERG CLARK
The Ox-Bow Incident

~

The Ox-Bow Incident is a classic Western novel. It has all of the basic genre ingredients—horses, cowboys, a saloon, a tough-talking woman, cattle rustlers, and more—and Walter van Tilberg Clark uses them to propel a story so gripping that it is almost impossible not to read this book in a single sitting. At the same time, this novel so far transcends the conventions and clichés of the Western genre as to turn into something else altogether.

The story is an account of the lynching of three supposed cattle rustlers and murderers, as experienced by an eyewitness. The action takes place in the eastern foothills of the Sierra Nevada, on the border between Nevada and California, in the spring of 1885. As the book opens, the narrator, Art Croft, and his friend Gil have arrived in the little town of Bridger's Wells after months taking care of cattle in winter pasture. They stop in at Canby's Saloon and soon hear that the valley is in an ugly mood over a spate of cattle rustling. Then news comes that a local cowhand has been murdered and more cattle are missing. Quickly the men of the town form a posse. Art and Gil join the group, though just on the fringes; they are well aware that suspicion would quickly fall on them, as relative outsiders, if they declined to join the hunt for the killers.

A local shopkeeper, Davies, tries to persuade the men to bring in for trial any suspects they find, but it quickly becomes clear that the posse is well on its way to becoming a mob, and few people listen. Art and Gil, at Davies' request, hurry to the house of the local judge to enlist his aid in restraining the group, but meet with little success. Meanwhile a leader of the group emerges: Colonel Tetley, a former Confederate officer, now a prominent rancher. Tetley has the manner of command, and the men move out under his direction. He assures Davies that nothing will be done to any prisoners unless the facts clearly prove their guilt. But Tetley, it emerges, has an agenda of his own, which is to force his delicate and somewhat effeminate son to participate in this "manly" pursuit.

As the posse rides up into the mountains, darkness falls and a snowstorm begins. An encounter with a stagecoach produces some intelligence: A band of strangers has been seen at a camp a few miles ahead. But before the party reaches that spot other strangers are seen near an old cabin at a place called the Ox-Bow, and they are soon surrounded and taken prisoner. The three are Martin, a young man who claims to be a new settler in the valley; Hardwick, an addled old man; and Juan Martinez, a Mexican cowboy in Martin's employ. Things look bad for them, especially because they have with them fifty head of cattle with the brand of a local rancher, Drew. Martin claims to have bought the cattle to stock his new ranch, but he has no bill of sale.

A trial of sorts is held, with Tetley acting as prosecutor; eventually a vote is taken, and with a few dissenting voices, the prisoners are found guilty. Davies continues to object, asking only that the prisoners be brought back alive to face formal justice and a jury trial, but the men will have none of that. At dawn the three men are hanged. The men of the posse, in a sober mood, head back to town, and on the way they meet up with the sheriff and the judge, who have incontrovertible proof that the three dead men were innocent. The murder—one can hardly call it anything else—of Martin and his two cowhands leads to further deadly consequences and leaves an indelible imprint on the lives of many men.

This is a fast-paced, exciting, and disturbing story. Art Croft is a wonderfully low-key, calm-voiced narrator, and his account of these events (along with some side plots that enrich the tale) is enough to keep a reader engrossed in the book from beginning to end. But there is much more to this book than a good story.

The book is also an acute examination of mob psychology. From early on the mood of the townsmen of Bridger's Wells has been for revenge, not for justice. They have been wronged, not just individually but as a community, and someone is going to hang for that—preferably someone who deserves to hang, but a hanging there will be. Colonel Tetley's role is all the more despicable because he is an intelligent, forceful man who could have acted to restrain the crowd but chose instead to lead it. Davies, whom one admires, falls apart psychologically at the close of the book, convinced that whatever he did to try to stop the mob was not enough, and that he could and should have done more. We read on in fascination, perhaps as we would watch a distant plane crash, horrified but mesmerized by something that we can observe but cannot stop.

It is at that point that we realize how cleverly Clark has drawn us into the novel itself. We have been listening all along to the voice of narrator Art Croft, identifying with him, sympathizing with him. We like him, and he seems to be a voice of reason in the midst of mad events. But suddenly it hits us: Why are we going along with this man? He is part of the mob, too; he listens to and agrees with the opponents of the lynching, but in the end does nothing to stop the lynching or even to raise his voice against it.

Finally the message of the book emerges, in the form of a question that Clark forces us to ask ourselves: What response to evil is sufficient? And the answer is, nothing is sufficient that fails to halt the evil itself. We realize that this book is only on the surface a Western tale about a lynching. In the context of 1940, with war already raging between Nazi Germany and an embattled Great Britain, with credible reports emerging from Europe of atrocities inflicted on Jews and other groups designated by Hitler for extermination, Clark's question—what response is sufficient?—was a moral rallying cry to an America that was still trying to avoid entanglement in the widening war.

Walter van Tilberg Clark was born and raised in the East but spent most of his adult life in the country around Reno, Nevada—the setting for *The Ox-Bow Incident*. He wrote other books, but this novel was his one truly great work.

Walter van Tilberg Clark (1909–1971), *The Ox-Bow Incident* (New York: Random House, 1940). The Signet paperback reprint (1943) remains in print but is not easy to find.

EVAN S. CONNELL
Mrs. Bridge

~

When one looks back upon American culture from the 1920s to the 1950s, what seem to stand out are landmarks of vibrant change: the Harlem Renaissance, the novels of Fitzgerald and Hemingway, the music of Virgil Thompson and Aaron Copland, and Abstract Expressionism and the New York School of artists. At the time, however, most Americans lived in near-total unawareness of these manifestations of high culture. Cultural trends of a very different sort were quietly working their transformation of American society in burgeoning suburbs and in wealthy neighborhoods of cities and towns across the country. These trends amounted to a cultural revolution compounded of affluence, apathy, and ignorance, of two-car garages and gray flannel suits and corporate conformity, of bridge parties and country clubs and gentility. Some called it the American dream; it was a revolution of rising expectations, of a conviction that hard work and conservative values would make it possible for American families to enjoy hitherto unbelievable material abundance and thus be happy.

The protagonists of Evan S. Connell's novel *Mrs. Bridge* were in the vanguard of this revolution, for although the lifestyle portrayed in the novel seems like the quintessence of the Fifties (at least as that decade is remembered today), the actual time span covered is from the 1920s into the early 1940s. The novel follows the life of India Bridge from her marriage to the hardworking lawyer Walter Bridge (who, when he was courting her, quoted Ruskin and dreamed of visiting Europe, but after their marriage worked late every night at the office) to a time, some twenty-five years later, when she has become a middle-aged widow whose children have left home. Walter is a good provider, and they soon have an imposing house in which to raise their two daughters and a son. India tries very hard to be a perfect wife; she is always well groomed and agreeable, and leaves to her husband all matters that require strong opinions and serious decisions. She is a very nice person; her problem is that she is incapable of being anything but nice. Her world is bounded by domesticity and good manners. She is annoyed when her son actually dries his hands on a guest towel (which exists only to be seen, never to be used), and carefully explains to her daughter that the person who helps with the housekeeping is the cleaning *woman* ("A lady is someone like Mrs. Arlen or Mrs. Montgomery").

India Bridge socializes with a circle of friends who are all almost exactly like herself; she sometimes finds it hard to understand the one or two who don't quite fit in. (They read books that no one has ever heard of, for example.) India is far from unintelligent, but she is profoundly ignorant of everything beyond her immediate world. Sometimes she tries to expand her horizons (by learning Spanish or doing word exercises to improve her vocabulary), but nothing comes of this; although she has too little to do and is often bored, she somehow cannot find the time to devote to self-improvement.

This is a brilliantly written book. Connell reveals Mrs. Bridge's life to us in a series of very short chapters that are like snapshots passing before our eyes (in fact, like the photo album that she assembles near the end of the book). As these vignettes arrange themselves into a finely shaded portrait, we view her life with sympathy because she seems so bewildered by it; she would like to be happier, she would like to feel fulfilled, but she clearly hasn't a clue how to go about it. The final image that we have of her shows her literally trapped by the symbols of her affluence. It is hard not to shed a tear for her plight. (The two of us read *Mrs. Bridge* perhaps with particular sympathy and understanding, for we saw as teens in the Fifties too many lives lived according to the principle of "What will people think?") Evan Connell's portrait of Mrs. Bridge is low-key and nonjudgmental, but it is all the more devastating for that, because it rings so true. One remembers, after reading this book, why the turmoil of the Sixties (despite its excesses and youthful arrogance) had in some sense become necessary as a response to the failure of the American dream.

In 1969 Connell published *Mr. Bridge*, a companion to *Mrs. Bridge* that tells the whole story over again from the point of view of India Bridge's ambitious, confused, workaholic husband. We warmly recommend that you read the two novels back to back. Connell has had a productive and successful career as a writer, with many works of both fiction and nonfiction to his credit; we would also recommend his study of General George Custer and the Battle of Little Big Horn, *Son of the Morning Star* (1984).

Evan S. Connell (1924–), *Mrs. Bridge* (New York: Viking, 1959). The paperback reprint from North Point Press (now part of Farrar, Straus and Giroux) is in print, though not always easy to find.

JOSEPH CONRAD
The Secret Agent

~

Joseph Conrad is best remembered today for his tales of psychological conflict in exotic tropical locales, and justly so; his novels *Lord Jim* and *Nostromo* and the harrowing novella *Heart of Darkness* are well worth reading and rereading, and deserve every bit of their fame. *The Secret Agent,* set more prosaically in late Victorian London, is less well known except to serious Conrad fans and to literary scholars, who regard it as a landmark in the creation of modernist fiction. With its minute and psychologically relentless scrutiny of the circumstances surrounding a sordid and pointless crime and its aftermath, it shines a restless and uncomfortable searchlight into some of the darker recesses of the human soul. It is a book that deserves, and will repay, your attention.

Adolph Verloc, the secret agent of the title, lives the life of a barely respectable member of London's lower middle class. He runs a seedy bookshop in Soho, where from time to time he convenes meetings of a group of anarchists and revolutionary agitators from the Continent; he is accepted by them as a leading figure of their movement, a man of daring and integrity. Not part of the group, but well known to them, is the Professor, an anarchist bomb maker who ensures himself freedom from police interference by never leaving home—as the police are well aware—without wiring himself up with enough high explosives to kill everyone within a radius of fifty yards, his hand on the detonator in his raincoat pocket.

Despite the company he keeps, Verloc is no revolutionary, but a double agent twice over. He supplies information on anarchists and revolutionaries to a police detective, Chief Inspector Heat; more seriously, he is in the pay of the embassy of an unnamed Eastern European country and reports to his controller there on the movements and activities of his leftist comrades. Outwardly respectable, Verloc lives with his wife, Winnie, her mother, and her mildly mentally retarded brother, Stevie, whom Winnie shelters from an uncaring world with fiercely protective love. Winnie is careful to do nothing that will endanger the security of her small family, and she chooses to know as little as possible about her husband's activities and his odd associates.

Verloc, however, is suddenly thrust into a dangerous predicament. His controller at the embassy is tired of receiving routine and unhelpful reports from his agent; he also wants the British government to abandon its liberal attitude toward political activists and enact the sort of repressive police measures that had already become routine on the Continent. In short, the embassy secretary needs an anarchist outrage, and he commissions Verloc to supply one. Verloc, his livelihood threatened, resolves to comply despite his total lack of experience in revolutionary violence. He acquires a bomb from the Professor and makes plans to blow up part of the Greenwich Observatory. But Verloc's plan goes horribly wrong.

All of this we learn early in the novel. What makes the book so much a work of modernism, embedded in the worlds of Marx and Freud, is how Conrad then turns to scrutinize every aspect of the crime, every contingency that led to its planning and its failure, every tightening of the psychological tension springs of the main characters, every inevitability that carries the story to its fatal conclusion. This book is so fundamental to the whole genre of the psychological thriller that it is quite difficult to imagine, say, a cold-war classic like John Le Carré's *The Spy Who Came in from the Cold* had Conrad not written *The Secret Agent* many years before.

Joseph Conrad led an adventurous life in his youth before settling down in middle age to accomplish the difficult feat of becoming a novelist in a language that he had learned only as an adult. Jozef Teodor Konrad Korzeniowski, as he was originally named, was born into a family of aristocratic patriots in Russian-occupied Poland. When his parents were exiled for their political activities, young Jozef was raised by his uncle; he left home for France as soon as he was old enough to manage on his own. He worked as a sailor on French merchant ships, and barely escaped serious political trouble of his own when he became involved in smuggling arms to revolutionaries in Spain.

Still barely into his twenties, Korzeniowski moved to England. For nearly two decades he made his living in the British merchant fleet, rising through talent and hard work to win his ratings as mate and then as master. His extensive voyages in the Indian Ocean and the South Seas provided him with ample material for his novels and short stories, beginning with *Almayer's Folly* in 1895. In his new guise as Joseph Conrad, he became one of England's most respected writers, and although he always found the work of writing to be an agony, the very fact that he was not a native user of English made his creative work in that language all the more painstaking, subtle, and exact. With a gift for vivid description, a deep understanding of how people behave under extreme psychological pressure, and his own powerful, supple prose, Conrad became one of the great modern masters of the novel. *The Secret Agent* is one of his greatest works.

The Secret Agent, though not lengthy, is a book to read with care and attention; it is a long one-night read, and a grim one. This is not a book to read for easy entertainment after a hard day's work, but it is one that will reward you richly when you bring to it a rested mind and the mood to respond to a brilliant writer at the peak of his creative power.

Joseph Conrad (1857–1924), *The Secret Agent* (London: Methuen; New York: Harper and Brothers, 1907). The Modern Library paperback edition (1998) is widely available.

JILL KER CONWAY
The Road from Coorain

~

Jill Ker Conway, an Australian, received her Ph.D. in history from Harvard and has been a distinguished historian and academic leader in Canada and the United States, including her service as president of Smith College. In *The Road from Coorain*, Conway has given us a beautifully written memoir of growing up in the Australian outback with family tragedy, the cruelty of drought, and, later, the challenges facing a successful young woman in a male-dominated society. Coorain (an Aboriginal term meaning "windy place") is her family's sheep-herding station in the Australian outback, five hundred miles from Sydney, the country's largest city.

The book takes us from the settlement of Conway's family in the outback through her final departure for the United States. Conway begins her story with an evocative description of the western plains of New South Wales, where her father took up his land in 1929 as a "settler soldier" (his right as a veteran of World War I). He was an experienced manager of sheep stations; his wife, a nurse who headed up a hospital, had lived as an independent woman for ten years prior to their marriage. There soon followed two sons and, a few years later, a daughter.

Raising sheep in these distant plains, with a fragile ecology not evolved for the grazing of sheep and cattle, and at the mercy of the weather for desperately needed water, was a chancy enterprise. It offered large gains in good times and economic misery in bad times, and Conway's family experienced both. It was a harsh world for the ranchers and their families; they became inured to difficulties and shy about showing emotion. For them there were only two places: the bush, which was their immediate world, and Sydney, at the end of a long train journey to the southeast coast, where wool could be sold and luxuries purchased when circumstances permitted. In the way of learning for the young daughter in the Ker household there was education at home and books that came a dozen at a time for her mother from a lending library in Sydney. Work was usually allocated by gender, but there was more than enough work for everyone, male and female. With the author's brothers away at school, she became her father's ranch hand at the age of seven. She rode sometimes with him and sometimes on her own as work demanded, although she had trouble getting the sheepdogs to listen to her childish voice and was too small to get back on her horse easily after dismounting to take care of a task.

The family prospered at first, but a long drought that began in 1940 spelled the end for them in the outback. Even the best-managed small station eventually fails if a drought is long enough. The slow failure of the Ker station was an increasingly bitter experience for everyone. Her father was overworked and heartsick keeping the farm together, and one day he drowned trying to repair a pipe in a depleted reservoir so that water could be pumped. It is uncertain whether he died from an accident or from his own depression; Conway's memory of running after her father's car as he left the house on his final journey, trying to catch him and go with him, is indelible. She was not allowed to cry when told of her father's death.

The family moved to Sydney, with the mother determined to hang on to the farm, with a resident manager, until times improved. She pulled her family through hard times, making good guesses on sheep prices and the weather, and Coorain prospered once more. But tragedy struck again with the loss of one of Conway's brothers, and then her mother's progressive physical decline and increasingly unbalanced mental state created a crushing dependence on her daughter.

After a false start, Conway began a distinguished student career at the University of Sydney. She experienced the struggles and outright discrimination facing a woman in an intensely male society. When Conway and two other bright university friends were interviewed for posts in the Australian foreign service, her two male colleagues received offers, and she did not because she was female. We read of her well-justified shock and anger but also see, ultimately, the adult incarnation of the seven-year-old girl figuring how to get back on her horse by standing on a stump. There is a year in England and Europe with her mother, work for an M.A., her first publications, and then teaching, including a large lecture course on American history. This is a turning point in her life, and after the emotional ills of her mother go beyond all bounds she decides to apply to Harvard for graduate school. She had lost her father, a brother, and (emotionally) her mother, and had no place as a woman and an intellectual in her own society. We leave her at the plane at Sydney airport, bound for Cambridge, Massachusetts.

What stands out about this exceptionally well-written book is the emotion without self-pity that informs it; it is understanding but not sentimental. Conway has the historian's ability to see her own past in perspective. In writing this volume, she has performed a remarkable service in describing so well what she experienced and learned as a child and young woman. While Conway's early life had more than its share of challenges, the ways in which she understood, grappled with, and overcame them are familiar to some extent to all of us. Her ultimate success is admirable.

One of us was acquainted with Conway when she was a graduate student. She was the new wife of John Conway, a historian, Canadian war hero, and beloved master of Leverett House at Harvard. She was his match as an impressive personality: a few years older than most graduate students, tall, composed, friendly, and very bright, altogether the model of what a soon-to-be-successful academic should be. But there was a preternatural wisdom about her that could just be glimpsed and which had no evident explanation. When this book was published we learned why, and at what cost, Conway seemed so much wiser than her fellow graduate students.

If you enjoy *The Road from Coorain*, as we think you will, you will also like its sequel, *True North* (1994), a memoir of Conway's life after her marriage and completion of her doctoral work in women's history, through her work at the University of Toronto and up until her acceptance of the presidency of Smith College in 1975.

Jill Ker Conway (1934–), *The Road from Coorain* (New York: Alfred A. Knopf, 1989). The Vintage Departures paperback reprint edition (1990) is readily available.

F. M. CORNFORD

Microcosmographia Academica: Being a Guide for the Young Academic Politician

~

F. M. Cornford was one of the successful and connected figures who seem to define life at England's two great ancient universities, Oxford and Cambridge. He was the son of a priest of the Church of England, the husband of a granddaughter of Darwin, the Laurence Professor of Ancient Philosophy, and a Fellow of Trinity College. Perhaps you have already come in contact with Cornford's academic work in the field of classical philosophy: His edition of Plato's *Republic*, still wonderful to read today, may well have been part of your coursework in college. Unlike most of his fellow cloistered academics, however, he had the ability to see things as they actually are in organizations, and to write down his observations in a way that is both amusing and insightful.

Cambridge—where, as we learned as visiting fellows at one of the Cambridge colleges, there is a problem for every solution—is a place rich in ancient tradition and sometimes arcane customs. Cornford used his experience there, and his easy familiarity with classical literature, to formulate wise and accurate observations of academic decision making. He placed these in a framework of facetious advice to ambitious young academics, but in this fine book Cornford, like Parkinson (p. 213), transcends the particular time and place in which he wrote. His perceptions on the functioning of organizations, and the endless impediments to innovation in them, relate amazingly well to modern business and government as well as to academics.

The book begins with a warning to the young about the hazards of the career on which they are about to embark. This is followed by witty assessments of groups and their behavior, the need for innumerable rules (the more pointless the better), and the process of decision making (or, most of the time, the lack of it). His illustrations of these ideas have great charm, even at this distance. He notes, for example, that the purpose of rules is to relieve the young of any need to think about right and wrong. One that he cites is that on Sundays no one shall walk to the village of Madingley unless he is wearing black academic robes. (This was a real regulation; as Dave Barry might say, Cornford is not making this up.)

Cornford goes on to describe the many strategies that academics and others use to ensure that the innovations that might disrupt contented lives and careers go nowhere. The central part of the book is about arguments regarding proposed policies, mostly against. Cornford sagely observes that there is only one reason for doing something, which is that it is right; but of course there are many reasons not to do something. His categorization of reasons not to act is splendid. Our favorite is the Principle of Unripe Time, a general-purpose stalling device. When at last a proposal is made that is of obvious merit, is entirely right, and should be done, there is no recourse but to acknowledge the quality of the idea and then to argue that, most regrettably, the time is Not Yet Ripe. Among others there is the invaluable Principle of the Wedge, according to which any useful action should be avoided; it may, after all, be the thin edge of the wedge that, once implemented, would unduly raise expectations for the future. Nor are organizational measures to be neglected in the noble cause of preventing innovation. It is well, for example, to have various boards, on which no one is allowed to act without consulting at least twenty others, all of whom are accustomed to regard each other with well-founded suspicion. (In our own time, certain governmental review procedures have come to serve this function with great effectiveness.)

There are less lofty measures available as well, such as wasting time until tea is about to be served (in modern life, the imminent departure of the airport limo would be a rough equivalent), an infallible way of ending any further consideration of proposed measures. Cornford cleverly concludes the book with advice on how to actually make things happen. This involves seemingly casual but really subtly planned encounters between individuals strolling on Kings Parade, the road directly in front of many of the colleges at Cambridge. You will no doubt be able to point to the Kings Parade in your own office.

Of course, much of this, as you read it, will seem entirely familiar from your own work experience, and perhaps also familiar from your reading—many of the foibles identified by Cornford were still going strong a century later and were skewered again by Scott Adams in his *Dilbert* books. *Microcosmographia Academica* is so right-on that—who knows?—an evening spent with it may well be more effective in advancing your career than the two years it takes to earn an M.B.A. At a minimum, you will get through meetings of the local school board with a much improved sense of humor.

F[rancis] M[acdonald] Cornford (1874–1943), *Microcosmographia Academica: Being a Guide for the Young Academic Politician* (Cambridge, England: Bowes and Bowes, 1908). A modern reprint is from MainSail Press, Cambridge, England, 1993.

PATRICK DENNIS
Auntie Mame

~

Although the copyright page of *Auntie Mame* includes a disclaimer, often found in works of fiction, to the effect that "any resemblance between the characters in this book and actual persons is wholly coincidental," most readers have tended to assume that the book is closely based on its author's life. That turns out not to be true; *Auntie Mame* is a novel, not an autobiography. Nevertheless, it appears that the book was written in part in response to the author's own experience as an artistic, imaginative boy raised in a stodgy Midwestern family. Even if the most outrageous parts of the story turn out to be too good to be true, this is a very funny fantasy of the unconventional upbringing Patrick Dennis wished he had.

The book is related in the form of a memoir by its protagonist (named, like the author, Patrick Dennis), who, when we first meet him in 1928, is the ten-year-old son of a wealthy but emotionally remote Chicago businessman. Soon he is an orphan, with his father's considerable fortune placed in a trust fund for his eventual benefit. After his unlamented father's funeral, he travels with his Irish nanny, Norah Muldoon, to New York City, where he is to be raised by his legal guardian, Mame Dennis. Mame is a splendidly eccentric woman whose life is a continual round of parties and cultural happenings; Patrick is intrigued by her, and even Norah, who regards most of Mame's enthusiasms as heathenish or worse, cannot resist her charm. Mame soon loses most of her fortune in the stock market crash of 1929 and has to move from her fancy Beekman Place apartment to much more modest quarters; her attempts to actually earn a living (as a receptionist, switchboard operator, and department store saleswoman, among other things) end in abject failure. Patrick, whose trust fund purse strings are held by the unpleasant banker Mr. Babcock, is packed off to boarding school, and things look bleak for Auntie Mame.

Salvation comes in the form of Beauregard Burnside, a fabulously wealthy Southern oilman. He is immediately charmed by Mame, who in a matter of days becomes Mrs. Burnside. On a trip to the Old South, Mame, first seen by the locals as an upstart, gold-digging Yankee, even manages to charm Beau's numerous relatives. But the idyll does not last long. In little more than a year Beau dies in a riding accident, and Mame is a very rich widow. Patrick, rapidly growing up, wants nothing more than a conventional childhood; his flamboyant aunt often embarrasses him, and it takes a while—it takes, perhaps, all the years of hindsight that preceded the writing of this book—for him to appreciate fully what a treasure she is. (Exactly the things that embarrassed Patrick the most are, of course, sidesplittingly funny when we read about them in these pages.)

In most ways this book remains as fresh and charming as when it was first published. The one feature that does not hold up well is a framing device for the story that now seems very old-fashioned. The opening paragraphs of each chapter of the book are explicitly modeled on stories that regularly appeared in *Reader's Digest* on the theme of "The Most Unforgettable Character I've Met." Fifty years ago *Reader's Digest* was an important part of American middle-class culture, and using one of its best-known features as a way of setting up a memoir of an amusing and eccentric character would have struck contemporary readers as clever and instantly recognizable. Today the *Digest* is much less widely read, and for a modern reader the device falls flat. But this is a minor flaw, easily overlooked. On the other hand, the contrast that the book draws between Auntie Mame's free-spirited, freethinking lifestyle and the narrow conformity of much of American life has lost none of its power.

The book's defining episode comes when the protagonist, Patrick, is grown up and engaged to be married to Gloria Upson, a pretty but shallow and utterly conventional young woman of whom Mame deeply disapproves. With great subtlety Mame provokes Gloria and her ghastly family (who live in a rich, "exclusive" Connecticut suburb) into revealing just how bigoted they are, and then denounces their narrow-mindedness in a stirring speech that still rings true today. When the book was written half a century ago, this passage would have shocked many readers (whose views on blacks, Jews, and others would likely not have been so different from those expressed by the Upsons). Auntie Mame may be flighty, sometimes reckless, and a pigeon for fads and frauds, and she is not very good at planning or being prudent. But although she gets into some very funny escapades, she is not herself a ridiculous figure. She is not only lovable, she is admirable for being the passionate upholder of the best American values of individuality and tolerance, and the enemy of whatever is mediocre and meretricious.

The 1958 film of *Auntie Mame* follows the book relatively closely but is overall a bit sweeter; the book has more bite. The film nevertheless is worth seeing because it features Rosalind Russell in the role of a lifetime as Mame Dennis; this is a brilliant performance. Interestingly, the film's most famous line—"Life is a banquet, and most poor suckers are starving to death"—is not from the book at all, but is original to the screenplay by Betty Comden and Adolph Green. Nevertheless, it captures Auntie Mame's philosophy very well indeed.

Patrick Dennis wrote a number of other books, but *Auntie Mame* made him famous, and (with the book's various theatrical and film adaptations) wealthy, too. This one book is ample reason for readers to feel grateful to him.

Patrick Dennis [Edward Everett Tanner III] (1921–1976), *Auntie Mame* (New York: Vanguard Press, 1955). There is no paperback edition currently in print; there is a hardcover reprint (1995) from Buccaneer Books. See also the very good new biography of the author by Eric Meyers, *Uncle Mame: The Life of Patrick Dennis* (New York: St. Martin's Press, 2000).

Maria Dermoût
The Ten Thousand Things

~

Maria Dermoût was born in 1888 in Java, the child of a family that for many generations had been employees of the Dutch East India Company and its successors. There were many such colonial families of merchants, sea captains, and administrators whose roots went deep into the islands of the Indies (now Indonesia). Maria married at an early age into another old colonial family and lived, as she said, "in twenty different houses, not counting bungalows and guest houses," all over the archipelago. After World War II, she retired to Holland and at the age of sixty-three published a brief memoir of her girlhood in Java. It was well received, and that first foray into writing encouraged her to complete *The Ten Thousand Things*, a magical, dreamy novel of the Spice Islands. (The title is from a Chinese poetic phrase meaning "everything in the world.")

The Ten Thousand Things is set on one of the Moluccas—the group of islands of eastern Indonesia once known as the Spice Islands. (The island is never identified by name; it is always and only "the island," but it is recognizably Ambon, site of the chief town and seaport of the Moluccas.) Most of the story takes place either in the island's principal town, on the outer bay, or at a spice plantation called the Small Garden, several hours by *proa* (outrigger canoe) from the town. The Small Garden has been run by the same colonial family, whose name we do not learn, for generations. The plantation's occupants, as the story opens, are a little girl, Felicia, her parents, and her grandmother, along with a small number of servants and workers. The story follows Felicia through her lifetime, but the novel is as much about the plantation and the island as it is about any individual person.

Felicia loves her grandmother's stories of the past and is entranced by the older woman's curio cabinet, full of shells and mysterious remedies (such as a snakestone that can remove venom). She loves to wander around the extensive gardens and orchards of the plantation and is fascinated by the three small graves, side by side, that stand near one of the fields; they are, she knows, the graves of three sisters of a previous generation who died all on the same day. (Were they poisoned by their nanny? No one knows for sure anymore.)

Felicia's happy life on the island is disrupted when her mother and her grandmother quarrel; her parents depart for Europe, where Felicia grows up. We learn that she met a handsome stranger and married him quickly; he left her before their son was born. With the family fallen on hard times, she returns to the Small Garden to live with her grandmother again. Felicia throws herself into the work of the plantation, making it more of a commercial success (despite her grandmother's distaste of appearing to be "in trade," an unsuitable occupation for an old colonial family); we gradually understand that she now has little happiness in her life and that her hard work fills the place where she might have wished love to reside instead.

Her great consolation is her young son, Willem, who grows up on the plantation in a way that seems to replicate her own carefree childhood. But Himpies, as the son is called, is after all a boy and therefore must be educated, so he is soon sent away to boarding school, first to Java and then to Holland; for years Felicia knows him only through letters.

When Himpies returns as an officer in the colonial armed forces, Felicia is delighted to have him nearby again. But the spell of the three little girls in their graves has never left her, and death is a strong presence on the island. As the book ends we see Felicia, now an aged eccentric of whom people are a little bit afraid, preparing a banquet for the many ghosts who haunt the Small Garden.

The one word that comes insistently to mind to describe this lovely novel is *magical*. Dermoût does not so much tell a story as weave a spell. Her descriptions of the Small Garden, with its groves of nutmeg and kenari nut trees, its crumbling old house ruined in an earthquake generations ago, its palm trees and brilliant birds, evoke one of the most beautiful and fascinating places in the world. It is no paradise—too much danger and death lurk beneath the surface for that—but it is a place of wonder.

The East Indies—an enormous country ruled by a tiny one—had a tremendous impact on the culture of the Netherlands. Merchants and administrators of the Dutch East India Company had lived in the islands since the early seventeenth century, and many of them had retired back home to the old country; the textiles, spices, and even the exotic seashells of the Indies were found in every bourgeois house in Holland. Many of the founders of modernism in Dutch art and literature were children of the islands. In the works of these authors (for example, in Louis Couperis' seminal novel *The Hidden Force*) one detects the same feeling that one finds here in *The Ten Thousand Things*, of the beauty and mystery of the Indies and their rich indigenous cultures, a sense also that the islands will hold outsiders in the grasp of their mysteries and never yield up their secrets altogether. This sense of the unknowable, amounting even to a small but pervasive aura of fear, perhaps reflects both an unconscious sense of doubt on the part of these colonial intruders about the rightness of imperialism and an awareness of instability, impermanence, and impending change.

One of us has visited the Moluccas several times and knows Ambon well. It was a sad experience to reread this book, because it now stands as a record of a vanished world. In recent years, Ambon has been torn by terrible communal violence (part of the turmoil that followed the end of the long, corrupt Suharto regime in Indonesia), with fighting between Christians and Moslems claiming hundreds of lives and leaving the town of Ambon a smoking ruin. It is wonderful to have this novel to remind us of how beautiful it was, once upon a time.

Maria Dermoût (1888–1962), *The Ten Thousand Things*, trans. Hans Koningsberger (Amsterdam, 1958; New York: Simon & Schuster, 1958). Reprinted in both hardcover and paperback (1983) by the University of Massachusetts Press in the handsome Library of the Indies series, but that edition also is now unfortunately out of print. The Vintage paperback (1984) can sometimes still be found.

Edward Cameron Dimock

Mr. Dimock Explores the Mysteries of the East

~

Reading this little memoir by a bluff, exuberant, good-humored American who lived in India for much of his adult life is a refreshing and eye-opening experience. Edward Cameron Dimock spent his working career as a professor of South Asian languages at the University of Chicago; he lived in India for extended periods to pursue his research and, it becomes evident, for the sheer pleasure of being there. Here he relishes his experiences again in the telling, and we, his readers, appreciate anew the complexities of human societies.

Retired and living on Cape Cod (and having become too ill for further travel abroad), Dimock wrote this little book about his travels and adventures in the subcontinent, each chapter a gem of narrative style, wit, and instinct for the incongruous. It would be hard to find a more delightful companion for armchair travel than Edward Dimock, not least because he understands that in India as elsewhere, extraordinary events are everyday occurrences, to be taken with a grain of salt.

As many travelers have found, India is a complex place. Initial encounters are often confusing and sometimes almost overwhelming, not so much because preconceptions turn out to be either true or untrue as because they all seem true simultaneously. In India as much as anywhere else on the planet, contradictions coexist—sublime spirituality rubbing elbows with crass materialism, exquisite beauty cheek by jowl with dehumanizing squalor, maddening bureaucratic arrogance and delightfully old-fashioned courtesy, delicious food and repulsive stenches, a shifting array of baffling, disorienting impressions and sensations. It is much to Dimock's credit that he does not try to hide these contradictions and problems of life behind a facade of Orientalist prettification, but rather devours them all with an unquenchable appetite and savors every part of the experience.

Mr. Dimock Explores the Mysteries of the East is not a conventional, chronological memoir. In fact, there is very little sense here of time passing; events occur in a sort of timeless present of the author's memory. Each chapter is organized around a theme, an idea, a person, or an experience, with diversions and digressions as they strike the author's fancy. One chapter tells of how he came to terms with sharing his living quarters with a troop of monkeys. Another begins with an account of playing golf in India and segues into a meditation on karma. Another is about curry and food lore more generally. Every chapter is illuminated by Dimock's keen eye for details, his capacity for taking pleasure in all of the small things in life (even things that turn out other than as hoped and planned), and his love of a good story.

Here are a few vignettes to give the flavor of the book:

Despite his great affection for India, the author is not entirely immune to the occasional frustrations of life. Once he is driven beyond endurance by the prolonged nondelivery of furniture for his rented house in Calcutta. After an especially dreadful night in the bare house, he hears a creaking bamboo handcart arriving with the missing items. While two men carry the furniture upstairs, Dimock corners the foreman of the crew and lets out his pent-up anger in a torrent of invective; curses and abuse that he was hardly aware of having learned pour fluently from his tongue. After some minutes of this, as Dimock pauses for breath, the astonished foreman says, "in a voice soft with wonder, 'Sahib, what beautiful Bengali you speak.' "

At a religious festival, held in a typically hot and dusty Indian setting, Dimock slakes his thirst by downing one delicious coconut yogurt milk shake after another, only gradually realizing (as his Indian companions knew all along, to their great amusement) that the refreshing beverage is heavily laced with hashish. The result is a series of quite startling visions of the ferocious goddess Durga, and a headache.

On riding an elephant named Gopal: "Gopal's eye showed intelligence, a sad wisdom, a kind of mild curiosity, and a knowing humor that I have come to associate with older people who have seen a good deal of life and loved some of it and hated some of it but don't want to talk about any of it anymore. The elephant seemed very much, in fact, like my father." The kinship that Dimock feels for this wise, tolerant fellow creature makes one feel, in turn, what a truly special person the author must be.

This book is not in any sense a travel guide. It is not necessary to have an intention to go to India, or even any particular interest in India, to take pleasure in reading it. In the end perhaps its greatest reward for the reader is that of spending time with a man wholly at home with himself, and therefore at home anywhere in the world.

Edward Cameron Dimock (1929–2001), *Mr. Dimock Explores the Mysteries of the East* (Chapel Hill, N.C.: Algonquin Books of Chapel Hill, 1999).

HUGH DUNDAS

Flying Start: A Fighter Pilot's War Years

~

Hugh Dundas was a World War II British fighter pilot who enjoyed an unusually successful career both during and after the war. He was rapidly promoted as a very young pilot, but what was really extraordinary was that he survived five years of combat flying duty. Many of his fellow pilots, including a beloved brother, were killed in action, and it took both skill and luck for pilots to make it through the war alive. It is our good fortune that, after a long and successful postwar business career (including the chairmanship of Thames Television in the United Kingdom), Dundas reread his wartime letters and log books and wrote this memoir. It is an exceptional example of the first-person narrative of war, combining the feeling of being on the spot with a mature distance that makes the dilemmas of wartime deeply convincing.

Dundas grew up in Yorkshire, the child of minor landed gentry somewhat down at heel but firmly a part of a world that even then was vanishing: large estates, manners and daily schedules straight out of Victorian times, hunting parties, and fancy cars. Unable for financial reasons to follow his brother to Oxford, he became attached to a solicitor's (lawyer's) office for training and pursued a childhood fascination with aviation to become a member of an auxiliary air force unit. Somewhat the reverse of the situation in the United States, the auxiliary units were rather gentlemanly and their members looked down upon the regular Royal Air Force pilots. As real war dawned these distinctions faded into the background.

Dundas saw combat first during the evacuation of Dunkirk, in France, from which defeated British troops were reembarked for England. Dundas had a rude introduction to fighting, blacking out in rapid turns and losing his bearings on the return flight. Dunkirk was followed by air defense missions over the British Isles and the climactic Battle of Britain in the summer of 1940, in which Dundas was shot down and wounded, just managing to crawl out of the cockpit and parachute to safety before his plane crashed in an English field. Then there was further fighting over France, the desert war in North Africa, the invasion of Italy, and finally the end of German resistance in Italy. All of this was followed by Dundas' perhaps unoriginal feeling of relief at still being alive.

Writing from the vantage point of maturity, Dundas is able to bring out more clearly than someone in the midst of it the fear of war and the constant battle in the pilot's mind between two pressing desires: the desire to live, by going into some less hazardous line of work such as staff duty, and the desire to serve. The latter may be a little hard for us to recapture in our prosperous and protected times, but in fact no one knew, especially in 1940, if Britain would survive; to our good fortune, in Dundas' mind the desire to serve won out. We read of Dundas' pride in his combat successes, and his immense feelings of responsibility at his rapid promotion to combat command posts. There is his constant struggle to maintain the will to fight, and professional errors as well, such as his wrong recommendation on the tactical use of a new plane, the Typhoon, which later threatened his career.

Nor does Dundas shirk description of the personal problems in his young life. He often dealt with the immense pressures of warfare by drinking himself blotto, resulting in car accidents and a fatherly warning by a superior officer. At one point in Italy, one of his superiors thought him (incorrectly, as it turned out) incapable of further fighting. We see a young man, in other words, rather like a star athlete in our own time, who succeeds marvelously well at a skill but fails to grow up as an adult because there is no time for that.

The book brings out the importance of technology in warfare, as indeed in many areas of life, which we often take for granted. For British fighter pilots, the most important element of technology was the constant competition between the Spitfire and Messerschmitt designers and manufacturers to obtain air superiority, with various improvements being made in both planes throughout the war. The key for the British was a seemingly arcane advantage: The Spitfire had a smaller turning radius than the Messerschmitt and therefore had the advantage in dogfights, where the most important maneuver was to turn on the enemy's tail, closing and firing at just the right moment. Other things, such as the fact that the Spitfire could use high-octane gasoline brought in from the United States, were important, too, as were the improved perforated steel mats used for landing fields in the desert. The young pilots learned to improvise, buying rearview mirrors, a key bit of hardware forgotten by the manufacturer in early Spitfires, at local auto stores and screwing them into the cockpits. Dundas deals also with larger issues of war, including the endemic suspicion between branches of the service—the RAF thinking that it had done the maximum in a particular campaign, and the harried ground troops under withering enemy fire wondering where the air force was.

Among the raft of war memoirs, this one is special because of its remarkable combination of immediacy and perspective. The direct writing style enhances the impact of a truly impressive story. Dundas is able to quote from some of his letters and logs without mawkishness and to good effect, and he uses later information well to illuminate problems and incidents that were not fully clear at the time. We are in Dundas' debt for turning, at the end of his career, to this book. It is clearly written, fast-paced, and highly informative, and reminds us that if there is something truly special in our own lives, each of us should consider writing it down for our own and others' benefit.

Hugh Dundas (1920–1995), *Flying Start: A Fighter Pilot's War Years* (New York: St. Martin's Press, 1989). Out of print.

Freeman J. Dyson

The Sun, the Genome, and the Internet

~

This book is the physicist Freeman Dyson's guide to technology, fairness, and the future. The title reflects the technologies that he believes will be most important within the lifetimes of our children: solar energy, genetics, and the Internet. Dyson, one of the most articulate scientists of our time, is an unusually helpful guide for the layman because his own contributions have ranged across many fields and he is practiced at making connections between science and policy. This is a graceful book, based on lectures given at the New York Public Library that we were fortunate enough to be able to attend.

In his introduction, Dyson provides some background about himself and discusses what it means to think about the future. He was born in Crowthorne, Berkshire, England, and has had a notably successful career. Armed with a degree in mathematics from Cambridge University, he went to Cornell as a professor of physics and since 1953 has been at the Institute for Advanced Study in Princeton. He correctly (and disarmingly) notes that "Experts, when they try to forecast the future, are usually wrong." What can be done is to examine reasonably possible futures; Dyson's aim, in conformity with his view that humans must try their best, is to sketch out ways in which society might use technology for the betterment of all.

In the first of three linked essays in the book, Dyson presents a fine discussion of scientific change. He discusses the two main approaches: that changes come through new theories, or from new tools. His own view is that most recent scientific changes have been tool-driven, such as the discovery of the double-helix structure of DNA (Watson, p. 283), which relied heavily on the technique of X-ray crystallography.

Throughout the book, he teaches us a great deal about the methods and techniques of science. For example, in discussing the first discovery of extrasolar planets, he notes in passing that the evidence studied was indirect: The existence of planets was inferred from patterns of radio-wave pulses. We see immediately from this example that much of science is based on inference rather than on direct observation of the objects of interest. Dyson also does not shy away from taking on sacred cows. He thinks that the unsustainable funding requirements of the Apollo manned space program set space science back twenty years. Dyson may be wrong, but he raises a crucial issue, that of resource allocation for big science. That is his style; he comments later that it is "better to be wrong than to be vague," because others can then engage one's argument more effectively.

It is in his second essay that Dyson describes the three technologies that he thinks will be most important from an earthbound perspective (space is left for the last essay) over the next fifty years: solar energy, genetic engineering, and the Internet. He begins by telling stories about various technological changes in the past, some in the context of his family history. This is Dyson's way of bringing the nonscientist aboard, and it is very effective: We feel the immediate relevance of science and technology as we would not if faced with technical drawings, graphs, and equations.

Dyson is especially concerned with the possibilities of using technology in the interest of social justice, that is, to help the least advantaged in society, rather than to make the better-off still more privileged. Here is where his three chosen technologies are effective. Solar energy can be used to bring electricity to villages distant from central generating stations and power lines, although costs must still be brought down further. Dyson likes the case of a village on Guadalcanal that has electricity from solar energy but is still only accessible by canoe, a wonderful time warp of technologies. Dyson thinks that it will be possible to genetically engineer trees so that they will be much more efficient in converting solar energy to fuel, and perhaps so that they will produce liquid fuel directly. (He believes that trees might also be bred to use solar energy to generate useful products such as silicon chips for computers.) With solar energy and fuel from genetically engineered trees, places everywhere will have the energy they need to connect with the Internet, Dyson's third defining technology. He characteristically finds memorable phrases to set out our remaining tasks for the Internet: We have to find the right large-scale architecture (the right combination of land lines and satellite links), and we have to find out how to go the last mile, that is, how to reach the most disadvantaged.

Looking further into the future in the book's third essay, Dyson distinguishes between two purposes of space exploration, scientific investigation on the one hand and human exploration and adventure on the other, on the basis of time scale. Development and operation of technologies for the first relate to a relatively short time scale, say ten years; technologies for the latter involve a longer time scale, on the order of a century. (The manned shuttle that the United States now uses is an uneasy compromise, Dyson thinks, that isn't very good at achieving either objective.) Dyson's discussion of novel launching methods for spacecraft that might be developed (laser, ram jet, and "slingatron") gives us a good sense of how choices are made in technology on the basis of costs and practicality. Many will find the most exciting section of the book to be the discussion of human settlement of other parts of the solar system, notably comets in the Kuiper Belt (outside the orbit of Neptune). Comets are largely ice and therefore better suited to settlement than something made of rock. One of the main techniques of settlement would depend on genetic engineering: the development of plants that grow their own greenhouses.

For the longer future, Dyson also considers problems of genetic engineering in humans. For him an area of particular concern is the technology of "reprogenetics" that would enable parents (wealthier ones, in a market system) to produce "better" children with the right genes. On artificial intelligence, Dyson ponders the defeat of the chess champion Gary Kasparov by the computer Big Blue in 1997 and recognizes that we cannot think in sterile fashion of human versus machine, but rather must be creative in seeing that humans are assisted by machines.

This is a fine volume for readers generally interested in science and policy. Dyson's folksy manner enables him to provide the layman with an extraordinary amount of information and insight in a brief book; we come away with our appreciation of his ideas enhanced by knowing that his grandfather, a blacksmith, made boilers for steam engines, while three generations later his daughter earned some of her medical school fees by helping to compile DNA information. Especially at a time of extraordinarily rapid scientific and technological change such as our own, one might wish to discover a volume of this quality every few years.

Freeman J. Dyson (1923–), *The Sun, the Genome, and the Internet* (New York: Oxford University Press, 1999).

BOB ELLIOTT AND RAY GOULDING

Write If You Get Work: The Best of Bob and Ray

~

Bob Elliott and Ray Goulding met as young radio announcers at the Boston station WHDH (both were from Massachusetts), hit it off with their inventive sketches and friendly humor, and made a long career together in radio and television. Their routines, capturing the wonder, vexation, and silliness of the human condition, were shared among friends much as those of Garrison Keillor's *A Prairie Home Companion* were in a later generation. For most of their fans, Bob and Ray were simply uproariously funny guys whose characters and routines became part of one's own life. For professional writers and entertainers, they were renowned for their perfect timing and grasp of the possibilities of their media. It is thus no surprise that the introduction to this volume is by the writer Kurt Vonnegut.

Write If You Get Work contains some four dozen beautifully structured, very funny short sketches. One of the many nice things about this book is that, good as it is, you don't need to feel you should hold back from reading it all in one sitting—the sketches hold their quality so well that you can enjoy them again and again. Fans will find their favorites here, including the hapless ace reporter Wally Ballou, who never quite manages to have the mike switched on at the right moment and thus always comes on the air as "—ly Ballou." Among our favorites in this volume are several episodes of Bob and Ray's soap opera parody, *Mary Backstayge, Noble Wife* (heartrending episodes galore, a takeoff on a genuine radio program that had an audience of millions in its heyday); an interview with Fentriss Synom, an entertainer who does food and drink imitations (at the suggestion of his agent he moved on from tree and furniture imitations); and the Charley Chipmunk Club, in which friendly Uncle Edgar's (Ray's) earnest efforts to teach the kids outdoor skills are interrupted by Bob, the smarmy spokesman for the commercial sponsors.

A typical piece is Wally Ballou's late-breaking story from Times Square, an interview with a cranberry grower. Ward Smith is, it seems, a great grower but not much of a salesman. For some reason, setting the berries in boxes and trying to sell them for folks to eat like strawberries doesn't work. He is amazed and grateful to a somewhat impatient Ballou for telling him that cranberries work well in juice (that's *j-u-i-c-e*, according to a mildly miffed Ballou, while Smith laboriously spells it out in a notebook) and in sauce. This piece shows Bob and Ray's style perfectly. Everyone is trying hard—Smith is, after all, a fine grower, and Ballou is doing his best to give the folks in radio land this late-breaking story from Times Square. And no one gets overly angry—Ballou evinces only a mild vexation at Smith, to whom he is so helpful. Moreover, Bob and Ray's characters and their situations stay with us for a long time. It's hard to walk through Times Square without thinking of —ly Ballou, or to drive past a cranberry bog without recalling the earnest cranberry grower.

Bob and Ray's humor moved easily between platforms, as we would say in the computer age. In part this is due to their careful craftsmanship, and in part because their humor deals with fundamental human situations rather than, say, with visual effects. From a technical standpoint, their start in radio gave them insights into the importance of understanding the medium, and they moved very well to television. Perhaps more surprisingly, their comic sketches transfer beautifully to the printed page. (Some of the sketches in this book include radio soundman instructions—"theme music: establish and under"—that are used to frame the situations.) We happened to see their Broadway show of some years ago, *Bob and Ray: The Two and Only,* and they were effective on the stage as well. They managed to overcome—or to use effectively—the artifice of the theater to project themselves as the same old Bob and Ray, just two guys telling funny stories.

Reading *Write If You Get Work,* we realize that the deepest impact of Bob and Ray's humor is its reflection of the human condition. We come to see that there is probably something of Ward Smith in all of our lives—some piece of our existence where, in fact, we've been trying to sell cranberries in boxes like strawberries, and we are grateful to Elliott and Goulding, the two old Boston radio men, for showing us this.

Bob Elliott (1923–) and Ray Goulding (1922–1990), *Write If You Get Work: The Best of Bob and Ray* (New York: Random House, 1975). Out of print.

RALPH WALDO EMERSON
"The American Scholar" and "Self-Reliance"

~

Ralph Waldo Emerson was the most prominent and influential American intellectual of the nineteenth century. Born in Boston, the son of a well-known Unitarian minister, he attended Harvard and then, as expected, followed his father's footsteps to the pulpit. He soon resigned his ministry, however, when he found that he was unable to administer the Christian sacraments with full faith and conviction. Thereafter, for the rest of his long and agreeable career, he was famous as a poet, philosopher, essayist, and, especially, as a spellbinding public speaker.

The "Sage of Concord," as newspapers liked to call him, was a source of particular American pride as a home-grown thinker who could hold his own with the great minds of contemporary Europe; he was known to be a friend of the great Thomas Carlyle and to be well thought of by Coleridge and Wordsworth. He was a visible symbol that America (still a very young country) had arrived on the stage of world influence in arts and letters.

In American intellectual circles, Emerson was known particularly as an advocate and spokesman for transcendentalism. This was a rather loosely defined religious and philosophical doctrine that argued that God was to be found primarily in nature and the individual soul, rather than in specific deities or individual religious leaders such as Jesus and Muhammad. Transcendentalism drew from a number of philosophical sources, including European Romanticism, the radical religious doctrines of Emanuel Swedenborg (famous at the time, though now largely forgotten), and classical Indian religion and philosophy. (Emerson, a multiculturalist ahead of his time, was fond of reading the *Bhagavad Gita*.) Emerson was for several years in the early 1840s the editor of the transcendentalist journal *The Dial* and a friend and supporter of another prominent transcendentalist thinker, Henry David Thoreau.

Emerson's reputation and influence lasted well beyond his lifetime (he died in 1882), but nowadays his works are no longer widely read, and he has become more a topic in American-studies courses than a vital presence in American thought. This, we think, is unfortunate, because Emerson still has much to offer. He was a very good writer whose works can be read with real pleasure.

We recommend that you begin your reading of Emerson with two short pieces, "The American Scholar" and "Self-Reliance." These together amount to only about fifty pages of text, but they are enough to occupy an evening. There are several reasons to take them slowly. One is their language. American English has changed enough in the past century and a half so that Emerson's language takes a bit of getting used to, and even when they were composed these pieces would have been recognized as being in a high rhetorical style that was quite different from everyday speech. On the other hand, the language of these essays is one reason for reading them: Emerson regarded himself as first and foremost a poet, and in his prose, as in his poetry, he paid careful attention to the rhythm and music of language. Give yourself time to savor his sentences.

Another reason for taking these pieces slowly is that Emerson's style of argumentation owes more to the pulpit than to the court of law: His aim is to persuade you to his opinion, not to prove a case. His reasoning is not always airtight or consistent, and he will sometimes drop one thread of argument and pick up another in ways that require the reader to join him in leaps of reasoning. No matter. With Emerson, in the end one feels that one is in the presence of a powerful preacher and a formidable intellect, and that he has things to tell us that are both interesting and important.

"The American Scholar" is an oration (how much more impressive than a mere speech!) delivered to the Phi Beta Kappa honor society at Harvard in 1837. In it, Emerson presents a declaration of American intellectual independence from Europe and urges his young listeners to guard against simply ingesting the received knowledge of the past. He argues that there are three sources of true scholarship, nature, books, and action, and that all three are necessary for creating new knowledge for the present and the future. This rousing call to a vigorous life is a fine antidote to the passivity of much of our leisure activity today.

"Self-Reliance" (1841) is a more ambitious essay that argues for the rejection of all external influences on individual action. Self-reliance here does not simply mean, as one might think, being independent of external financial support (as parents might use the term in urging their child, recently graduated from college, to get a job), but a far more comprehensive doctrine that depends on the transcendentalist idea of God manifested in the individual soul. Emerson believed that the soul intrinsically knows what is right, and therefore the key to both individual and social perfection is for people to cultivate their own nature regardless of the opinions and influences of others. This is a stern and demanding doctrine, and also a wildly optimistic one; many will disagree with it, but Emerson argues his views powerfully and invites one to wrestle with them in a way that truly stimulates the mind.

If you would like to spend another evening with Emerson after you have read these two essays, we recommend "Nature," "Experience," and "The Divinity School Address," a commencement speech that, in its disregard for conventional Christian dogma, so shocked the faculty of the Harvard Divinity School in 1838 that forty years would pass before Emerson was invited to speak at Harvard again.

Ralph Waldo Emerson (1803–1882), "The American Scholar" and "Self-Reliance." Various nineteenth-century editions, collected in *The Complete Works of Ralph Waldo Emerson* (Boston: Houghton Mifflin, 1903–4). Many modern hardcover and paperback editions of Emerson's works are available. All of the speeches and essays mentioned above are included in the convenient Penguin Classics paperback (1982) *Ralph Waldo Emerson: Selected Essays.*

F. SCOTT FITZGERALD
The Great Gatsby

~

The Great Gatsby is frequently found on college reading lists; of our one hundred books, perhaps it is the one that most of our readers have already read. It is by common consent one of the best American novels ever written. It is worth reading again free from the pressures of essays and examinations that surround it in a college English course. On reacquainting yourself with the book, you will be surprised at how short it is: F. Scott Fitzgerald was at his pinnacle in combining tautness and lyricism in *The Great Gatsby*. The structure and integration of the novel are exceptional, and as you read you will find that there seems to be something quotable on every page.

The story takes place in the wealthy suburbs on the North Shore of Long Island, to the east of Manhattan, and in the city itself, during the summer of 1922. The summer, and especially the summer evenings, can be truly beautiful in this area, filled with flowers, light breezes, and the view of boats on the water. Through his narrator, Nick Carraway, Fitzgerald moves the novel along smoothly and knowingly. Nick is a Midwesterner, a Yale graduate, and a veteran of World War I; he has come back East to learn the bond business. By chance he rents a small house next to the palatial mansion of Jay Gatsby, in West Egg (in fact Great Neck). Across the bay to the east lies the more fashionable East Egg (Manhasset), where Daisy, Nick's second cousin once removed, lives with her husband, Tom (an enormously wealthy former Yale football star). Gatsby hides his blighted small-town past, and has a real war record as well as highly successful if shady and dangerous operations of the sort that seemed integral to the freewheeling Twenties. He has purchased his mansion, and made it a center of endless parties, in a doomed attempt to impress and recapture Daisy, whom he loved as a young army officer before she married Tom. The boorish and prejudiced Tom creates problems for himself and everyone else with his womanizing; indeed, most of the characters, including a young woman golfer, Jordan Baker, with whom Nick has a brief relationship, are troubled.

Fitzgerald deftly weaves the pieces of the story together with artful asides by Nick. Hope as we will for matters to work out with a measure of grace, Gatsby and others either meet disastrous fates or, perhaps worse, march on in life wallowing thoughtlessly in their flaws. Summing up, Nick makes the observation about Tom and Daisy that is the most famous quote from the novel: "They were careless people . . . they smashed up things and creatures and then retreated back into their money or their vast carelessness or whatever it was that kept them together, and let other people clean up the mess they had made."

A charming aspect of rereading *The Great Gatsby* is knowing that much of the physical setting of the novel remains as it was. If you are in New York and have time, you can visit the wealthy suburbs of the North Shore with their enormous houses, and you can drive into Manhattan across the Queensboro Bridge or take the train into the city. Manhattan is of course very different in some ways (*Gatsby* predates most of the famous skyscrapers), but there are parts of Fifth Avenue, Park Avenue, and the Wall Street area that echo closely the look of the city at the time the characters drove and walked about. (And the bond business is still in Manhattan.) The Valley of Ashes, which the characters cross by train or car when going into the city, is now the site of Flushing Meadows–Corona Park, Shea Stadium (where the New York Mets play), and the National Tennis Center.

This is a truly beautiful book; once you have read it outside of the structure of a college course, you will make it one of the books you read several times over the course of your life. In returning to *The Great Gatsby* (or, indeed, any fine book), we deepen our appreciation and understanding both of the book itself and what it says about the lives and circumstances of ourselves and those we know. The novel has been the subject of endless analysis, some of which you might wish to look into. However, the best thing is just to read—this is superb writing. A special treat is to read *The Great Gatsby* and then immediately move on to Ernest Hemingway's *The Sun Also Rises* (p. 105), a book that in some ways is its only competition from the Jazz Age.

F. Scott Fitzgerald (1896–1940), *The Great Gatsby* (New York: Charles Scribner's Sons, 1925). Widely available in various hardcover and paperback editions.

JANET FLANNER

Paris Was Yesterday: 1925–1939

~

Janet Flanner was born in Indianapolis, attended the University of Chicago, was a reporter on the *Indianapolis Star*, and then joined the crowd of young Americans in Paris in the 1920s. Harold Ross, the editor of *The New Yorker*, asked her to accept an assignment that some would think the best job on the planet: writing a fortnightly "Letter from Paris" for the magazine.

Paris Was Yesterday is a collection of Flanner's best work from the first years of her assignment, from 1925 through 1939. Flanner's letters (under the pen name Genêt) were written in the context of a very different time. The cultural and literary worlds were much smaller than they are now, and Paris (and London as well) was much more important to American cultural life than it or other foreign cities are today.

The American expatriates went to France for culture, because of experiences in World War I (which was to have been the war to end war), for good food (and drink, since Prohibition was in force in the United States), and for freedom in personal life. It was a time of cultural, personal, and financial optimism. Communication, other than by direct personal contact, was primarily by the written word, so that those who were lucky had friends in Paris who would write to them about life there; those who were very lucky subscribed to *The New Yorker* and read their letters from Janet Flanner. She had the gift of writing as if each reader were the individual recipient of her letters, and this ability to include everyone in the conversation was an important element in her success. Even now, we feel in reading Flanner's work that we are there, too.

The cultural dazzle of Paris in the 1920s was, in retrospect, almost too great to comprehend. There was Diaghilev's Russian Ballet, with sets by what seems to be the whole roster of modern artists; there was George Gershwin at the piano for the Paris premiere of *Rhapsody in Blue*; there was Josephine Baker in her sensational revue; there was Sylvia Beach, proprietor of the bookstore Shakespeare and Company and publisher of James Joyce's *Ulysses* (p. 130); there were Gertrude Stein and Alice B. Toklas; there was Ernest Hemingway at the time of the publication of *The Sun Also Rises* (p. 105); and dozens of other luminaries. Flanner knew most of the people involved, and she seems to have recorded everything. Her style was appreciative but usually came with an edge of critical assessment that provided depth, and it was well adapted to the needs of journalism. For example, she had the knack of using the occasion of a birth or death anniversary or a funeral to write compellingly about an individual and his or her cultural impact. (The essay in this collection on the great American dancer Isadora Duncan, buried in Père-Lachaise, is lovely and sad; the essay at the death of Edith Wharton (p. 296) is a fine example of Flanner's incisive critical intelligence.)

While not shy of putting her native land in perspective (she reminds us that when the Pilgrims were still roughing it in Massachusetts the Duc de Saint-Simon was stepping it at fancy balls at Marly and Versailles), Flanner always kept a sharp eye out for the idiosyncracies of the French. To take merely the topic of interment, a substantial matter in France, we learn that Clemenceau, twice prime minister and France's representative at the Paris Peace Conference, wished to be buried upright, a position that Flanner notes suited the great combatant's moral qualities. (She leaves it to the reader to infer that few other French politicians of the time could claim the same.) The coffin of Claude Monet, tireless fighter for his art and man of the people, is taken to his grave in Giverny, the village in which he had the marvelous garden that he painted so often, by two peasants using a handcart. And Lucienne Bréval, the great French Wagnerian soprano, gets in last licks at her enemies (cultural wars, then as now, being of surpassing importance in France) by leaving a detailed list of those who were to be invited to her funeral.

After the stock market crash in 1929, political infighting in France, the rise of Hitler, and preparations for war, Flanner's reports remain rich and incisive, but their tenor changes: There is less glitter and more apprehension. Her reports of the developments of the 1930s can be frightening, and our dismay at reading these pieces is greater because we know the outcomes of the events of which she writes. Her description of Nazi anti-Semitism and Jews fleeing Germany in 1933 could hardly have left anyone in doubt that worse was to come. She reports both on subsidiary but terrible happenings, such as the flood of Catalan refugees into southern France after the collapse of the Spanish Republic, and on the main event. She writes, in a tone both hopeful and disappointed, of the 1938 "Peace in Our Time" conference in Munich, in which the unprepared democracies showed themselves all too willing to temporize at others' expense. She writes of rapid preparation for war and of the possibility of the United States coming in sooner this time. The last piece in the book is entitled simply "War in Our Time"; it is dated a few days after the German invasion of Poland. Flanner left France for the United States and returned in 1944, the year of the Liberation. The great years of Americans in Paris were gone, but we are grateful to Flanner for preserving them for us. Her letters were the product of an acute intelligence focused on culture, society, and politics with wit and sophistication.

Most of Flanner's marvelously rich and evocative work has been collected in books of essays and reportage; we like especially *Janet Flanner's World: Uncollected Writings 1932–1975* (1979). Flanner also wrote a novel and translated works from the French. A reminiscence of Flanner and her longtime love, Natalia Danesi Murray, by Murray's son William, was recently published.

Janet Flanner [Genêt] (1892–1978), *Paris Was Yesterday: 1925–1939*, ed. Irving Drutman (New York: Viking, 1972). The Harvest Books paperback reprint (1988) is in print but not easy to find. William Murray's memoir is *Janet, My Mother, and Me* (New York: Simon & Schuster, 2000).

E. M. FORSTER

Where Angels Fear to Tread

~

E. M. Forster was born in London, the only child of a comfortably wealthy family. His father died when he was still an infant, and he was raised by his mother in the attractive country house he would later celebrate in his novel *Howards End*. He attended King's College, Cambridge, and after graduation lived for several years in Italy and Greece. His early experience with the open emotionalism of Mediterranean culture, compared to the British habit of emotional restraint, influenced him deeply. He lived in India from 1912 to 13; after serving with the Red Cross in Alexandria, Egypt, during World War I, he returned to India for another extended visit in the early 1920s. These experiences, too, had a profound effect on his outlook on life.

Forster's reputation as one of the greatest novelists of the twentieth century is based on only six novels, written over the course of a twenty-year period early in his life. *Where Angels Fear to Tread* (1905) was the first; the last and arguably the greatest of his novels was *A Passage to India* (1924). (*Maurice,* which deals openly with homosexuality, was written in 1913–14 but was suppressed by Forster during his lifetime; it was published posthumously in 1971.) Following his early burst of literary creativity and frequent travel and residence abroad, Forster settled down to live quietly in London and Cambridge, where he became loosely associated with the Bloomsbury group of artists and writers. His later writing focused on literary criticism, essays, and biography; his *Aspects of the Novel* (1927) remains a brilliant guide to both the writing and the reading of fiction.

Where Angels Fear to Tread, like the better-known *A Room with a View* (begun at around the same time but not published until 1908), draws heavily on Forster's youthful years in Italy.

As both of us have observed during extended periods of living abroad, few things can create so jaundiced a view of one's own countrymen as seeing them in action as tourists. Forster's upbringing had taught him all that he needed to know about the hypocritical, narrow-minded gentility of Victorian England; in Italy he had ample opportunity to observe, and feel embarrassed by, English travelers behaving in ways that were boorish, overbearing, ignorant, and generally appalling. One of the most powerful themes in Forster's novels is the propensity of the British (rulers of an empire, as they liked to remind themselves, upon which the sun never set) to trample on the sensibilities of "foreigners." (A foreigner, of course, was anyone who had the bad luck or bad judgment not to be born an Englishman; it would not have occurred to many English travelers abroad that they themselves were, for the time being, foreigners.) Forster, whose views were much more broad-minded, used his novels to hold up a mirror to his English audience in which they could see their attitudes and behavior reflected. Even today these images remain compelling.

Where Angels Fear to Tread starts as a domestic comedy but soon develops into something much more substantial. The book begins with Lilia Herriton embarking for a year's sojourn in Italy, accompanied by a plain, sensible young paid companion, Miss Abbott. Lilia is the young widow of Charles Herriton and the mother of little Irma, and it is for the sake of Irma's future that Lilia has been taken in by her disapproving mother-in-law. Mrs. Herriton, a fiercely narrow-minded exemplar of the British upper middle class, presides over the social life of her small town of Sawston with an iron hand and dominates the lives of Lilia and her own two surviving children—sour, bigoted Harriet and ineffectual, romantic Philip.

Lilia is being sent abroad because she has developed an unsuitable affection for an impoverished clergyman, Mr. Kingston; it is thought that a year in Italy will induce her to forget about him. She forgets quickly, but for an unthinkable reason: She has met and fallen in love with Gino Carella, a young Italian of no social standing whatsoever. Philip is dispatched to Italy to rescue her, but by the time he arrives the marriage has already taken place; Miss Abbott has treacherously encouraged Lilia in her mad pursuit.

The marriage, not surprisingly, is an unhappy one; Lilia realizes sorrowfully that she has made a mistake. When she dies in childbirth, leaving Gino with a healthy son, Mrs. Herriton is appalled but washes her hands of the whole situation. When, however, Irma learns (via a postcard from Gino) that she has a little brother, and the news spreads throughout Sawston, Mrs. Herriton is forced to take action: Harriet and Philip are sent to Italy to save the child from the unspeakable fate of being raised as an Italian. The Herritons conduct themselves abominably (convinced all the time of the rightness of their course); only Gino retains his dignity, and only Miss Abbott her honesty, but they are powerless to stop the forces arrayed against them. What had begun as comedy ends in tragedy and uncomprehending dismay for all concerned.

All of Forster's novels have a bittersweet quality to them; he writes not so much of happiness as of people striving to be happy. All of them, in one way or another, exemplify Forster's most famous phrase (from *Howards End*), his plea to "only connect." We think you will want to read all of Forster's novels; we also recommend to you one of his least known but most charming books, *The Hill of Devi* (1954), an account of his youthful experience as private secretary to the ruler of a small Indian principality.

E[dward] M[organ] Forster (1879–1970), *Where Angels Fear to Tread* (Edinburgh: William Blackwell and Sons, 1905; New York: Alfred A. Knopf, 1920). Most of Forster's novels are readily available in various editions; the Bantam Classics paperback of *Where Angels Fear to Tread* (1996) is a convenient edition. The Harcourt paperback reprint of *The Hill of Devi* is in print but hard to find.

JOHN KENNETH GALBRAITH

Name-Dropping

~

John Kenneth Galbraith has been one of the best-known social scientists of our time and is certainly one of the best writers among them. Born in Iona Station, Ontario, Canada, he came to the United States for graduate work at the University of California, Berkeley, moved on to Harvard and government work, and has had a distinguished career spanning more than six decades. *Name-Dropping* is a series of linked remembrances of people he knew and (mostly) worked with, beginning with Franklin Delano Roosevelt and Eleanor Roosevelt, through Harry S. Truman, John F. Kennedy, Lyndon Johnson, and others. There are also reminiscences of Canadian leaders (especially William Lyon Mackenzie King and Lester Pearson) who deserve to be better known in the United States, and of British political leaders as well.

This collection of essays includes the trademark Galbraith wit and affectionate and less-than-affectionate memories, but it is more than that. It is an introduction to a range of political, social, and economic issues, including Galbraith's own ideas, and it provides as well insight into the actual process of government and politics as it proceeds through the influence and friendship of a large number of people.

Galbraith's career had several important elements: his distinguished work in the field of economics as a professor at Harvard; service in government during World War II as the deputy head of the Office of Price Administration, responsible for maintaining price stability amidst wartime pressures; later as President Kennedy's ambassador to India; and as friend, advisor, and speechwriter to the mighty. All of these provide material for his reminiscences in this book.

Franklin Delano Roosevelt and Eleanor Roosevelt, who may be said to be Galbraith's heroes, are remembered with great affection. He likes President Roosevelt for his ability to lead in complex and challenging circumstances both in depression and in war, and Eleanor Roosevelt for her concern for the disadvantaged. John F. Kennedy and Jackie are much admired, Kennedy for his hardheaded self-awareness and Jackie for her astute assessments of people on whom the president could rely. Lyndon Johnson is praised for domestic actions and heavily criticized for what Galbraith sees as his inability to understand the meaning and costs of war in Vietnam.

In all of his sketches, Galbraith brings to bear his aptitude for finding the remembered moment or phrase that captures a person or a situation. Galbraith has always been known for his wit and irony, and as one of us can attest from graduate days, even friendly criticism from the professor had its sting. The most quoted exchange from *Name-Dropping* is one that puts Galbraith himself in perspective. On his appointment as ambassador to India, Galbraith remarked to Kennedy that he couldn't see why *The New York Times* felt it necessary to call him arrogant. "I don't know why not," said Kennedy. "Everyone else does." Jawaharlal Nehru, the great Indian independence leader and prime minister, was a friend. Nehru was devoted to Trinity College, Cambridge, where Galbraith had also been in residence for a time, and said to Galbraith, "I am the last Englishman to rule in India." And there are the small ironies of history. Galbraith and President Richard Nixon had, it is fair to say, a relationship that fell well short of friendship, and Galbraith here takes perhaps more glee than he should in reporting that the former president, as an unknown young lawyer, drafted letters for Galbraith to sign at the Office of Price Administration.

Galbraith has useful comments on policy and process. He observes that seasoned public servants can sometimes put aside serious differences to work effectively together, and he reports a call from President Johnson, after Galbraith had broken with him on the Vietnam War, asking him to put aside differences for the moment and come to Washington for some speechwriting, which he does. His assessments of Adlai Stevenson make Stevenson's weaknesses as a candidate clear and show how a devoted core of supporters can bring about the nomination of candidates who are not the strongest from the standpoint of a general election.

And there is the occasional agreeable corner-cutting that some-times works out in politics. President Kennedy and Prime Minister Lester Pearson agreed to appoint a bilateral commission of two mem-bers to work out the vexing question of air transit rights between the United States and Canada. To simplify matters, it seems, Kennedy ap-pointed the U.S. citizen Galbraith, and Pearson appointed the former Canadian Galbraith, thus making the professor the single member of a two-member commission. Galbraith deemed the commission's work highly satisfactory (very little dissension among the commissioners), and the results governed air transit between the two countries for some time.

It is fair to say that Galbraith has always leaned further toward government activism than most of his colleagues (no doubt in part because of the success of price controls in World War II), but in this volume the arguments and discussions touching on economic and so-cial issues are usually phrased so that one can see arguments on both sides. Published when Galbraith was past the age of ninety, *Name-Dropping* shows him not exactly mellowed, but endowed, one might say, with the long view; his favorable views of President Eisenhower and his realization of the limits of government intervention in India will be surprising to many.

What is so worthwhile about this book is that, in a very brief com-pass, we have portraits of leading figures and glimpses of key economic, political, and historical issues in a highly literate form that enables any reader to agree or disagree. If we had more books like this and fewer thousand-page tomes of ghosted remembrances by our public figures, we would all be much better informed.

Galbraith's most famous book is *The Affluent Society*, a considera-tion of economics in a situation of wealth rather than the grinding poverty that existed when much of early economic theory developed, but our favorite among his more than thirty other books is Galbraith's record of his service in India, *Ambassador's Journal*.

John Kenneth Galbraith (1908–), *Name-Dropping* (Boston: Houghton Mifflin, 1999).

GRAHAM GREENE
Our Man in Havana

~

Graham Greene was one of the most prolific and influential British authors of the twentieth century. A superb storyteller and literary craftsman, he was at home in several different types of novel, from light "entertainments" (his word) such as *Our Man in Havana* and *Stamboul Train* to serious and rather grim examinations of religious faith and moral failures such as *The Power and the Glory*. He also worked for long periods as a journalist and editor and produced a distinguished body of nonfiction work including literary, theatrical, and film criticism. Greene was widely read and admired by his fellow writers and had a correspondingly great influence on modern British literature. He led a psychologically conflicted and, by all accounts, not especially happy life, and it may be that his great outpouring of literary work should be seen as a lifelong, though unsuccessful, attempt to exorcize his own personal demons.

Greene was born in 1904, making him just too young to have direct military experience of World War I; he came of age in the period of disillusion that followed that bloody and inconclusive conflict. He attended Balliol College at Oxford University and after graduation embarked on a career as a journalist. In 1926 he converted from Anglicanism to Roman Catholicism, a key event in a long struggle with questions of religious faith and doubt. He traveled extensively and restlessly and lived abroad for long periods of time, which enabled him to create realistic settings for his novels in places as diverse as Cuba, Mexico, West Africa, and Southeast Asia.

Our Man in Havana is worth reading entirely for its own sake and also as a first taste of Greene's work. Its combination of cynical humor and biting contempt for political institutions and bureaucracies makes it distinctive, and it would be hard to imagine anyone else as the author of this book.

The plot concerns an inconspicuous and unimportant Englishman named Wormold, who for years has lived in Havana as the agent of a vacuum-cleaner company. He is not a happy man. His agency is doing poorly, because in unsettled times, when electric power has become unreliable, the market for vacuum cleaners has shrunk. His wife left him some years before, and he still misses her. His sixteen-year-old daughter, Milly, is an almost comically devout Catholic who nevertheless allows herself, with the careless indifference of the young, to be courted by the sinister Captain Segura of the political police.

One day, quite out of the blue, Wormold is accosted by a man named Hawthorne, who recruits him (or intimidates him) into becoming a British spy—"our man in Havana" for the British secret service. Hawthorne gives him a crash course in recruiting subagents, communicating in code, and various other aspects of spycraft; London is delighted to have Wormold on board.

Wormold finds it impossible to take any of this seriously. He is, however, well aware that the extra money he will be paid as a spy will make his life much easier. So he throws himself into the work with great energy, inventing a whole stable of subagents and filing reports from them, including alarming rumors of mysterious military construction projects in Oriente Province (supplemented with drawings of sinister-looking equipment, actually vacuum-cleaner parts drawn at gargantuan scale). Although he worries that his fraud will be detected, no such thing occurs; rather, his reports are received with utmost seriousness and his supposed importance as an agent soars. He is provided with a secretary (fortunately as cynical as Wormold himself) and a radioman (fortunately utterly bereft of imagination), and his career prospers.

Even lies can take on lives of their own, however, and some of the events that Wormold has fabricated become real through being taken seriously. Events lead to assassinations, an attempt on Wormold's own life, and a nasty confrontation with Captain Segura. Wormold's scheme finally collapses, but with no ill consequences for himself; this being an entertainment rather than one of Greene's more serious and pessimistic novels, all ends well for the people that we come to care about in the novel. This is, in other words, a comedy, but only barely.

The fact that Greene called this an "entertainment" does not mean that he did not wish it to be taken seriously in some respects. In particular, Greene, who had some personal experience working with the British Foreign Office, uses this novel to show his disdain for bureaucracies in general and intelligence services in particular. His portrait of the ignorance and credulity of intelligence "experts" is scathing, as is his (very accurate) depiction of how bureaucrats will do almost anything to avoid the appearance of being wrong.

This book also helps one to remember, after the passage of more than forty years, why Fidel Castro's Marxist insurgency found such fertile soil in which to grow. Greene portrays Cuba in the waning days of Fulgencio Batista's corrupt regime as being in equal parts an impoverished, oppressed agrarian backwater and a decadent, morally deracinated playground for foreign tourists. The portrait, if unflattering, rings uncomfortably true, and perhaps explains why some Cubans were willing to put up with privation and homegrown despotism in exchange for an end to foreign exploitation.

Greene was so prolific, and so good, that we feel hard pressed to limit our recommendations for further reading to just two or three books. For a diverse sampling, however, you might want to try a classic spy story, *Stamboul Train,* a more serious novel, *The Heart of the Matter,* and the *Collected Essays* and *Fragments of an Autobiography.*

Graham Greene (1904–1991), *Our Man in Havana* (London: Heinemann, 1958; New York: Viking Penguin, 1958). The Penguin paperback edition (1991) is readily available.

DASHIELL HAMMETT
The Maltese Falcon

~

Dashiell Hammett was born and raised near the shores of Chesapeake Bay in eastern Maryland. Like most American boys in the late nineteenth century, he received only an elementary education, leaving school at the age of thirteen to go to work. He drifted from one job to another before finding a niche to his liking as an operative for the Pinkerton Detective Agency. In eight years on that job, he acquired the experience, vocabulary, and point of view that would sustain him in a literary career as one of America's premier popular writers, and indeed as virtually the inventor of a new genre of crime fiction.

Prior to the 1920s, the detective novel was mainly a specialty of English writers in a tradition extending from Sir Arthur Conan Doyle through Mary Roberts Rinehart and C. K. Chesterton to Agatha Christie. The common element in the work of these writers is that every case is treated essentially as a puzzle to be solved by the detective, using mainly clever brainwork. The books of these authors were generally very decorous, with no sex, little violence, and few hints that crime in the real world was usually a gritty, nasty business far removed from the drawing rooms of English country houses. In his early pulp magazine stories, and then emphatically in his novels, Hammett reacted against this type of crime fiction, producing instead what came to be known as "hard-boiled" fiction, as gritty as one could want. (To some extent Hammett was taking the detective story back to its American roots, as his work contains clear echoes of the crime stories of Edgar Allan Poe.)

The Maltese Falcon was not Hammett's first published novel, but it is widely regarded as his best. It certainly is the book that brought him fame and fortune and established him as a major popular writer. (It was published in 1930, the same year in which Hammett began his lifelong relationship with the playwright and literary personality Lillian Hellman, a liaison that was the subject of much comment in the gossip columns of the time.) *The Maltese Falcon* featured one of Hammett's finest creations, San Francisco private eye Sam Spade.

Sam Spade is, as the genre requires, a tough loner who tries not to be beholden to anyone. He is willing to push the envelope of the law to its limits but is personally incorruptible. He is very attractive to women and not averse to sexual entanglements when opportunities for them arise, but he remains in a sense morally chaste, because he never allows romantic impulses to interfere with his handling of a case. He makes his living as a detective, but his personal independence, his sense of honor, and his devotion to an ideal of justice are more important to him than money. Spade, like his fictional cousins Philip Marlowe (Chandler, p. 33) and Travis McGee (MacDonald, p. 167), reflects an American ideal of manhood (with roots going back to earlier iconic figures like the mountain man and the cowboy) that serves to reinforce for readers of these books notions of how a real man should act. If today the role model seems in some respects dated—for example, by incorporating elements of male chauvinism and homophobia that are now at least obsolete and sometimes outright unpleasant, and by portraying a world in which everyone drinks a literally stupefying amount of alcohol—it still speaks to us enough to make these *noir* crime novels fascinating and entertaining reading.

The Maltese Falcon begins with a scene that would eventually become a cliché of the hard-boiled detective novel. Sam Spade is in his office doing nothing in particular when he is interrupted by the arrival of a new client, a very beautiful and mysterious woman. The woman in this case uses a number of different names, though eventually we know her mainly as Brigid O'Shaughnessy. She spins an implausible tale about wanting to rescue her sister from evil companions, and offers Spade a large retainer. He asks his partner, Miles Archer, to shadow whoever comes to Miss O'Shaughnessy's hotel that night. By the end of the night, Archer has been shot dead, as has the thug he was following. (Spade is notably unmoved by his partner's death; we learn that he didn't like him much and had earlier had an affair with his wife.) Miss

O'Shaughnessy disappears temporarily, and Spade's life is made uncomfortable not only by the inevitable police enquiries into the death of his partner, but by the arrival of several unpleasant characters. One is Joel Cairo, a floridly gay Middle Easterner (portrayed with the casually homophobic stereotypes of the time), who wants Spade to reveal where the lady has gone, and a weightier bad man in all respects, Mr. Gutman, who is accompanied by his bodyguard, the nasty young punk Wilmer.

With this cast of characters in place, we learn that everyone is after a fabulous relic, a solid gold, jewel-encrusted statue of a falcon (enameled black to disguise its value) made on the Mediterranean island of Malta centuries before by one of the Crusader knightly orders. O'Shaughnessy, Cairo, and Gutman had been allies from time to time in trying to acquire the falcon by fair means or foul, but there is no honor among these thieves, and each is trying to cheat the others out of their share. Several corpses later, the falcon is in fact recovered, but not without a surprise twist in the story. In the end, Sam Spade arranges the outcome in accordance with his own sense of justice, in part to avenge the unlamented Miles Archer. ("When a man's partner is killed he's supposed to do something about it. It doesn't make any difference what you thought of him. He was your partner and you're supposed to do something about it.") Sam Spade, his own man to the end, has little patience for unfinished business.

The 1941 movie version of *The Maltese Falcon*, which marked John Huston's directorial debut, is a wonderful example of a hard-boiled novel translated to the silver screen. Humphrey Bogart is in fine form as Sam Spade, and the film also features great performances by Sydney Greenstreet as Gutman and by Peter Lorre as Joel Cairo. As with Chandler's *The Big Sleep*, rent the movie after you've read the book.

Dashiell Hammett (1894–1961), *The Maltese Falcon* (New York: Alfred A. Knopf, 1930). Vintage Crime paperback reprint, 1992.

HELENE HANFF
84, Charing Cross Road

~

This charming memoir recounts one of the most heartwarming and improbable friendships in modern literature. The friendship, between a New York book lover and a London bookstore clerk, was carried out entirely by letter during a period of twenty years. Helene Hanff's book consists of a selection of a few dozen of those letters, reproduced exactly as sent and received, without further comment. By framing the book in that way, she gives her story a vividness and immediacy that perhaps could not have been achieved otherwise; certainly one finishes the book with a sense of having reaffirmed some deep truths about the nature of friendship and love.

Helene Hanff was born in Philadelphia but lived in New York City for her entire adult life and made her career there as a working writer. She seldom enjoyed any great success, but managed to make a living writing screenplays, television scripts, children's books, and short pieces for magazines such as *Ellery Queen's Mystery Magazine* and later (in more prosperous times) *The New Yorker* and *Harper's*. She was also a voracious reader, and it was through her appetite for books that she began to correspond with Frank Doel. Her first letter to the firm of Marks & Co., of 84, Charing Cross Road, London, dated October 5, 1949, begins: "Your ad in the *Saturday Review of Literature* says that you specialize in out-of-print books. . . . I am a poor writer with an anti-quarian taste in books and all the things I want are impossible to get over here." This elicited a prompt, polite response, assuring her that two of the books she had asked about were already on their way to her; the reply was signed simply, "FPD for Marks & Co." She was hooked as a customer; he became, probably mostly by default, the clerk principally responsible for dealing with her requests; and so letters flowed back and forth across the Atlantic. Before long "(Miss) Helene Hanff" became "HH" and then "Helene" (though if she was annoyed, it reverted to "MISS Hanff to you"); after a somewhat longer period (allowing for British reticence) "FPD" became "F. Doel" and then "Frank."

Friendship blossoms as we read. Sight unseen, she becomes a steady customer of the shop and comes to know its other clerks. She asks a friend in London to describe the shop for her and is delighted with the reply ("It is the loveliest old shop straight out of Dickens"). She has parcels of fancy food sent from Denmark to the bookshop staff, and they are received rapturously (in postwar Britain, everything was scarce and many things were rationed; the arrival at Marks & Co. of a tinned ham and some jars of preserves was a cause for genuine rejoicing). The staff in turn send her a book as a thank-you present; she is overwhelmed ("I've never owned a book before with the pages edged all round in gold").

As a writer, Hanff's best creation was herself, and her letters to Marks & Co. do not just reveal a person, but flaunt a persona. She loved being a New Yorker and played the city girl to the hilt: brassy, loud, opinionated, uninhibited, unafraid of anything. Part of her charm for her London audience must have been her unpredictability. Would a newly arrived letter be a purr of thanks for the latest treasure received, or a manic rant? "WHAT KIND OF A PEPYS' DIARY DO YOU CALL THIS? this is not pepys' diary, this is some busybody editor's miserable collection of EXCERPTS from pepys' diary may he rot. i could just spit." Cecily, Megan, and the other shop assistants must have wondered if they had suddenly been thrust into the presence of a madwoman, and as always it was up to Frank to frame a response: "Dear Miss Hanff, First of all let me apologize for the Pepys. . . ."

Always Frank is there, patiently replying to every demand ("SLOTH, i could ROT over here before you'd send me anything to read"), and as we read these letters we watch the blossoming of an extraordinary friendship. He takes infinite pains to find the books she wants and to educate her about book collecting and the antiquarian book trade. Gradually he begins to share his life with her—his wife, Nora, their daughters, their vacations. Nora joins the correspondence with thanks for holiday packages and occasional pairs of nylon stockings. We see, just beneath the veneer of professional detachment and reserve that he thinks his business letters must maintain, Frank's strong and growing attachment for his irascible, demanding, demonstrative American correspondent. And Helene is totally smitten with her English friend.

Come over for a visit, urge Frank and the other shop workers. Travel plans are made, fall through, are postponed until another year; meanwhile the correspondence goes on for twenty years until . . . But we will not tell you what comes after that "until." This is a book to be read as an unfolding tale, one with a momentum and trajectory that must be discovered in the reading.

And truly it is a book that you must read; it would not be fair to deny yourself the pleasure. It is our great good fortune that Helene Hanff saved these extraordinary letters and was willing to share them with us.

Helene Hanff (1916–1997), 84, *Charing Cross Road* (New York: Grossman, 1970). Paperback reprint, Penguin Books (1990); there is also an attractive Moyer-Bell hardcover reprint (1995).

JOSEPH HANSEN
Fadeout

~

1970. Barely a year since the Stonewall riot. The gay pride movement was not much more than a hope. The idea that respectable bookstores such as Barnes & Noble would have gay and lesbian books sections would have seemed a joke. And in that year, Joseph Hansen created the first openly gay private investigator in the history of mainstream American crime fiction. It is hard to imagine now just how revolutionary that seemed at the time. But long after the novelty has worn off, the Dave Brandstetter mysteries continue to be exceptionally good reading, not because the hero is gay, but because he is a great character in an unusually interesting and intelligent mystery series.

Dave Brandstetter is in many ways a most unlikely crime-fiction hero. He is a middle-aged, well-to-do, cultivated death-claims investigator for an insurance company. He doesn't make a big deal about being openly gay; it's just who he is. He hates guns and is deeply averse to violence. His job consists of investigating suspicious deaths on behalf of his clients, insurance companies that will not pay a death claim if the terms of a life insurance policy have been violated. Without really intending to, in each novel he winds up discovering that things are not as they seem; usually he succeeds in identifying a murderer no one else suspects.

Throughout the series, he spends a fair amount of time on domestic pursuits: dining well at his friend Max Romano's restaurant, buying and remodeling a ramshackle house in the hills above Los Angeles, dealing with his insurance-executive father's death, and staying friends with several of his young, beautiful ex-stepmothers. We follow him through the trajectories of two serious, long-term love affairs. Reading about his life from book to book in the series, we realize that if Dave Brandstetter were a real person, we would very much like to have him as a friend. Few writers manage to create such a well-liked and well-rounded character, one who continues to interest readers decades after his first appearance in print.

Fadeout is the first of the Dave Brandstetter novels, and it sets the tone for all of the others. We meet Dave at the wheel of his company car, on his way to begin a death-claims investigation. Fox Olsen, a popular singer and radio personality, is missing and presumed dead. His car has been found in a riverbed, apparently washed off the road by a flash flood. But Olsen's body has not been found, and Brandstetter believes that he may have faked his own death. Olsen, also a talented painter, has left behind a hint of a drastic change of mood—a painting, quite unlike any of his other work, of a looming, ominous wooden structure. Putting together a string of small and subtle clues, Brandstetter tracks Olsen to a nearly deserted town on an unfrequented stretch of the southern California coast, where a ruined entertainment pier looms over the scene just as Olsen had painted it. Olsen, we learn, had fled there with a long-lost love who suddenly reappeared after an absence of many years, but this attempt to recapture his youth quickly ended in tragedy. Olsen indeed is dead. For Dave, the adventure has an unexpected bright side: The handsome lover, Doug Sawyer, is destined to play a big part in his life (as is a young television reporter, Cecil Harris, who makes a brief appearance in these pages) in future books in the series.

With *A Country of Old Men*, the eighth of the Brandstetter books, Joseph Hansen decided to bring the series to a close; he ends that book with a dramatic finality that precludes any further installments. To his unhappy fans, he explained that he had said all he had to say in the Brandstetter series and that he wanted to leave the crime genre and devote himself to writing other kinds of novels. This perhaps was not a good decision. Hansen, who also had a career teaching writing in California, was a prolific author, with several more novels in his own name as well as under such pseudonyms as Rose Brock and James Colton, but none of his mainstream novels gained anything like the commercial and critical success of the Brandstetter books. In hindsight, it seems certain that Hansen's literary reputation will rest on the character and adventures of Dave Brandstetter.

Greedy for more as always, fans wish that Hansen had kept the Brandstetter series going for many more books, but it would be churlish not to express thanks for every one of the eight books in the series that he did give us. *Fadeout* is a great one-night read, and you may well wish to move right on to the other seven.

Joseph Hansen (1923–), *Fadeout* (New York: Harper and Row, 1970). The Holt, Rinehart and Winston paperback reprint (1980) can sometimes still be found; there is a new paperback edition from Alyson Publications (2000).

SEAMUS HEANEY (TRANS.)
Beowulf

~

Beowulf is the founding work of English literature, but it is a book that more people have heard of than have read. Some readers will remember struggling through it in a college English-lit course, slaving miserably over its nearly impenetrable Anglo-Saxon (a language closer to Danish than to modern English). Others may remember looking at older English translations, full of lines like "Oft Shield of the sheaf from scathing hordes / From many meinies their mead-stools tore," and thinking that they might as well be in Danish. Students accepted their professors' assurances that this is one of the most important classics in the literary canon, but it was pretty hard for them to actually understand how that could be so. And the editors of the fourth edition of *The New Lifetime Reading Plan* (one of us, in collaboration with Clifton Fadiman) reluctantly left *Beowulf* off their list of essential books, despite its obvious importance, for lack of a translation that they felt they could recommend with any enthusiasm.

Suddenly all that has changed. Seamus Heaney, the winner of the Nobel Prize for Literature in 1995, has produced a brilliant new translation of *Beowulf* that brings the poem fully to life for the modern reader. The publication of Heaney's *Beowulf* became a major literary event. The book spent weeks on the bestseller lists in both Great Britain and America and won England's prestigious Whitbread Prize for best book of the year. Heaney, an Irish poet from Ulster who writes in English and has been in recent years a professor at Harvard, is acknowledged as a master of poetry that crosses boundaries of time and culture; with his translation of *Beowulf*, he was acclaimed anew as the creator of a modern masterpiece.

Beowulf tells the story of a king whose long reign is marked at both its beginning and its end by battles with daunting monsters. As the tale opens, we learn of the plight of King Hrothgar of Denmark, whose splendid feasting-hall at Heorot has been ravaged by the depredations of the water monster Grendel. The beast comes to the king's feasting-hall by night, killing several of his warriors each time and carrying them off to eat. The narrative then tells of a boat full of heavily armed men crossing the wave-swept sea from Sweden to Denmark. Beowulf, king of the Geats, is on his way to help his neighbor and ally Hrothgar, both from a sense of obligation and to win the fame that a victory over the monster will bring. After a night of feasting and boasting, Beowulf stays alone in the hall to await the monster. Soon Grendel appears, and after a prolonged and bloody battle is overcome by the hero. (Grendel is immune to metal weapons; Beowulf mortally wounds him by tearing his arm off at the shoulder.) Grendel's mother, a monster as fierce as her son, arrives a few days afterward, seeking revenge on her son's killer, and Beowulf must fight and defeat her as well. Beowulf then returns home to enjoy a long and honored reign in his own kingdom.

Fifty years after his battle with Grendel, however, he is fated to fight again, this time against a dragon disturbed on the pile of gold on which it sleeps. Beowulf triumphs once more, but the battle drains his strength, and he dies soon afterward and is given a hero's funeral.

Beowulf was first composed by an Anglo-Saxon bard around A.D. 800; the oldest surviving version of the original is a manuscript dating from about 1000, now kept in the British Museum. The plot of the poem is fairly straightforward and uncomplicated, but the tale is one of immense power and dignity. What makes Heaney's version such a stunning achievement is that he does not gloss or paraphrase, but rather finds ways of cloaking the bones of the original in new literary flesh and sinew. His translation is masterly but unobtrusive; its main effect is to let the reader understand, at last, how truly great a poem *Beowulf* is—how beautiful the language, how artful the narrative technique, how exciting the story. Also, Heaney's version gives the reader a sense of the original by sticking close to its formal properties without ever sounding strained or artificial.

Anglo-Saxon bardic verse followed strict conventions that must be preserved if a translation is to give any sense of the original, and Heaney does this brilliantly. Each line is divided into halves, each half with two stressed syllables, and moreover with one of the stressed syllables of each first half line alliterating with a stressed syllable of the second (so, for example, *shield . . . scourge; wrecker . . . rampaging; foundling . . . flourish,* and so on). Anglo-Saxon poetry, like all Norse verse, is full of *kennings,* or poetic descriptive terms (a well-known example is *whale-road* for *sea*), and Heaney's *Beowulf* succeeds in making these terms seem fresh, lively, and well integrated into the richly rolling English of his translation.

This is a book that affords many pleasures. Readers of Tolkien's *The Hobbit* (p. 272) will find *Beowulf* a special treat, for the fight with the gold-hoarding dragon Smaug that is the climactic episode of *The Hobbit* is modeled precisely on Beowulf's final battle with the dragon that disturbs his realm. (This is hardly an accident, as Tolkien spent his whole career as a professor of early English literature at Oxford.)

In his long and very interesting introduction to the book, Heaney notes that he began his translation of *Beowulf* some years ago, but the project soon bogged down and he felt unable to complete it. Only when he realized that the language of the Anglo-Saxon original was in many respects similar in cadence, and even in vocabulary, to the speech of the blunt, plainspoken older men of his family in Ulster was he able to take up the project again, turning the ancient language of the epic into a mode of expression that he had known since childhood.

In the skillful hands of Farrar, Straus and Giroux, Heaney's *Beowulf* is published as a bilingual edition, a nice touch that allows the reader, if so inclined, to read, or even recite, the Old English text and compare the translation to it. The peculiar orthography of Old English, which contains several letters no longer in the English alphabet, takes some getting used to, but once that obstacle has been overcome it is fun to try to read the original poem aloud. Heaney's *Beowulf* is a book to savor.

Seamus Heaney, trans. (1939–), *Beowulf* (New York: Farrar, Straus and Giroux, 2000). For a definitive collection of Heaney's own verse, see his *Opened Ground: Selected Poems, 1966–1996*, published by Farrar, Straus and Giroux in 1998. A fine biography of the poet is *Seamus Heaney* by Helen Hennessy Vendler (Cambridge, Mass.: Harvard University Press, 1998).

ERNEST HEMINGWAY
The Sun Also Rises

~

Ernest Hemingway was born in Oak Park, Illinois, near Chicago. After high school, he worked as a reporter on the *Kansas City Star* and then joined a World War I volunteer ambulance unit in Italy. He was severely wounded, returned to Chicago as a journalist, and then left for Paris to work as both a reporter and a writer. He was a prolific novelist whose prose style at its best is taut, clear, and beautiful; *The Sun Also Rises* is his greatest work. A short novel, it is deceptively simple and straightforward, but it embodies layers of meaning and allusion that grow with each reading. Like Fitzgerald's *The Great Gatsby* (p. 77), with which it is often compared, it is a book that many of our readers have gone through in college; you will want to read it again.

Jake Barnes, the narrator, has been wounded in the war and has lost his sexual functioning as a result. Coming to terms with this in the intensely masculine framework of his world seems impossible, especially as he and Brett (Lady Ashley) allow themselves to think, at least sometimes, that if he were whole, life would be wonderful for them. It is not, however. Brett, an Englishwoman who lost her first love in the war, is a fearsome drinker, as is her current (unlikeable) fiancé, a Scot. Robert Cohn, a former Princeton boxing champ, hangs about as a minor writer; Bill Gorton, a friend and writer, visits from the States. The first part of the novel takes place in Paris, and then Jake and Bill go to Burguete, Spain, to fish in the Irati River. They meet up with the others at the fiesta and bullfights in Pamplona. (Here, Hemingway's love of bullfighting provides some of the best writing of an immensely well-written novel.) During the fiesta, Brett causes serious trouble for the great young torero, Romero.

Jake, a more or less practicing Catholic, is a sympathetic character, although we wonder quite why he likes Brett, other than her beauty, her need, and his own dislocation. The other characters are not especially likeable, most being prejudiced, self-referential, and heedless. One of Hemingway's gifts is that we are intensely interested in them even though we might not like them.

The setting of the novel is important in reading and understanding it. It is a post–World War I story. For the Europeans, this war meant tragic losses in men and women killed and lives destroyed; to Americans, it meant that also, but perhaps more: It was a great overseas adventure, a kind of coming of age of the country, rescuing Europe from its decadence, fighting a war to end war. Despite the psychological dislocations of the time, it was an age of financial strength and prosperity. And it was an age of newspapers—Jake Barnes' profession of newspaper reporter out of Paris was among the most important and privileged of the time. There was something else, too, that frames the action: In the Twenties, the wealthiest lived with an elaborate and well-functioning public transportation and communications system. As in the novel, lives were planned around train and boat departures, telegrams were sent, letters were delivered on time and forwarded as directed.

Hemingway's great gifts show in this book in his mastery both of description and of dialogue. The geography of European cities and countrysides is part of the story. The walk that Jake and Bill take one evening through Paris has surely inspired innumerable American students to retrace their footsteps, and in an age when travel writing that focused on great monuments was in vogue, Hemingway made intensely real for Americans the quiet European landscape of woods and farms (for example, in his description of the fishing trip). His dialogue is crisp and seems to say everything with a careful economy of words.

He ventures into humor here, too, with his depictions in English of conversations originally in French and Spanish. Jake's discussion with the manager of a bicycle racing team is marvelous ("Paris is the town the most *sportif* in the world"). Moreover, the masculinity and sexuality that Hemingway lost control over in his later writing, almost to the point of parodying himself, are just right here. Jake's wound is not often mentioned, given its seriousness, and we are left to draw our own conclusions about Jake, bulls, steers, and toreros.

The freshness of the novel is astonishing: It was published, to great acclaim, seventy-five years ago (1926) and with few exceptions reads perfectly today. Rereading it over the course of your career as a reader, you will see new things in it (and yourself) every time. We also like, as do many, Hemingway's short stories; for a second novel, we recommend *A Farewell to Arms*.

Ernest Hemingway (1898–1961), *The Sun Also Rises* (New York: Charles Scribner's Sons, 1926). Widely available in paperback in various editions.

George V. Higgins
The Friends of Eddie Coyle

∼

George V. Higgins began his career as a journalist, writing for the *Providence Journal* and other New England newspapers before deciding to become a lawyer. Following law school, he joined the Massachusetts District Attorney's office, and after several years became an Assistant U.S. Attorney in Boston. All the while he kept working at what he felt to be his true vocation, writing novels; reportedly he wrote fourteen, none of them published, before making a spectacular debut in print with *The Friends of Eddie Coyle*. Many critics at the time commented that Higgins' book seemed much too accomplished for a first novel, and they were right; it was his first published book, but he had been working up to it for a long time. (Once he broke into print, he continued to write prolifically; though he died at the comparatively young age of fifty-nine, he published a total of twenty-five novels.)

At some point during his long apprenticeship, he learned to create a truly distinctive style that combined his reporter's skill at compressing a story to its essentials, his prosecutor's sense of the shady, intertwined worlds of crooks and cops, and his own phenomenal ear for dialogue. These qualities give *The Friends of Eddie Coyle* its richness and depth and explain why its appeal extends well beyond the circle of crime-fiction fans to readers dazzled by the author's sheer virtuosity in the use of language. A Higgins novel is almost literally a feast of words.

Higgins had an extraordinary ability to capture on paper the sounds and cadences of Bostonian English in all of its subtle flavors and variations. *The Friends of Eddie Coyle* is written almost entirely in dialogue. Part of Higgins' genius was to know how to let his characters' voices carry a story through from beginning to end; the effect for the reader is like listening in on a series of private and somewhat scandalous conversations—a series of wiretaps, perhaps. Consider this sample:

> "Eddie don't like jail," Dillon said.
> "Well," Foley said, "very few guys do. I know quite a few that went to jail at one time or another and there wasn't more'n one or two of them that you could really say, that actually liked it, you know?"

That is precisely how guys talk to one another. Notice, too, how within two sentences Higgins captures exactly the right tiny nuance of distinction between the working-class criminal Dillon and the better-educated federal agent Foley. Boston, as both of us know from years of residence there, is a city where ethnicity looms large and where distinctions of class, wealth, neighborhood, and accent determine to a surprising extent how people relate to one another. Employing his skill in conveying such distinctions through a meticulous reconstruction of the way people actually speak to each other, Higgins was able to create for his readers a remarkably vivid sense of his city and its diverse inhabitants.

The Friends of Eddie Coyle tells of the downfall of one petty crook. Eddie Coyle does indeed have friends, but they don't trust him entirely, nor does he trust them, and all with good reason: In their world there is little honor among thieves. Eddie is willing to try his hand at most kinds of nonviolent crime to make a living. At the moment, his main racket is procuring guns for a group of more serious and violent criminals, but Eddie has a problem, too, and he thinks he may be able to develop a sideline to his gun business. He has recently been convicted in a truck hijacking and is facing sentencing; anxious to stay out of jail, he thinks, correctly, that a tip-off aimed at the right federal agent might earn him a good word with the prosecutor. Eddie manages to sell out an important gunrunner without implicating any of his own customers, but when a bank robbery goes wrong, some heavyweight bad guys also begin to think of how Eddie might have had an incentive to rat out his friends. These are people who are used to solving their problems in a fairly direct and uncomplicated way, and Eddie is suddenly in very deep trouble in a world where one tends not to get second chances.

The Friends of Eddie Coyle manages to seem like an absolutely authentic crime documentary and to be an artfully crafted entertainment at the same time, somewhat like a virtual-reality thrill ride where the thrills are incredibly real but you know that you can turn off the simulator when the game is over. This is a book to read first for its gripping story, and to reread from time to time for the pure pleasure of savoring its art.

George V. Higgins (1939–1999), *The Friends of Eddie Coyle* (New York: Alfred A. Knopf, 1972). Paperback reprint, Owl Books, 1995.

PATRICIA HIGHSMITH
The Talented Mr. Ripley

~

The Talented Mr. Ripley was published in 1955, and for most of the time since then it has enjoyed a modest but persistent success, a book best known to a devoted audience of fans of Patricia Highsmith's particular brand of creepy suspense fiction. Then the book's hero, Tom Ripley, suddenly became famous, thanks to the enormously popular film version of the novel released in 1999.

The basic story of the book is simple enough. Dickie Greenleaf, heir to a commercial fortune, is living in Italy with his girlfriend, Marge, and refuses to come home to take up his family responsibilities. Dickie's father mistakes Tom Ripley, a supreme egotist who for all his ambition is really not much more than a con man and a drifter, for an old friend of Dickie's, and bankrolls Tom for a trip to Italy to persuade Dickie to come to his senses. Tom (nothing if not a plausible liar and improvisor) ingratiates himself with Dickie, who finds him a nuisance sometimes but tolerates him enough to try to teach him about the finer things in life.

As Tom gains self-confidence, he begins to feel that he is Dickie's equal; more and more he resents Dickie's condescension, and eventually he decides that he would make much better use of Dickie's life than Dickie himself is doing. So Dickie has to go, and soon Ripley has, without much bother, committed his first murder. Thereafter, despite almost paralyzing fears of discovery, he switches back and forth between identities, being either Tom or Dickie as the need requires, killing again when he needs to, and finally, with the help of some inept police work, getting away with the whole caper. This story raises interesting issues of personal identity and how the normal assumptions of life can be threatened by someone who is willing to act in a wholly amoral way.

It also raises familiar but important questions about the relationship between books and films. While fine films can be made from novels (*The Godfather* comes to mind), in this case the film, with added characters, plot incidents, and even an extra murder, doesn't remotely reflect the quality of the novel. The reason goes to the heart of the meaning of books. Highsmith's novel succeeds far more than the film because of the powerful ability of the printed word to evoke the imagination and the emotions. Highsmith makes us feel to a startling degree how dangerous and menacing Tom is, how deeply mentally disturbed he is beneath the bland exterior that he puts on for the world to see, how he gets away, literally, with murder because no one he deals with can imagine what a monster this attractive young man really is. The available techniques of film, especially for a popular audience, make this much harder to achieve. The film version of *Ripley* thus cannot convey the psychological impact of the novel; this is true even though it will now be difficult for most people to imagine Tom Ripley without thinking of Matt Damon's handsome, troubled visage.

Menace lurking beneath a bland exterior was Patricia Highsmith's specialty. Born in Fort Worth, Texas, in 1921, she began her career as a struggling, impoverished member of the bohemian literary culture of Greenwich Village in the years just after World War II. She had a successful debut as a novelist in 1950 with *Strangers on a Train*, which was (in an exception to the rule) made into a celebrated film by perhaps the all-time greatest director of crime movies, Alfred Hitchcock. A macabre tale of two strangers who agree to commit murder on each other's behalf, the book and movie won Highsmith a lot of attention, but critical opinion was mixed—some reviewers found themselves unable to praise a book with so disturbing a moral tone. *The Talented Mr. Ripley* soon followed, with two sequels—*Ripley Underground* and *Ripley's Game*—again to great acclaim from Highsmith's fans but again condemned by some reviewers. In the case of the Ripley series, which continued with *The Boy Who Followed Ripley* and *Ripley Under Water*, it seems clear that some of the critical unease was a response to their subtheme of muted but obsessive homoeroticism. (Highsmith herself was gay.) Realizing that her work was selling better in Europe than in America and that she herself also felt more comfortable there than at home, she moved to Switzerland in the late 1960s and lived there until her death in 1996.

In the years since her death, Patricia Highsmith has gained increasing critical and public recognition as a master of psychological crime fiction. Her novels are hypnotically compelling, disturbingly entertaining, and hard to put down. *The Talented Mr. Ripley* and its sequels are a good introduction to the work of this underrated master.

Patricia Highsmith (1921–1996), *The Talented Mr. Ripley* (New York: Coward-McCann, 1955). A convenient edition is in *The Mysterious Mr. Ripley*, containing the first three novels of the Ripley cycle and published in paperback by Penguin in 1985.

JAMES HILTON

Lost Horizon

~

Few books succeed in adding a new word to the English language; *Lost Horizon* is one of them. *Shangri-la,* meaning a remote paradise of comfort, exotic beauty, and spiritual enlightenment, is the sort of word one might assume was incorporated into English a long time ago, perhaps on the basis of early European accounts of voyages of trade and exploration in the romantic East. In fact, it was invented by James Hilton as the name of the remote, and entirely imaginary, Tibetan monastery that is the setting for his fantasy adventure novel. *Lost Horizon* was a huge bestseller when it was first published in 1933, and it soon led to an equally successful film; the name, and the concept, of Shangri-la quickly passed into British and American popular culture.

Lost Horizon broke other new ground as well: It begins with what is almost certainly the world's first (though fictional) skyjacking. In other respects it is a traditional fantasy adventure in the footsteps of Jules Verne and H. Rider Haggard. Like many of the works of those authors, Hilton's novel is set within a framing story of several men sitting together (over drinks and cigars, of course) recounting the tale of an adventure that had befallen a mutual acquaintance. The reader is invited, as it were, to join the small group to hear a tale wherein truth is stranger than fiction, a tale vouched for by the reliability of the gentleman telling it to his friends.

Here we begin with a group at dinner in Berlin's Tempelhof Airport, where the talk naturally turns to aviation. Someone brings up the strange case of a plane that had been hijacked in the course of an operation to evacuate Europeans from Afghanistan to India in the midst of some disturbances in 1931. Another member of the group, Rutherford, claims to have encountered Conway, one of the passengers from the hijacked plane, in a remote part of China recently, and to have heard from him the whole story. Conway, says Rutherford, was in a mission hospital, ill, worn out, and suffering from amnesia. Rutherford helped to nurse him back to health and was rewarded by hearing a story stranger than he could ever have imagined. At that point, the group at Tempelhof breaks up; as he is leaving, Rutherford takes out of his bag a manuscript and hands it to the unnamed narrator of the book. What we are reading in the rest of the book is supposedly that manuscript.

The flight begins normally enough, but the four passengers soon realize that they are veering badly off course. An attempt to question the pilot is met with the silent display of a pistol; clearly the plane has been commandeered by someone other than its authorized pilot. When, many hours later, the plane crash-lands in a valley in what appears to be Tibet, the passengers are escorted to a remote temple and treated kindly. Their host at the temple is an elderly Chinese monk, who tells them that a supply caravan is expected to arrive soon; they make plans to return to the outside world when the caravan departs from the temple again. But after a while it becomes clear to them that this remote valley is a very strange place indeed (for one thing, the temple's abbot is well over two hundred years old) and that the monks of Shangri-la have no intention of letting their reluctant guests leave—ever.

The effect of this realization on the four hijacked passengers is at the heart of the story of *Lost Horizon*. The calm, competent Conway regards this development mainly with interest; Mallinson, a young British foreign service officer, begins to crack up; and Bryant (who early in the book we know as Barnard) is quite cheerful, for reasons of his own, to be a long way from conventional civilization. Miss Brinklow, of the Eastern Mission Society, confidently makes plans to find a way to leave and then return someday with fellow missionaries to convert the temple's monks, whose religious ideas she regards as highly unsuitable. But Shangri-la holds many surprises. As Clifton Fadiman wrote in *The New Yorker* when *Lost Horizon* was first published, this is "a yarn all aquiver with the most artful kind of suspense"; readers today, too, will race through these pages to see how things turn out.

But what makes *Lost Horizon* especially appealing is the concept of Shangri-la, which Hilton develops with great skill. He clearly took the trouble to learn something about Tibetan Buddhism and Chinese philosophy. Even the name *Shangri-la* is possibly derived from *Shambala*, which in Tibetan mythology denotes a hidden paradise. More important, the ideals of moderation and contemplation that the monks of Shangri-la advocate are entirely convincing, and as one reads, one becomes gradually aware that this is not only an adventure novel but an argument for a particularly broad and appealing spiritual vision. (One fine bit of wisdom from the abbot of Shangri-la: "Many religions are moderately true.") This is a book that offers an exciting and well-told tale as well as a satisfying and thought-provoking intellectual encounter.

Hilton published his second spectacularly successful book, *Goodbye, Mr. Chips,* in 1934, just a year after *Lost Horizon*; it is a sentimental (and, for modern readers, rather too saccharine) portrayal of a beloved English schoolmaster. In 1935, Hilton moved from England to Hollywood to work on the scripts for the movie versions of *Lost Horizon* (1935) and *Goodbye, Mr. Chips* (1939); both were highly successful.

Lost Horizon also deserves a footnote in American publishing history that attests both to its popularity and its influence: It was the first book published by Pocket Books, the pioneer publisher, and virtually the inventor, of the inexpensive paperback reprint. The success of that venture helped to make great books widely available in very inexpensive editions to unprecedented numbers of readers.

James Hilton (1900–1954), *Lost Horizon* (New York: William Morrow, 1933). The Pocket Books paperback reprint, first published in 1939, is now in its one-hundredth printing.

SHIRLEY JACKSON
The Haunting of Hill House

~

Shirley Jackson exploded onto the literary scene in 1948 with the publication in *The New Yorker* of her short story "The Lottery." In the intervening half century, "The Lottery" has become known as one of the best and most memorable of American short stories, but when it was first published it was greeted with shock, outrage, and almost universal condemnation. It tells what at first seems to be the ordinary and innocent tale of an annual lottery (the purpose of which is unclear) in a small New England town; the tale gradually takes on an indefinably threatening air of mystery, until finally we realize that the lottery is a rite of human sacrifice, with the "winner" stoned to death by the other villagers. Because the story offers no reason for the lottery and the killing, Jackson seems to be saying that random unfairness and murderous feelings exist as a matter of course beneath the surface of our normal, placid lives; for apparently holding those views, she was accused of gratuitous bad taste, slandering the traditional New England way of life, Satanism, and much else besides. She herself declined to explain anything about the story's meaning, and throughout her career as a writer of gothic horror tales and stories of psychological suspense she resisted writing or talking about her work, preferring to let it stand on its own and affect its readers as it might.

If Shirley Jackson's name is inextricably linked to "The Lottery," *The Haunting of Hill House* also plays a significant part in her enduring reputation as a fine and memorable writer. This is a short novel, and a fast one to read because the story impels the reader through the pages at a breathless pace. As with all of Jackson's work, it is not always entirely clear what is going on in the story, and most of the events depicted have more than one possible explanation; that quality of ambiguity is central to her talent as a writer.

As the book opens, Dr. John Montague is pleased to have discovered Hill House, an abandoned mansion on the outskirts of a scruffy New England village. A university professor who does research on psychic phenomena, he had been in search of a haunted house that he might investigate at length, and Hill House seems perfect for that purpose. He leases it for the summer and assembles a small research team to assist him: Luke Sanderson, nephew of the elderly owner of the house (who insists to Dr. Montague that a member of the family be present); a beautiful young woman known only as Theodora, reputed to have the power of extrasensory perception; and Eleanor Vance, from whose perspective the story is told. Eleanor is at best a rather neurotic personality and perhaps is much more psychologically disturbed than that. As we follow her in her drive from the city where she lives to Hill House, her eerie introspection makes us wonder whether anything perceived through her point of view can be relied upon.

No villager will come near the house (which has a reputation for driving people to commit murder or suicide) except for the maid, Mrs. Dudley, and she will not stay there after dark; she herself is an odd figure, almost mechanical in her speech and movements. The house (in many ways the main character of the story) chills and disturbs all of the researchers when they arrive there. When Eleanor first sees it, she thinks, "Hill House is vile, it is diseased; get away from here at once." But of course the house fascinates as much as it repels, and no one from the party leaves. They settle in uneasily and soon are more than rewarded in their quest for ghostly phenomena; Hill House is more malevolent, and more frightening, than they could have imagined.

But is that really so? A week passes, we are told; to the reader, though, the events of the book seem to have taken place over a longer period than that. Perhaps time itself is elastic in the warped environment of Hill House. Anxiety mounts among the members of the research group, exacerbated by subtle sexual tensions that enmesh Eleanor, Theodora, and Luke (Eleanor obsessively thinks of the line "Journeys end in lovers' meeting," from Shakespeare's song "O Mistress Mine").

Near the end of the novel, Dr. Montague's wife arrives to join the party for a few days. Mrs. Montague is a bossy, domineering harridan, laughable and disagreeable at the same time, but she is no fool, or at least not a fool in every way, and with her arrival some of what we thought we knew about Hill House is called into question. If Mrs. Dudley is such a creepy figure, why do she and Mrs. Montague find it so easy to converse in perfectly ordinary and civil terms? Why is Mrs. Montague so immune to the ghostly racket that shakes the house at night? Is it true, after all, that everything that has occurred is a figment of poor Eleanor's overwrought imagination? But then it turns out that Hill House is going to claim a victim after all. . . .

Even if one is not disposed to believe in ghosts, this is a book that will send a shiver up one's spine. It is a fine entertainment, in the way that spooky stories told around the campfire were part of the fun of camping trips in one's youth. But it is more than that; Jackson is asking us to look at the nature of fear and the irrational by setting us, as we empathize with Eleanor, in a situation that does not seem to admit of conventional, rational explanations. She does not make things easy for us by explaining what is happening. We have to figure it out for ourselves. But she does perhaps provide a clue, in the words of Dr. Montague: "No ghost in all the long histories of ghosts has ever hurt anyone physically. The only damage done is by the victim to himself."

The Haunting of Hill House was made into a very good and successful film, *The Haunting,* in 1963; a 1999 remake of the film was a forgettable flop. If you enjoy reading this novel, as we think you will, we would also recommend to you Jackson's other famous gothic tale, *We Have Always Lived in the Castle.*

Shirley Jackson (1916–1965), *The Haunting of Hill House* (New York: Viking Penguin, 1959). The Penguin paperback reprint (1984) is widely available.

HENRY JAMES
Washington Square

~

Henry James is a magisterial presence in American literature, the master of finely honed novels of the individual in society. James' grand-father emigrated from Ireland in 1789 and became a notable personage (he was official orator at the opening of the Erie Canal) and exceed-ingly wealthy, with a fortune thought to be inferior in New York State only to that of John Jacob Astor. James' father was a well-known theo-logian and philosopher, and his older brother, William, achieved emi-nence as a psychologist and philosopher in a long career as a professor at Harvard.

Amid this wealth and success, Henry James lived and worked in grand style. Friends with many of the literary and social luminaries of the day, including Edith Wharton (p. 296), he spent most of his adult life in Europe, living for many years in the house later occupied by E. F. Benson (p. 21) in Rye, England. He became a naturalized citizen of Great Britain just before his death. *Washington Square,* like much of James' work, resonates with the novelist's own background: He was born at 21 Washington Place on the Square. (The James house, unfor-tunately, no longer exists.)

The principal characters of *Washington Square* are Dr. Sloper, a well-regarded and prosperous physician; his daughter, Catherine; his sister Mrs. Lavinia Penniman; and a suitor for Catherine's hand, Morris Townsend. The history of the Sloper family provides the background to the story. Dr. Sloper married one of the prettiest and wealthiest girls in Manhattan and they had a son who died as a child, to the profound and lasting distress of the father. Then their daughter was born, and just one week later her mother died. Dr. Sloper, always remembering his wife fondly, did not remarry. After some years in a house in the neighborhood of City Hall, near the southern tip of the island, Dr. Sloper, Catherine, and Mrs. Penniman, who had come to stay with them, moved to a house built for the family in Washington Square, then a neighborhood at the height of fashion. (The house in the novel bears a distinct resemblance to the house in which the James family lived.)

Dr. Sloper is a man of great prestige in the city, and one of substantial character and wisdom as well. His daughter is a relatively plain and simple woman, or so we are told at the beginning by the unnamed narrator; Catherine is respectful of her father. Mrs. Penniman, the widow of a clergyman and childless, is a romantic sort given to ideas of overwrought drama in personal relations, at least in those of others.

The principal events of the novel are rooted in a party honoring the engagement of one of Catherine's cousins (one of the many children of Dr. Sloper's other sister, Mrs. Almond) to a Mr. Townsend. Morris Townsend, a distant cousin of the groom-to-be, has been out of the country; he has no money and no prospects, and is descended from a somewhat disreputable branch of the Townsend family. Nevertheless, he begins a determined, apparently well-thought-out courtship of the wealthy, quiet Catherine.

Dr. Sloper sees quickly that Morris is not a suitable man for his daughter and is actually out for her considerable wealth. He confirms this by a visit to and discussion with Townsend's widowed sister, who lives with her five children (and Morris, who is staying with her) in an unfashionable neighborhood "in the Second Avenue." Dr. Sloper is joined in his view by Mrs. Almond; Mrs. Penniman thinks Townsend is wonderful, and throughout the story she engages in witless plots allegedly in the interest of her niece. Catherine herself is very taken by Townsend, who is exceptionally handsome and articulate, and happily accepts his declarations of love and eternal devotion. She agrees to marriage, against her father's wishes.

In the fashion of the times, father and daughter go to Europe for a year in the father's hope that Catherine will "throw over" Morris. She returns still determined to marry him. The characters rise and fall in our estimation, sometimes page by page, as we observe their conflicts described in James' rich, complex, and exacting psychological detail. We are pained by the deep gulf between father and daughter, angry at Morris, and exasperated by the antics of Mrs. Penniman; we are surprised by the way the story turns out. We learn then where considerable moral strength lies among people who are highly constrained by the social structure in which they live.

This fine short novel is a pleasure to read because of its exceptionally acute delineation of character and James' intimate knowledge of the customs and mores of the upper classes in nineteenth-century New York. He knows exactly how and when people are supposed to call on other people, for example, and what they must say, and he knows, too, just which neighborhoods are fashionable as the great city expands northward. (New York's history was one of constant change throughout the nineteenth century, as New York grew from a town of twelve thousand people at the end of the Revolutionary War to a city of millions by 1900.) James' portrait of old New York will resonate with many readers who have family roots in the city.

Washington Square today is still the heart of the Greenwich Village neighborhood in Manhattan, and the buildings on the north side have a pleasant nineteenth-century quality. When you are next in New York, you might want to visit there. On a misty spring afternoon, one can almost imagine Dr. Sloper coming back from his rounds, or Morris Townsend wiling his way into a meeting with Mrs. Penniman.

Henry James' novels are intricately plotted and filled with emotional tension, but they require a slow and careful style of reading that most of us are no longer accustomed to in this modern era of the short attention span. James was interested in nuance; he liked to hold ideas up and look at them from every side, and he was a master of the subordinate clause. James represents exactly what Hemingway (p. 105) was reacting against in his invention of a direct style of prose. James' writing now takes a bit of getting used to, but it repays the effort. Of his many other works, often dealing with the interactions of Americans and Europeans, we like especially *The Ambassadors* and *The Portrait of a Lady*.

Henry James (1843–1916), *Washington Square* (New York: Harper and Brothers, 1880). James' novels are available in a wide variety of modern hardcover and paperback editions, including a handsome hardcover omnibus edition from the Library of America. Two convenient paperback editions are from Viking (1985) and Oxford University Press (1998). A fascinating collective biography of the James family is by R. W. B. Lewis, *The Jameses: A Family Narrative* (New York: Farrar, Straus and Giroux, 1991).

SARAH ORNE JEWETT

The Country of the Pointed Firs

~

Sarah Orne Jewett was born in 1849 into a well-to-do family in South Berwick, in southern Maine. It may seem unlikely in our time that a writer of such grace would hail from what is often regarded as a rural part of the country, out of the mainstream. In fact, however, at the time of Jewett's birth this region was one of the most prosperous parts of the United States. South Berwick lies a short distance upriver from Portsmouth, New Hampshire; with sea and later rail connections, the town was well within the orbit of Boston and participated fully in the extensive foreign trade and the industrial development of nineteenth-century America. Jewett's ancestors included an array of distinguished citizens, such as a governor of New Hampshire and a secretary of war for President Jefferson. She had a comfortable upbringing and an excellent education, both through her cultivated family life and at Berwick Academy, which she attended with her friends, cousins, and siblings.

At the same time, Jewett grew up with an acute and enduring knowledge of rural life. Afflicted with an illness of the joints that lasted all of her life, she was often too unwell to attend school, but instead went on trips into the countryside with her beloved father, a physician. Listening to and observing her father talk with and treat his patients, Jewett learned to understand and to appreciate the dignity and hardiness of rural people. She also acquired a lifelong habit of prescribing herbs and other remedies (some of doubtful efficacy) for friends and family. In truly understanding and partaking of country life, but at the same time growing up in an educated family that was at ease with the cultural riches of Boston, Jewett had a childhood that combined the disparate elements that are the foundation of her work.

Jewett seemed to understand early that she preferred friendship and writing to the then-conventional choice of marriage, and her decision to become a writer was fully supported by her father. She was successful almost immediately, beginning primarily with children's stories and very quickly publishing fiction for adults in well-known journals. Her talents enabled her to support herself comfortably by her writing, and an inheritance gave her an additional sense of material security.

After her career began to blossom, she became friends with the leading lights of the Boston literary world. She was especially close to James and Annie Fields; James was perhaps the most important publisher of the day, and Annie, who wrote and published poetry, also served as hostess to a large circle of literary friends at the Fields' Charles Street home in Boston. When James died, Jewett began to live part of the year with Annie in Boston; the two women also traveled extensively together and with friends. This relationship became the most important of Jewett's life and was deep, affectionate, and committed. In Boston, Berwick (where she always lived part of the year), and elsewhere, Jewett remained throughout her adult life surrounded by friends and relatives, primarily but not exclusively women. The maintenance of these friendships was one of the crucial elements of her existence.

Jewett and her friends were part of a distinguished group of literary celebrities in the United States and Europe. Her fame was such that during a visit to the World's Columbian Exposition in Chicago with friends late in life, she found a portrait of herself in the State of Maine pavilion. In Boston, friends included John Greenleaf Whittier, Oliver Wendell Holmes, the Longfellow family, the artist Sarah Wyman Whitman, and many others. (In the younger generation, Willa Cather [see p. 30], as a writer still forming her style, visited Boston and sought and received valuable help from Jewett.) And few of us enjoy as elevated an event in our first visit to Europe as Jewett did, when, during an extended tour in 1882, she and Annie Fields paid a visit to Lord Tennyson and his wife on the Isle of Wight, off the south coast of England. Jewett's literary gracefulness certainly owes something to the company in which she moved; at the same time, her down-home origins keep her writing from nineteenth-century ornateness.

Much of Jewett's work seems dated, but she has left us with one sparkling masterpiece that seems as fresh now as when it was published in 1896, *The Country of the Pointed Firs*. In this, her best-known work, Jewett presents us with a civilization that is now vanished—the coastal towns of Maine and the country people who lived in them, fully shaped individuals who interconnected in a society that depended on the quality of human relationships. The book is a series of linked chapters; the narrator is a woman who visits the small seaside town of Dunnet Landing for a summer to, as she hopes, write, but instead finds herself learning, observing, and coming to care deeply for the people of the town. The narrator boards with Mrs. Almira Todd, the central personality of the book, whom in the course of the summer she befriends. Mrs. Todd is herbal physician, friend, and mentor to her neighbors; she, like the other characters, is sketched in a remarkably complete and complex way.

Although the book is short, we come to feel that we know Mrs. Todd and other people in the narrative well. These include Mrs. Todd's mother, the doughty Mrs. Blackett, living on Green Island, off the coast; Mrs. Todd's shy brother, William; a retired sailor, Captain Littlepage, haunted by his memories; and many other well-drawn characters. In the course of the story, the narrator becomes friendly with the people of Dunnet Landing, goes on excursions, and attends events. Notable among these is the reunion of the large Bowden family, to which many of the characters are linked; we see at this gathering the importance of personal contacts—people remember encounters from years ago and exactly what was done and said. The narrator also brings out in a fully convincing way the everyday life of the people in Dunnet Landing, including their hard-won skills in seacraft and farming. The novel, although carefully (but unobtrusively) constructed, does not have a conventional plot, which allows the author to depict clearly the full quality of her characters' existence in a relatively few pages, presenting us with an entire way of life.

Even for someone who visits Maine often, this book is a revelation. It presents a culture that, while gone, still seems to stand behind the character of the modern New England coast. This lovely short volume embodies both the country and the literary parts of Jewett's life but, in the way of great art, transcends and becomes something more than both of them. Jewett wrote four additional stories about Dunnet Landing after the success of *Pointed Firs*. Some posthumous editions included several of these, sometimes awkwardly interpolating them between chapters of *Pointed Firs*. However, there is no evidence that Jewett thought of these additional stories, well written as they are, as part of the original novel, and they are best read separately.

South Berwick is worth a visit; it still has the marks of a wealthy nineteenth-century town, including large houses and a Victorian business block. The Jewett House (1774) can be visited in season, and Sarah's childhood home, next door, is now the town library. If you stop in and read a book there, you will come to know more deeply something of the life that made Jewett a writer whose best work still speaks to us.

Sarah Orne Jewett (1849–1909), *The Country of the Pointed Firs* (Boston: Houghton Mifflin, 1896). This is widely available in several paperback editions, most of which include the four additional Dunnet Landing stories printed after the original work. The Norton edition (1994) is especially attractive. We also like the handsome Modern Library hardcover edition (1994).

JAMES JOYCE
Dubliners

~

James Joyce is one of the iconic figures of twentieth-century literature, known for his stylistic innovations in works firmly rooted in the Dublin of his youth. The eldest son and one of ten children of an impoverished gentleman and his wife, Joyce nonetheless benefited from a good Jesuit education and attended University College, Dublin. He was a precocious writer; his first article, published while he was still in his teens, was an appreciation of the Norwegian playwright Henrik Ibsen in the *Fortnightly Review* in 1900. In 1902, after college, he went to France; he returned periodically to Ireland, and then left for good in 1912. The self-exiled writer made a precarious living in Trieste as a language teacher and lecturer, had a family with his longtime companion, Nora Barnacle (they were finally married in 1931), and later lived in Zurich and Paris.

Dubliners was his second book (a volume of poetry, *Chamber Music,* was published in 1907). Astonishingly, given its power and exceptional writing, *Dubliners* was written between Joyce's twenty-second and twenty-fifth years. Its publication was long delayed because of fears of legal action (its sexual references were at the time considered rather frank) and fears of libel (some figures were identifiable), and it finally appeared in print in 1914. The book is composed of fifteen stories, which Joyce intended as a "moral history" of the city. The stories are arranged generally in an order that goes from childhood through adulthood and public life. Each story focuses on different characters, but the stories do indeed read as part of the same history, of the (mostly Catholic) lower middle class of Joyce's youth. The stories share exact descriptions of Dublin and its people, and also share a penetrating psychological insight into the characters they depict. Reading this collection, we have the impression that Joyce must have spent all of his young life observing. The quality of the writing makes us feel that we ourselves are the observers, so acute and exact is the physical and psychological description.

The people of whom Joyce writes did not live in an optimistic city, politically, religiously, and economically. The drive for Irish Home Rule (partial independence from Great Britain), under which people such as Joyce's own family expected to play a substantial part, had suffered a shattering blow with the failure and death of the great nationalist leader Charles Stewart Parnell in 1891. The city was dominated by a Protestant, English, and English-supporting elite, and in addition, some thought, Catholics were oppressed by their own church. Economically, Dublin was constantly diminishing as a port and productive center; Belfast, in the north, was growing larger, and Cork, in the south, was prospering as a port. Joyce's characters have modest jobs, when employed, in clerking, trade, the church, or the lower civil service. They live in a perhaps impossible web of social, economic, religious, and national expectations, are frequently in debt, and suffer a pervasive abuse of alcohol, leading to problems with employment, and the abuse and bullying of wives (or husbands). Even when there is some happiness in family or friendship, it is always shadowed—perhaps Freddy will arrive drunk at the dance again and ruin things, or a night out with friends will cost a job or grievous financial loss.

Each of the stories has its own special qualities, although they all fit within Joyce's overall framework of moral history. "Araby," one of the earlier stories, depicts the self-concern, confusion, and wild hopes of a young boy thinking of a girl, matters that perhaps have not changed a great deal since Joyce's time. In "Two Gallants," two men (the title is ironic, as the men are less than gallant), one of whom is involved with a servant in an upper-class house, scheme to get a favor from her. We are surprised to learn what is being asked for, and perhaps even more appalled at the moral squalor of the men than if our initial reading had been correct. "A Little Cloud" is a study of disappointed hopes. A chance encounter gives a clerk a balmy notion that he, too, could publish a poem—perhaps the critics would think him "Celtic" because of a suitably melancholy note—before the thought is quashed by an angry wife and squalling child. In "A Painful Case," a lonely bank cashier throws away the only chance in his life for real human relations, and several years later the woman involved is a drunken suicide. In a story of despair in public life, "Ivy Day in the Committee Room," we see a pitiful group of election canvassers scrounging drink, discussing their ineffective efforts, and listening to a poem that one of them has written about the fallen chief. (The day happens to be October 6, the day of Parnell's death, when the faithful wear a sprig of ivy.) The contrast couldn't be more marked between great civic hopes and squalid, sold-out wardheelers.

This is not a hopeful book, but it is an exceptional one. It is the most accessible work of a great writer and, with its rich layers of meaning and powerful writing, provides us with an entire new world. And somehow we come away thinking that despite all, there may be hope for human relations—they just can't be conducted as they were at the end of the nineteenth century in Dublin. In order to blossom, people need a freer social and political climate and more prosperity than Joyce's characters had—perhaps this was the reason for Joyce's self-exile.

We recommend also *Portrait of the Artist as a Young Man*. Joyce's later and more complex works are *Ulysses* and *Finnegans Wake*, which have many devoted fans.

James Joyce (1882–1941), *Dubliners* (first published in 1914; the 1926 Modern Library edition was the first to gain wide distribution). Widely available in various hardcover and paperback editions, including the Penguin Twentieth-Century Classics edition (1993) and the Viking Critical Library edition (1996), with helpful criticism and notes.

George Kates

The Years That Were Fat

~

George Kates enjoyed a privileged childhood of nannies and tutors, travel and elegance. It was entirely natural that he would be educated at Columbia and Harvard, completing his education with a D.Phil. in European history and fine arts at Oxford. He was an aesthete by upbringing, by education, and by natural inclination, well placed to pursue a life of study and connoisseurship. Thus we are not surprised to learn, in the opening pages of this memoir, that his first venture into the world of gainful employment, working for a major motion-picture studio as an expert advisor on costumes, sets, and matters of historical and artistic authenticity, quickly began to seem to him a Philistine and unsatisfactory way of making a living. Despite the easy money (no small thing, in the early years of the Depression), the big houses, and the endless parties, Kates could see stretching before him a Hollywood career that, little by little, would draw him into a life he would neither want nor respect. He decided, in the spring of 1932, to give it all up and spend some time finding out what he really wanted to do.

A period of solitary reading and study led him to Chinese poetry, which made such an impression on him that he began to read more widely in Chinese history and culture and to take the first steps toward learning the language. Soon it came to seem inevitable to him that he must go to China; as this book opens, we find him in a carriage of the Shanghai-Beijing express, ready to begin what would turn out to be the defining experience of his life.

He describes the details of getting settled in Beijing (in the book, the name is, of course, spelled in the old style, Peking), hiring servants, finding tutors in modern and classical Chinese, and, above all, finding the ideal house—which turned out to be a neglected, and thus never "improved" or modernized, courtyard house near the Forbidden City, rented from an elderly eunuch who had served in the imperial palace before the 1911 revolution. Having settled in, he began the long and endlessly rewarding process of learning to live the life of a traditional Chinese scholar, in tune with his surroundings and the passing seasons. What lifts this account from the routine to the sublime is a quality of humane wisdom that illuminated his experience in Beijing. Many people have spent long years abroad in bovine ignorance of the culture and values of their adopted home; Kates sought transformation and found it, because his mind was already prepared to perceive and absorb the riches around him.

Much of the book simply tells of Kates' life in Beijing as he learned his way around the city's neighborhoods and explored its fabled palaces and temples and the nearby countryside and hills. The author lived a quiet life, and these accounts are quiet, too, owing their absorbing interest to the author's marvelous powers of observation and his deep feeling for beauty and the meanings of things, rather than to dramatic events or personal crises. There were dramatic events in China in the 1930s, to be sure; Kates tried to ignore them as much as he could. When, in early 1941, it became clear that he could no longer remain in Beijing in the middle of a war between China and Japan, leaving his adopted home was a wrenching experience that stayed with him for the rest of his life.

Kates continued, on the surface, to lead an interesting life. He returned to China in 1943 as an advisor at the wartime American embassy in Chungking, and he worked on the Chinese text of the United Nations Charter after the war. Later he served for a time as curator of Oriental art at the Brooklyn Museum before retiring early to study and write. He was an immensely well read, learned, and accomplished man, whose life exemplified how spiritually rich one can become through being open to experience. Yet having found what for him was a perfect life in a time and place that vanished forever after just a few short years, he was left, in the end, with the feeling that he had outlived himself. This book is a celebration of his years in Beijing, but it is an elegy as well.

We were fortunate enough to know George Kates in Boston in the late 1960s, when he was in his early seventies but seemed older (partly because we ourselves were then young and partly because, with his grave, dignified good manners, he may perhaps always have seemed older than he was); we remember with pleasure and gratitude the kindness he showed to his much younger friends. Although he was living in modest circumstances (occasionally selling off a piece of his superb Ming furniture to supplement his income), he was in every way a man rich in experience and wisdom; his demeanor radiated the Confucian moderation and sense of harmony that he had learned in Beijing decades earlier. He lived to a very great age, and while he grew physically quite frail, he retained to the end of his life both his quiet dignity and his humane serenity. He was a man to remember; even if one was not lucky enough to have met him, his qualities animate the pages of this book.

George Kates (1895–1990), *The Years That Were Fat* (New York: Harper and Brothers, 1952). The original edition is long out of print, as is the later MIT Press paperback reprint, but both can be found in used-book stores or via the Internet.

YASUNARI KAWABATA
Snow Country

~

Japanese literature is, generally speaking, unexplored territory for most Western readers, and at first glance it does not always seem very welcoming. Like the Japanese language itself, Japanese fiction is often indirect, allusive, even occasionally obscure, preferring to let meaning emerge from unspoken hints rather than saying things straight out. (This Japanese habit of indirection has driven countless Western businessmen to the brink of despair in the course of commercial negotiations in Japan.) But Japanese literature also offers great rewards of beauty and insight to those willing to persevere in exploring it with an open mind. Among modern Japanese novelists, we find the work of Yasunari Kawabata especially appealing.

Kawabata was born in 1899 in Osaka and grew up during a time of intellectual and artistic ferment. During the last third of the nineteenth century, Japan, having been substantially isolated from the rest of the world for more than two hundred and fifty years, went through a period of very rapid modernization and Westernization in an attempt to avoid the kind of domination by Western imperial powers that had been the fate of other Asian nations. By the time Kawabata was a young man, many Japanese intellectuals had begun to question the previous generation's enthusiasm for all things Western and were moving toward a more balanced position that sought to use Western literary and artistic techniques to create a literature that would be both modern and distinctively Japanese. Kawabata, who was a leader of this movement, developed a personal literary style that was rooted in the traditional Japanese seventeen-syllable haiku poetic form but also strongly influenced by the avant-garde literature of post–World War I France. Kawabata's work is characterized by a spare, allusive narrative technique and great emotional subtlety. He won early acclaim as a major writer and, capping a long and successful career, became Japan's first winner of the Nobel Prize for Literature, in 1968. Despondent over the public, politically inspired 1971 suicide of his younger friend and protégé, the writer Yukio Mishima, Kawabata committed suicide himself in 1972.

Snow Country is one of Kawabata's most famous novels and typical of his work. It is short and superficially easy to read, but readers coming to it for the first time are likely to find it somewhat puzzling. It is the kind of book that can be enjoyed on some levels at first sight (for example, the sheer beauty of its language, which comes through even in translation) but which yields deeper meanings only after repeated readings. Even then, its atmosphere of emotional repression and things left unsaid seems to convey a sense that one will never uncover all that lies beneath its surface.

The novel's protagonist is Shimamura, a wealthy and rather idle Tokyo intellectual (it says much about his character that through reading and collecting memorabilia he has made himself an "expert" on Western ballet but has never seen a ballet performance). Shimamura has fallen into the habit of going for prolonged vacations, without his family, to a small hot-spring resort inn on the northwestern coast of the island of Honshu, in Japan's remote and isolated "snow country," where Siberian storms deposit many feet of snow every winter. There he has drifted into an affair with a young geisha, Komako, who against her own better judgment begins to fall in love with him.

There has been much misunderstanding in the West about the status of the Japanese geisha. The word itself means "artistic person," and geishas were always first and foremost entertainers, hired to sing, dance, and generally provide feminine companionship at the otherwise all-male teahouse parties that formed the core of traditional Japanese social life. (Wives were expected to stay at home and had no role to play in evenings out.) Geishas might, and often did, become mistresses of wealthy patrons, but they were not prostitutes in the usual sense and were not expected to provide sexual services on demand for payment. Country geishas at hot-spring resorts could seldom afford to be so aloof, however. The inns where they worked were typically places to which men came, alone or in groups, in search of relaxation and sex, and geishas, maids, and waitresses alike were expected to make themselves agreeable to the paying customers. Japanese readers of *Snow Country* would understand, though it is never clearly spelled out, that however attracted Shimamura and Komako feel to each other, their relationship is fundamentally one of sex for hire: She is under contract to her employer, who bills Shimamura for the time they spend together.

Shimamura certainly has no illusions about Komako's occupation. He is, however, flattered by how much she likes him; he enjoys her company, while she takes every opportunity to spend as much time with him as possible. It is not out of the question that he might become a long-term patron who would support her as his mistress. Apparently in hope of some such outcome, Komako allows herself to relax the tight rein she keeps on her emotions for self-protection. Trouble appears, however, in the form of another young woman, Yoko, who has already been Komako's rival for the love of a young man who has since died of tuberculosis. Yoko, we understand, is mentally unstable and obsessed with any man with whom Komako herself forms an attachment. The book ends ambiguously, but we sense that Yoko's intervention has broken the tenuous threads that bind Shimamura's relationship with Komako. Komako becomes, finally, a figure that every Japanese reader will recognize from dozens of traditional novels and plays: a young geisha seduced into falling in love with an unattainable man.

Kawabata's work is often beautiful and intensely moving, but it is seldom happy. Much of his work deals with themes of disappointment and death, and with emotional coldness and inability to express love—characteristics common to many of his male fictional figures. Much of the emotional content of his novels is expressed indirectly, in hints and allusions, which is why his books seem to ripen with successive readings. The effect is similar to the delicate aesthetic of haiku, in which both meaning and emotional impact are conveyed in a single, unexpected turn of phrase.

Some critics have traced Kawabata's fascination with emotional remoteness to his own childhood—he was orphaned at a very early age—but that kind of easy psychological explanation strikes us as superficial. Kawabata was a great literary artist, and we do not assume that his work was simply an expression of his unconscious impulses. His books are a taste well worth acquiring; other works that we recommend are *Beauty and Sadness* and *The House of the Sleeping Beauties and Other Stories*.

Yasunari Kawabata (1899–1972), *Snow Country* (*Yukiguni;* Tokyo: Shinchosha, 1948; English trans. Edward G. Seidensticker, New York: Alfred A. Knopf, 1956). Vintage International paperback, 1996.

ALVIN KERNAN
Crossing the Line

~

In the early spring of 1941, Alvin Kernan, a seventeen-year-old who had never seen the ocean, left the remote, bankrupt Wyoming ranch where he had grown up and enlisted in the United States Navy. He went through basic training and then took advanced training in San Diego as an aviation ordnance specialist; he arrived in Pearl Harbor in mid-November for assignment to the aircraft carrier *Enterprise*. The huge ship went on maneuvers at the beginning of December and was prevented by heavy seas from returning to port until late in the day on December 7. Kernan thus missed being bombed, and probably killed, in the Japanese raid on Pearl Harbor that morning; he served in the Pacific throughout World War II, surviving without a scratch but transformed into a person that the young ranch boy he had been could hardly have imagined.

To our great good fortune, Kernan, like his British counterpart Hugh Dundas (see p. 64), after a long and very successful postwar professional career, decided to write about his wartime experiences, at first thinking only that they might be of interest to his grandchildren. He was prevailed upon to publish these memoirs as a book, and the result is a stunning success. To read these pages is to spend time with a person of deep and humane wisdom who can look back on the extraordinary experiences of a young man at war without either romanticizing the comradeship and exotic adventures of wartime or being bombastic about the dangers and hardships he faced. He writes with wonderful candor about his experiences in the war, how they felt at the time, and how he sees them in hindsight. Kernan had what the English like to call a "good war." He was never wounded, but several times escaped death by inches; he conducted himself well, was awarded the Navy

Cross and a number of other distinguished decorations, did scutwork and hard duty without complaining very much, and even managed, sometimes, to have a good time.

Kernan saw plenty of action. He was in the thick of the Battle of Midway with the *Enterprise*, and he was aboard the same ship in April 1942 when General Doolittle's bombers made their famous carrier-launched raid on Tokyo—doing little real damage but raising American morale and shocking the Japanese. A few months later, Kernan survived the sinking of the *Hornet* at the Battle of Santa Cruz. He served on a couple of so-called escort carriers, slow, dangerous tubs converted from merchant ships to warships of a sort, and was happy to get off them alive. He saw some duty ashore in the Pacific islands, where life sometimes was as pleasant as a chorus of *South Pacific*, sometimes a misery of heat and bugs.

In the first years of the war, Kernan's work mainly involved servicing guns, ammunition, bomb racks, and bombs for the planes aboard the carriers on which he served; later he became a radioman-gunner in a carrier-based squadron of dive bombers. Among his other aviation adventures, a faulty catapult launch once sent his plane straight into the water off the carrier's bow, making him and the other crew members scramble to get out and be picked up by a destroyer doing sweeper duty. As with every young man at war, perhaps the hardest and most vivid lesson he learned was how thin the line is between life and death. At one point he describes a plane making a low pass over the deck of a carrier, its two crewmen smiling in the prime of vigorous youth; suddenly a wing tip grazed one of the ship's catwalks, and seconds later the plane was over the side, its fliers dead in their harnesses, sinking without a trace. One readily believes Kernan when he says that to have survived the war seemed like a miracle and that every year since then has been a gift.

Kernan left the Navy in 1945 as a chief petty officer and promptly took advantage of the opportunity that the G.I. Bill offered to continue his education. He had left the ranch for good. He earned a doctorate in English literature at Yale and embarked on an academic career that saw him rise to become director of Humanities at Yale, dean of graduate studies at Princeton, and finally director of the Graduate Fellowship

Program at the Andrew W. Mellon Foundation. Even if one knew none of those details, it would come as no surprise to learn that he had an exceptionally distinguished career after the war; the wisdom and insight of this book would lead one to suppose exactly that.

Perhaps what strikes the reader most forcefully in reading this book is Kernan's intelligence and his equanimity. As a young sailor, he learned his tasks quickly and easily, was happy to do pretty much whatever the Navy ordered him to do, and had the good sense to understand that doing his job well was the best way to try to stay alive (to the extent that one's own actions had anything to do with it) under very dangerous circumstances. One feels that he would have made a very agreeable and pleasant shipmate, and in fact he treats his readers almost as shipmates, or at least as people who can be trusted to understand, and vicariously share, the experiences he describes. This is a book to be read with enormous satisfaction, not just for its information and its insights, but for the pleasure of the author's company.

Alvin Kernan (1924–), *Crossing the Line* (Annapolis: Naval Institute Press, 1994). The 1997 paperback reprint edition from the Naval Institute Press is still in print, though not easy to find.

RUDYARD KIPLING

Kim

~

Rudyard Kipling was, during the first years of the twentieth century, one of the most famous authors in the English-speaking world. Born in Bombay to a family stationed in India, he spent part of his childhood there, with the requisite miserable years back "home" in England. After completing his schooling, he returned to India at the age of sixteen to make a career as a journalist, poet, and writer. He succeeded early and was the recipient of the Nobel Prize for Literature in 1907. Kipling married an American, lived for many years in Brattleboro, Vermont, and enjoyed financial and popular success. He had an intimate familiarity with India and the interrelationships between Indians and the British Raj, or rule, of the Indian subcontinent, and this knowledge informs *Kim*.

Much of Kipling's output, which was considerable, is now largely forgotten, although one of us had to memorize as a schoolchild his inspirational poem "If." He is sometimes dismissed now as a "patriotic" writer or derided as an apologist for imperialism, but this understates his merit, notwithstanding that much of his work is hard to read today. *Kim,* in particular, has endured and is one of the very few books that can be thoroughly enjoyed by both adults and young people. It is a fine tale of adventure, history, and fantasy all rolled into one, featuring a central character with whom we can all empathize.

Kim is the story of the orphan son of an Irish soldier and his wife; his true name is Kimball O'Hara. He grows up in the care of a woman in Lahore, speaking the local tongue much better than English and learning the ways of Indian city life. The story begins when Kim meets and befriends an old Tibetan lama, who has come from his snowy homeland on a spiritual quest, and becomes his *chela*, or disciple. They wander together toward central India along the Grand Trunk Road,

141

sometimes using trains, more often walking and begging (Kim is expert at this). Kim runs into his father's old regiment and is recognized by some papers he carries in an amulet. He winds up at school in Lucknow under the aegis of Father Victor, the Roman Catholic chaplain of the regiment, the lama, and Colonel Creighton, nominally of the Ethnological Survey, whose real business is the Great Game, pitting England against Russia for control of central Asia. Kim learns his lessons well in St. Xavier's in Partibus school at Lucknow, and plays his part in the game.

The characters are well drawn: Mahbub Ali, the wily Pathan horse trader and intelligence agent for the British; Hurree Babu, a pompous Bengali; Lurgan Sahib, with his jewelry shop in Simla; Colonel Creighton; and other vivid figures such as Father Victor and the Woman of Shamlegh in the hills. Those who know India will enjoy the stock character of the sharp-tongued widow of a hill rajah, constantly talking, berating her retainers, watching her property, and wishing for more grandsons. Kipling catches well the vast mix of peoples and religions, the restless movement among cities, and the petty trading and sharpness that are still a part of Indian life; the tales, fantastic and otherwise, shared by travelers; and the incredible number of languages. Although the tale is set more than a century ago, it is still possible (as both of us know from personal experience) to recapture some of the wonders of the story—the first entrance of Kim to the princely city of Lucknow, the business of northern towns such as Meerut, the very different and almost magical qualities of the hill stations such as Simla.

It is helpful to remember that *Kim* takes place in British India, when the subcontinent was united under British hegemony. Thus Kim moves easily from Lahore, now in Pakistan, to the marvelous towns and cities of the plain of the Ganges River, a journey that would be much more difficult today. We should also remember that India was very much less populous than it is now, so that the descriptions of open space are more realistic than they might seem to visitors today. An interesting element of the book is its quite infrequent references to England; it really is an Indian story.

The book ends with Kim, having grown up in two worlds, still young and with some success in the Great Game under his belt; we are able to imagine much more to come. While the historical reality of the British/Russian conflict frames the novel and its outcome, the real story is of Kim and, more, of inexhaustible India, this "great and beautiful land," as Kim says. The story has just the right combination of mystery, fantasy, and the cares of the young boy. While few of us will have had the childhood of Kim, the writing is so good that we feel ourselves able to relate our own (much less exciting) childhood experiences and wonders to those of Kim himself: his endless curiosity, his enthusiasm, his successes and failures. You will take away from the book the characters—in addition to Kim, who embodies part of all of us as young people, who can forget Hurree Babu or Mahbub Ali?—and the physical and historical details, such as the unrelenting tumult of a third-class railway carriage and the streams of ritual abuse loosed upon each other by travelers of different castes and ethnic groups. This book will give you the gift of an entire new world. Of Kipling's many other writings, we especially like *The Jungle Book*.

Rudyard Kipling (1865–1936), *Kim* (London: Macmillan; New York: Doubleday, Page, 1901). Widely available in paperback; a convenient and inexpensive version is the Bantam Classic edition (1983).

WILLIAM KOTZWINKLE

The Bear Went Over the Mountain

~

This novel is a hilarious send-up of the American cult of celebrity, and of the publishing industry in particular. The plot is improbably zany— the book's hero is a talking bear—but you will find yourself completely enthralled by it. We promise you that by the time you are a few pages into the book you'll be laughing so hard that the tears will run down your cheeks, and you will have to be careful not to fall off your chair. (And remember that books featuring talking animals are not necessarily for children—this is very grown-up humor.)

As the book opens, a cabin in the Maine woods is burning down, taking with it the manuscript of a novel called *Destiny and Desire*. No great loss, even to the author, a misanthropic, chronically depressed professor named Arthur Bramhall, who realizes that it was a derivative and worthless piece of hackwork. But then Bramhall feels a burst of inspiration; he writes the novel again, with the same title but with completely new content. The result is brilliant. Drained, he puts the manuscript in his briefcase and hides it under a tree—no fire is going to burn this masterpiece.

Unfortunately for Bramhall, the briefcase is found by a bear, who carries it off. The bear, who has learned to read in the course of licking old pizza boxes and jelly jars at the local dump, recognizes the book manuscript for what it is and knows that this is his big chance to make something better of himself. By the next day, he has broken into a store to get a new wardrobe and has headed off to the city to become an author.

Of course, the fun here is that nobody recognizes that Hal Jam (as he names himself) is a bear; everyone he deals with just takes him at face value as a big, macho new writer from the Maine woods. He can talk, of course, but he is very laconic, and his answers to questions are so cryptic that people think he must be brilliant. He finds an agent, who thinks the book is wonderful (it is; the unfortunate Bramhall put everything he had into writing it), and the literary sensation of *Destiny and Desire* snowballs its way to New York, Hollywood, and the White House.

Hal Jam is a very smart bear, but there is a lot about human society that puzzles him (including the human fondness for mating much more often than once a year). He learns very quickly, though, that once he is a celebrity, people are so eager to please him that fame makes its own rules. It's not that Hal isn't obviously a bear, it's just that people choose not to notice; when he behaves oddly, they make allowances. As far as Hal is concerned, as long as he has a steady supply of Cheesy Things, his favorite junk food (his publicist negotiates a huge endorsement contract), he's very happy. And he gets more and more suave all the time.

Trouble looms, however: Bramhall is suing Hal for plagiarism and theft of his manuscript. But poor Bramhall has been living in the woods for a long time, and he is beginning to seem more like, well, a bear; he is getting hairier and starting to smell pretty rank. When it comes to a jury trial, who are the jurors going to believe, a famous author or a dim-witted bumpkin?

Hal faces another difficulty, though: His editor is pressing him for his next novel while the publicity for *Destiny and Desire* is at its peak. The problem is that Hal can write only about enough to sign his own name. But fortune favors the well-prepared mind, and Hal is quite aware that manuscripts sometimes can be found in briefcases. . . .

This is not on the whole a book with profound lessons to teach, though it does lead one to ponder how people see what they want to see, and anyway are so self-centered that they don't see very much. This is mainly an entertainment, and it is marvelous fun to read. It would be hard to find a more inventive book than *The Bear Went Over the Mountain*.

William Kotzwinkle is in any case an author whose work you will want to become better acquainted with. Although he is a versatile and prolific writer, very few people recognize his name, but everyone knows Kotzwinkle's most famous character: He is the author of *E.T.: The Extraterrestrial*. In his own way, Hal Jam is as endearing and memorable as E.T. himself, and you will very much enjoy spending an evening with him.

William Kotzwinkle (1938–), *The Bear Went Over the Mountain* (New York: Doubleday, 1996). Paperback reprint, Henry Holt (1997).

PÄR LAGERKVIST
Barabbas

~

Therefore when they were gathered together, Pilate said unto them, Whom will ye that I release unto you? Barabbas, or Jesus which is called Christ?

. . . They said, Barabbas.

—MATTHEW 27:17, 21

The story of Barabbas, told in similar terms in each of the four Gospels, adds drama to the New Testament account of Jesus' trial and crucifixion. But Barabbas himself is hardly more than a bit player in his own story. The Gospels do not even agree about his crimes: Was he an insurrectionist, a murderer, a robber? In any case it doesn't matter, because his job was to fulfill a role: The chief priests of the temple, who orchestrated Jesus' execution, preferred to see a dangerous common criminal go loose than tolerate the seditious teachings of a religious rival, and Barabbas happened to be available.

It was the Swedish playwright and novelist Pär Lagerkvist who noticed that Barabbas was an interesting figure, or rather that he *became* an interesting figure when he suddenly, and for no particular reason, was spared his appointment with death. Barabbas, as Lagerkvist imagines him, is a hard man but not necessarily a bad man. He is a loner, used to thinking of himself first. He has had no advantages in life and looks for no favors. He has lived largely outside the law and is not at all fazed by knifing a man to death when it seems expedient to do so, yet we do not condemn him.

Lagerkvist, over the course of his writing career, had worked his way from a sort of pessimistic radicalism (he was a socialist who despaired of there ever being a true socialist revolution) to a more accommodating philosophy that acknowledged that people could at least strive toward goodness. Many of his stage works explored the propensity of people to judge and condemn others, and this fascination apparently led him to ponder the fate of Barabbas, the condemned man spared. What, he wondered, would happen to a man who bore such a burden of guilt? And how could such a man find redemption?

This is a very short novel, and it is written in a style of deceptive simplicity—deceptive because the unadorned, straightforward narrative perhaps seems too spare and slight for the emotional impact that it conveys. Its power accumulates slowly and unobtrusively, until by the end one realizes that one has been deeply moved. It helps, too, that the book is not at all preachy or didactic. Lagerkvist is very respectful of the religious convictions of the early followers of Jesus that he portrays in these pages, but religion here is the context, not the text. One certainly need not be a believer in any particular creed to read and enjoy this book.

Pär Lagerkvist was little known outside Scandinavia before the publication of *Barabbas*, which quickly was translated into many different languages and became a bestseller throughout the Western world. When he was awarded the Nobel Prize for Literature in 1951, just a year after *Barabbas* was published, it was not as an obscure Swedish playwright but as a world-famous author.

Still, Lagerkvist's international reputation is based almost entirely on this one slender book. The only other novel by Lagerkvist that achieved considerable attention in the English-speaking world is *The Dwarf* (1944), a chilling portrait of a malevolent retainer at the court of a Renaissance Italian prince.

Pär Lagerkvist (1891–1974), *Barabbas* (Stockholm: Albert Bonniers, 1950; New York: Random House, 1951). Vintage International paperback reprint, 1989.

LAURIE LEE

As I Walked Out One Midsummer Morning

~

On a summer day in 1934, at the age of nineteen, Laurie Lee left his village home in Gloucestershire, in the west of England. Several of his siblings had gone before him, and others remained at home. His last view of his village home was of his mother, hip deep in grass, waving to him. This memoir poignantly describes his two years of wandering, mostly on foot, in England and in Spain, and captures three distinct parts of his life: walking to London and working there as a laborer; traveling in Spain, earning his keep by playing the violin; and finally, observing the bitter first months of the Spanish Civil War.

Lee, in common with many English children of the time, had left school at fifteen; he worked as an office boy and led a local dance band. In contrast to our own times, when people in their late teens are just on the threshold of higher education, nineteen was grown-up in those Depression days. Lee was equipped with office skills and a way to earn his living on the road: playing the violin. Yet he had also had what in our terms is an inconceivably isolated childhood. When he left home, he had never seen the sea, which was less than a hundred miles away. Nor had he seen Salisbury Cathedral, hardly more than fifty miles from his home. In any given group of our readers, it is possible that a larger percentage has been to Salisbury than was true of the people in Lee's village.

Although London bound, he decided to detour via Southampton to see the coast and the sea. He arrived within a week and quickly learned that he could scrape together a living playing his violin for coins in the street; this was the realization that allowed him to continue. Walking on to London, he traveled with tramps and the army of unemployed. After arriving in the great city, he had the good luck to be hired as a construction laborer, thanks to the father of his girlfriend. He spent a year in the city, living in rented rooms and exploring after work on his own. There are fine remembrances of the London of the day, including mugs of tea strong enough to trot a mouse on, the staple foods of lower-class England, Cockney rhyming slang, and a successful labor action on his construction site.

The second part of his journey began the next summer. Not being sure where to go but realizing that Europe was, for the most part, open for wandering, he chose Spain. He went by boat to Vigo, in the northwest, and walked on. He lived by playing the violin and learned Spanish as he went, his route taking him to Valladolid, Madrid, and then to the south: Seville, Cadiz, Gibraltar (where, rather scruffy, he was unwelcome to the British authorities), and finally to Malaga, on the south coast, and farther east to Almunecar (called Castillo in the book).

His encounters with the notorious Spanish bureaucracy are not onerous: In Valladolid, he obtains a license to play music, a marvelously elaborate document (including the provision that the player not cause riots), for half a peseta. He learns local songs to please his listeners, and stays mostly in small inns (or worse) along the way, places where elaborate manners and codes (generally) kept the peace. He had luck as well as charm, for those were days when the dog bites, minor accidents, and fevers of the countryside could be death. He has a fine sense for local characteristics: He notes that in Seville, the fountain in the house has the same role as a symbol of home and comfort as the coal stove does in the north. And he has a remarkable ear for language. Some of the formal oaths he hears are wonderful—"God's codpiece" and "May my testicles wither"—and the proverbs are equally good: "God always sends nuts to the toothless." This part of the book is the most colorful evocation of the classical young European's "wandering years." And, of course, he is not entirely cut off from home; in Madrid he receives a letter from his mother hoping that his feet are dry.

It is when Lee arrives in Castillo that the book enters its third phase and becomes very sobering indeed. Lee takes a job in a hotel run by a Swiss; he works in the kitchen, does odd jobs, and plays the violin in the evenings. In February, the Socialists win the national elections, and there is euphoria among those whose families, for centuries, have been at the bottom of the heap economically and socially. But rumors of challenges from rebels led by General Franco are heard soon. There is bitter division, retribution, and killing within the town.

Lee, the constant walker whose comings and goings will not be noticed, goes on a mission, carrying a message to a farmer about the arrival of grenades. Fighting begins with hope on the part of the townsmen, but their first battle against a neighboring town ends badly, and Lee notes that, not for the first time, the citizens learned that a people's army can be beaten. Coastal bridges are blown up, the town is isolated, and things begin to look bad. Then, in a comic-opera moment, a British warship complete with deck awnings and polite officers arrives to inform Lee and another English expatriate that it is time to go; the citizens of Castillo push them out, knowing that this is their only chance. In an epilogue, Lee describes his second thoughts about leaving, and explains his decision to return to Spain to rejoin the war. When he clambered over the Pyrenees from France back to Spain, his youth was gone for good.

Lee's entrancing style, direct, clear, yet intensely poetic, makes this a memorable and moving book. And, of course, it is appealing because it represents a kind of adventure that most people would like to have had (and to have survived) but which is essentially impossible in our own world. In addition to books of poetry, Lee wrote, late in life, a report on his return to Spain, but he is best known for his memory of his village childhood, *Cider With Rosie* (published in England as *Edge of Day*). If you enjoy *As I Walked Out One Midsummer Morning*, which we are sure you will, *Cider With Rosie* will be on your must-read list.

Laurie Lee (1914–1997), *As I Walked Out One Midsummer Morning* (New York: Atheneum, 1969). Out of print.

ALDO LEOPOLD
A Sand County Almanac

~

Aldo Leopold is one of the heroes of modern environmentalism, and *A Sand County Almanac* is one of the movement's classics. In the half century since it was published, this book has inspired readers with its impassioned call for radical change in human attitudes toward the planet that sustains us. Few books have had the power to inspire people to make far-reaching changes in how we live our lives; this is one of them. That it is also a work of notable literary merit is an added bonus. For many, it will be one of a handful of the most significant works encountered in a lifetime's reading.

The cleaner water, clearer air, and growing number of protected natural areas that now grace our lives stem ultimately from the work of Leopold and other giants of environmentalism, including Henry David Thoreau, the author of *Walden* (1854), and John Muir (see p. 191), the great advocate of national parks and founder (1892) of the Sierra Club. The modern, well-organized environmental movement based on their heritage was born from a growing sense, in the period after World War II, that wasteful and careless exploitation of the planet's resources was rapidly reaching the point of crisis. Like *Silent Spring*, by Rachel Carson (1962), which alerted the general public to the dangers of widespread and indiscriminate use of pesticides, *A Sand County Almanac* called upon concerned citizens to take positive action to preserve the natural environment.

Leopold was born in Iowa and had a long professional career as a resource manager and expert, beginning with the U.S. Forest Service in 1909 and ending at the University of Wisconsin. His beautifully written, pathbreaking work came out of a lifetime of deep involvement with the land. In *A Sand County Almanac*, Leopold was able to combine his experience with and love for nature, his powerful literary gifts, and his ability to distill a coherent philosophy of nature from his life's work. His foreword to the book nicely sets out its content and purpose and, unlike many forewords, is well worth reading before beginning the book itself.

The first part of the book is the almanac proper: observations from the Leopolds' family retreat arranged seasonally. The writing here is memorable; many books remain in one's consciousness only in general terms, but after reading *A Sand County Almanac* you will find yourself startled by the immediacy of the author's vision. When walking in the country, for example, a chorus of sound in the middle distance might bring to mind Leopold's precise comments on "the proceedings of the convention in the marsh" (March) or the virtues of the songs of the more elusive birds (September).

The second part of the book, "Sketches Here and There," collects some of Leopold's essays written about regions in the United States, Canada, and Mexico, describing perspectives and incidents that contributed to the formulation of his mature views. In this section, one of our personal favorites is "Thinking Like a Mountain," which gives a good idea of the flavor of the book as a whole. The book culminates with four essays setting out Leopold's ideas, including "The Land Ethic," with Leopold's famous statement that a land ethic involves "love, respect and admiration for land, and a high regard for its value. By value I of course mean something far broader than mere economic value; I mean value in a philosophical sense." This view has been cherished by countless readers.

If Leopold's work has any troubling quality, it is an excessive certainty of the moral wrongness of those who disagree with his views—perhaps his reaction to the era of feckless development in which he wrote. You will want to think about this aspect of his work; whether you consider it principled intransigence or ideological stubbornness will be a matter of personal preference.

Leopold died heroically, fighting a grass fire on a neighbor's land, shortly after having been appointed an advisor on conservation to the

United Nations. We are fortunate that he left behind his journals and essays—a precious body of work. This is a book that will be read for a long time, perhaps for centuries.

Aldo Leopold (1887–1948), *A Sand County Almanac* (1949). An easy-to-handle (and pack) edition is the Oxford University Press paperback, first published in 1968, reprinted innumerable times, and widely available in bookstores. A posthumous collection, *Round River: From the Journals of Aldo Leopold,* edited by the author's son Luna B. Leopold, is also of interest; it, too, is in an Oxford University Press paperback (1993).

C. S. LEWIS
Out of the Silent Planet

~

Clive Staples Lewis was born in Belfast, Northern Ireland, of a privileged background, and spent his entire adult life in the rarified world of England's elite universities. He graduated from Oxford and taught there for almost thirty years (and was a colleague and close friend of J. R. R. Tolkien; see p. 272). Then he moved on to Cambridge, where he taught for another ten years, until his death. He was a respected scholar and teacher of medieval and Renaissance literature but was best known to the public as a deeply committed Christian layman who spoke and wrote eloquently in the service of his faith.

Many readers will know Lewis as the author of the seven novels of *The Chronicles of Narnia* (*The Lion, the Witch and the Wardrobe* and six sequels), greatly beloved by children who are fortunate enough to encounter them just as they are learning to be independent readers. However, he is probably best remembered for his moving and brilliantly written works of Christian apologetics (arguments for the validity of Christian faith), especially *Mere Christianity* and *The Screwtape Letters*. His *Space Trilogy* (*Out of the Silent Planet, Perelandra*, and *That Hideous Strength*) is less well known today, but it remains a pioneering work of science fiction; all three of its parts are very satisfying to read.

Out of the Silent Planet begins with Professor Ransom on a walking holiday in a remote part of England. He soon finds himself kidnapped and taken aboard a spacecraft on its way to an unknown destination. The craft is a joint enterprise of Weston and Devine, two men who, in the small world of the British intelligentsia, are actually known to Ransom. This unsavory pair, we learn, are returning to the planet Malacandra (the one we know as Mars) with Ransom as a required item of cargo; an influential group of the planet's inhabitants, the Sorns, have refused to have anything to do with Weston and Devine until the two men have supplied them with a specimen Earth-dweller for examination. Weston and Devine are a frightening and ill-assorted pair, the former a sort of fascist idealist looking for new worlds into which humans can expand, the latter interested only in the mineral wealth of Malacandra. Ransom, fearing both of them, assumes that the Sorns want him as a human sacrifice, or worse, and escapes shortly after the spacecraft touches down again. Eluding his fellow humans, he begins to wander in Malacandra's weirdly beautiful landscapes.

Luckily, he falls in with a group of the local inhabitants, who treat him very kindly. They are, he learns, not Sorns, but Hrossa, large, amiable creatures (think of them as resembling the Cookie Monster from Sesame Street) who live by farming and fishing and are devoted to poetry and music. Ransom soon learns that the Hrossa are only one of several populations of intelligent beings on Malacandra. There are Sorns indeed, but they are not fearsome; rather, they are the planet's philosophers and theologians, and the reason they are interested in humans is that there has been no news from Earth, which they call the Silent Planet, for many ages, since, in fact, a rebel angel did great damage to his world by renouncing God. (Lewis, true to his interest in theology, is using Milton's *Paradise Lost* here as a framework for explaining the religious disarray of planet Earth.) There are also Pfifltriggi, who are small, nervous, and fond of making complex gadgets, and Seroni, almost invisible beings that are something like heavenly messengers. Ransom expects to find exploitation and conflict among these populations, but in this, as in many other ways, he is in for a surprise.

Knowing that Lewis liked to use his fiction as a vehicle for serious ideas about religion and philosophy, readers might perhaps worry that his books would be preachy and dull. That they are not is because Lewis writes with such intelligence and grace, and also because he has a nice sense of humor about his own work. For example, when Ransom discovers that the Malacandrans are apparently possessed of both intelligence and a moral sense, he wonders whether it might be his duty to instruct them in religion. He is somewhat put out to find himself treated to a series of lessons on religion and ethics instead. In fact, as

Ransom discovers, the religious life of Malacandra is in many ways in better condition than that of Earth. That circumstance, along with the planet's fantastic scenery and intriguing inhabitants, helps to explain why the book holds such interest to us as readers.

One should probably classify *Out of the Silent Planet* as "space fantasy" rather than as science fiction. The book in fact does not deal very much with science and technology. Lewis clearly had no notion of how a spaceship might work, and little interest in finding out; the heavy spherical ship in which Devine, Weston, and Ransom travel, and which supposedly works by "exploiting the less observed properties of solar radiation," is quite preposterous. Even granted that this book was written before the space age began, even before German V-2 rockets began to rain down on England during World War II, this is pretty feeble stuff. It seems clear that Lewis was interested in none of the technical details of space travel and wanted only to get Ransom off the surface of one planet (and into space, where he could feel a sort of rapturous identification with the infinite) and onto another, where encounters with other sentient beings would test the social and moral issues that the author really cared about.

This is a short book, and it packs a lot of food for thought into well under two hundred pages. At least since 1965, with the appearance of Frank Herbert's classic *Dune* (and its many sequels and prequels in later years), the trend in science fiction has been for books to get fatter and fatter and for series to seem endless; Lewis' *Space Trilogy* is in that respect a refreshing change. *Out of the Silent Planet* is a very easy one-night read; *Perelandra* and *That Hideous Strength*, though longer, are still of quite manageable size. And whether you are coming to C. S. Lewis for the first time or returning to him after a childhood reading of the *Narnia* books, you will savor his intelligence, literary imagination, and charm.

C[live] S[taples] Lewis (1898–1963), *Out of the Silent Planet* (London: John Lane, The Bodley Head, 1943). Available today in several paperback editions, including one from Scribner (1996).

SIMON LEYS
Chinese Shadows

~

Throughout the twentieth century, China was in turmoil. The century that began with the Boxer Rebellion, a xenophobic popular movement aimed at driving all foreigners out of the country, ended with a mood of intense nationalism and a virtual orgy of private investment aimed at building China into a modern industrial power. In between came episode after episode of warfare, destruction, and senseless violence; the victory, in 1949, of the Chinese Communists altered the course of this cycle of turmoil but did not bring it to an end.

A constant theme of reform and revolutionary movements throughout the century was the necessity of ridding China of its old culture, which was thought to be holding the country back from the benefits of modernization. What happened was paradoxical in the extreme. Much of China's ancient culture was indeed destroyed over the past hundred years, but it tended to be the best part of that culture—the gracious arts, the harmonious traditional architecture, the civility of Confucian etiquette, the social ideals of moderation and harmony, the veneration of classical learning. The worst aspects of traditional culture—despotism, bureaucratism, corruption, nepotism, repression of human rights—have proven to be much harder to get rid of; they flourish with undimmed vigor to the present day.

The destruction of much of what was best in traditional China was applauded by many foreign observers, including many who regarded themselves as friends of China and the Chinese people and believed China's Communist leaders when they said that the sacrifice of these traditions was a small price to pay for the liberation of the people from their traditional bondage. One of the few dissenters was the Belgian art historian, China scholar, and diplomat "Simon Leys" [Pierre Ryck-mans], who saw clearly what so many others wished not to see: that the destruction of China's past was in fact pointless, because the liberation that was supposed to accompany it had not occurred and was pre-vented from occurring by China's rulers (old despots in new revolution-ary clothing).

Especially after the opening of "Ping-Pong diplomacy" between China and the United States in 1971, dozens of foreign journalists and other observers visited China and returned to report breathlessly that China had abolished superstition, done away with infectious dis-eases, achieved equality between men and women, vanquished poverty, and, in fact, had succeeded in creating the "New Socialist Man," moti-vated not by economic interest and greed but by love for his fellow humans, under the guidance of the radiant sun of Mao Zedong Thought. Ryckmans, again, was one of the few who pointed out how much this sounded like the reports from Stalin's Soviet Union in the 1930s by Western observers who refused to see the evidence in front of their eyes of purges, executions, oppression, poverty, and uni-versal fear.

Ryckmans, writing under the pen name Simon Leys, published a number of articles highly critical of Mao Zedong and the Chinese Communist Party, culminating in the publication of *Chinese Shadows* in 1974. *Chinese Shadows* is an angry, corrosive indictment of the en-tire Chinese revolution and all its works. The book was greeted with howls of protest not only in China (which, of course, one would ex-pect) but in the West, where Leys, whoever he was (this was not known at first, until Ryckmans was "outed" by European Maoists), was denounced as an enemy of the Chinese people, a stooge of the political right wing, and so on.

It is fascinating, and important, to read *Chinese Shadows* today. A professional China scholar (as one of us is) will find some particu-lar details where Ryckmans was mistaken, some instances where his analyses were hasty or his predictions wide of the mark, but over-all what one learns from reading the book almost three decades after it was written is how right the author was. The enthusiasts of Mao's revolution were numerous and vocal, and Ryckmans was lonely and widely denounced, but he has the last word, and it is the enthusiasts who are embarrassed in retrospect, and who try to forget all of the foolish things they said after their state-sponsored, packaged, bogus tours of China in the last years of the reign of Mao. There is a very important lesson here, one that deserves to be repeated again and again. As George Orwell (p. 209; one of Ryckmans' favorite authors, naturally) long ago pointed out, doublespeak can be terribly persuasive, it is easy to believe what one wants to believe, and the bearer of bad news often finds himself criticized and his news denied. But the majority view is not always correct, and dissenters are often the best guardians of liberty and democracy.

Chinese Shadows is a fine book to read today not only for its enduring historical and political importance, but because it is a superbly written polemic; it is a book, paradoxically, to read for pleasure. Ryckmans is by turns scathingly sarcastic, eloquently persuasive, and deeply sad, and the feelings that animated the book when it was written continue to resonate. Many readers today (except for China specialists) will want to move quickly through some passages that deal in detail with now long-ago and obscure issues of Chinese politics, but those are easy to skim. One will want, on the other hand, to linger on passages that go straight to the heart, as when Ryckmans describes the wanton vandalism that motivated the destruction of hundreds of memorial arches that graced the streets of old Beijing, or the completely pointless demolition of its massive and noble city wall in the 1950s.

It is important to note also that although China today has changed—liberalized—in ways and to a degree that Ryckmans would not have thought possible in the early 1970s, the mechanisms of repression are no less present now than they were then: mass propaganda campaigns are still organized against supposed counterrevolutionaries, dissidents are still put in jail without trial and their writings are suppressed, and religious leaders who refuse to toe the line of the state are sent away for "labor reform." China's long revolutionary agony is not over yet, and *Chinese Shadows* serves as an important reminder of how bad things have been, and could become once again.

Pierre Ryckmans was barred from China, of course, after it became known that he was Simon Leys. He settled in Australia, and taught at the University of Sydney until his retirement in 1993.

Simon Leys [Pierre Ryckmans] (1935–), *Chinese Shadows* (*Ombres chinoises*; Paris: Broché, 1974; English translation, New York: Viking, 1977). Out of print; look for a copy in your local public library.

A. J. LIEBLING

Between Meals

~

There are only a few journalists whose work survives their times; A. J. Liebling is one of them. He began his writing career as a reporter with the Providence, Rhode Island, *Journal* and became a writer for *The New Yorker* in 1935. He continued to write for that magazine during its era of greatness until his death in 1963. He was a raconteur as well as a writer, and he had a wonderful sense of humor. One old friend recalled Liebling saying about himself that he wrote faster than anyone who wrote better, and better than anyone who wrote faster. As it happens, that is a pretty good assessment of his work.

His life was one of privilege; he was the son of an immensely successful Austrian immigrant to New York City. A defining period of his early manhood was the year 1926–27; he left his reporting job in Providence and spent a year at the Sorbonne, as the gift of his father. *Between Meals* is a poignant, unforgettable memoir of this time and of his other journeys to Paris. These latter include his first visit there as a young child, during a trip to Europe undertaken by his family in the grand manner, and his World War II and postwar visits. In 1926–27, Liebling attended practically no classes, lived adventurously (particularly in the culinary department, the joy of his life and the bane of his health), improved his French, and strengthened his lifelong Francophilia. Liebling's book tells what it was really like to live in the great Paris of the Twenties: not the Paris of legend and famous writers, but the Paris of real neighborhoods and struggling people.

One of Liebling's principal gifts as a writer is his startling immediacy. *Between Meals* focuses primarily on his love of French food and wine, especially the many regional variations that then could still be sampled in their genuine form in Paris. As we read this book, we seem to be at table with Liebling. We feel that yes, on that night in the modest Restaurant des Beaux-Arts in the rue Bonaparte, we would agree to choose the Tavel *supérieur* rather than the ordinary, even though it costs a few centimes more; we would choose exactly the same food, and we would take enormous pleasure in this young man's conversation. The immediacy of the work accentuates what is, for most of us, a lost world: one in which neighborhood restaurants with fine kitchens were a regular part of life. We might not all have chosen Liebling's set of activities (including a hilariously unathletic attempt at membership in the Société Nautique de la Marne, a rowing club), but we would all like to understand and to structure our lives and our times as well as he did, and to enjoy the transformative impact on a young person of life in a great city.

During his *New Yorker* career, Liebling was best known as an acute commentator on journalism and as a war reporter. On media, we think you will enjoy *The Press*, a collection of very insightful articles on reporting. On war, we like *Mollie and Other War Pieces*; in that collection, as in others, Liebling's command of the French language contributes to the accuracy and humanity of the work. Be forewarned: To many of us, as it may become to you, Liebling's fine work is addictive. *Bon appétit!*

A[bbott] J[oseph] Liebling (1904–1963), *Between Meals* (New York: Simon & Schuster, 1962; London: Longmans, Green, 1962). Paperback reprint, North Point Press, 1986; there is also a Modern Library hardcover edition, 1995.

JACK LONDON
The Call of the Wild

~

The Call of the Wild is often described as a young-adult novel. While it is quite true that this is a book that can be read with great enjoyment by young readers (as our own teenage sons will testify), it is unfortunate that the juvenile label has stuck to it so firmly, because that has undoubtedly influenced some grown-ups to pass up a chance to read this dazzling novella. *The Call of the Wild* was recognized as a very special book when it was first published, almost one hundred years ago; today it retains its power to draw the mesmerized reader of any age into its world of cold, danger, and raw emotions.

The Call of the Wild is the story of a dog: not just any dog, but a dog that is exceptional in every way, a dog that makes an impression on every human, and every other dog, that crosses his life's path. Buck, a big, powerful St. Bernard–Border collie mix, spent the first four years of his life in luxury as top dog on a rich man's ranch in California's lush Santa Clara Valley. As Buck would soon learn, just at that time the Klondike gold rush was on, and the demand for dogs to pull sleds across the Chilkoot Pass between Dawson and the goldfields was relentless and overwhelming; dogs were being stolen all over the western United States and shipped north to work. So it was with Buck, and, being a smart and savvy dog, he soon learned that a man with a club was to be obeyed, if not respected or loved; that a dog who could not fit smoothly into a sled team faced a hard, short, unhappy life; that a dog who could not dominate others was doomed to abject servility. Always, as he was passed from one human to another, Buck understood more and more about the ways of his distant ancestors. When his last, and only truly loved, master was killed at a remote cabin, Buck found it very easy to take the last step in hearing the call of the wild.

This is a simple story, but a very stirring one. Behavioral scientists today would caution readers that Jack London has made Buck into far too human a dog, with too strong an intelligence, too much understanding, and unrealistic powers of reasoning. That is undoubtedly true; yet anyone who has spent a lot of time around dogs will agree that in their own canine terms they are amazingly adept at picking up clues to others' intentions, quick to learn, and gifted with a strange sort of insight. Buck is, in these pages, a superdog, but not to an extent that the reader rejects as impossible. Throughout the book, London wisely keeps the focus firmly on Buck's story. Other dogs have important roles, and humans appear and disappear from the narrative, but even the most important human character, the strong and admirable John Thornton, who shares with Buck the best years of both of their lives, is subordinate to the one true hero of the tale. One would give a great deal to have such a dog as Buck.

Scenes from the sled trail and trailside camps, raucous boomtowns and heart-stoppingly lonely wilderness, sled teams in peak condition and teams collapsing with starvation and exhaustion, are recounted here with the vivid truth of recalled experience; Jack London had himself been a participant in the Yukon gold rush, and while he found little gold, he stored up enough experience to become one of America's most famous authors in the early years of the twentieth century.

Jack London was born in San Francisco in 1876, into what would now be described as a dysfunctional family. He was a bright boy who showed an early love of reading, but he also was wild and headstrong and did not spend a lot of time in school. He left home in his teens to work at various times on an oyster boat, as a mill hand, and as a journalist; for a while he dropped out altogether to travel across the country as a hobo. He decided to settle down and began attending classes at the University of California at Berkeley, but when news came that gold had been found in the Klondike, he quit school after only one semester and headed north.

He returned from the goldfields with no money but with a burning vocation to write about his experiences. In an early collection of brilliant short stories (including the classic "To Build a Fire"), London brought home to his audience what the experience of the gold rush had been. With the publication of *The Call of the Wild* in 1903, London's reputation as a major writer was established. His literary star thereafter would burn brightly, but not for long. London lived life without restraint, and the elements of recklessness and bravado that add vitality to his writing were hard for him to handle in real life. Always he drank too much, spent money he did not have, quarreled with people who cared for him, and generally lived an unruly and sometimes scandalous life while managing, somehow, to continue to write prolifically and well.

In 1916 London, depressed, unwell, and in financial difficulties, died of a morphine overdose that most of his biographers agree was deliberately self-administered. Perhaps, as some have argued, he was by then played out as a writer, that he had said everything worthwhile that he had to say, and knew it. It is hard not to look at London in his last years as a pathetic figure who squandered at least some part of his enormous talent. We are fortunate that *The Call of the Wild* and his other books survive as testimony to how powerful that talent was and how promising Jack London's life seemed in his early years. Of his other novels, we especially like *The Sea Wolf* and *The Valley of the Moon*.

Jack London (1876–1916), *The Call of the Wild* (New York: Macmillan, 1903). Several paperback editions are available, including one from Pocket Books (1982). We recommend the 1994 Macmillan hardcover edition with illustrations by Barry Moser.

JOHN D. MACDONALD
The Deep Blue Good-By

~

The invention of the pocket-sized, inexpensive paperback book in the late 1930s gave rise to a generation of immensely talented fiction writers who were not offended to be called hacks and who wrote "pulp fiction"—so called because the paperbacks and the popular magazines that preceded them were printed on cheap, newsprint-like pulp paper. The work paid badly, and the only way to make a living at it was to write magazine stories or paperback novels quickly, and vividly enough to keep editors and readers coming back for more.

The pulp writers produced a body of work that is recognized, in retrospect, as a lasting contribution to American literature. Elmore Leonard, Louis L'Amour, and Ed McBain made their living in pulps for many years and had the good fortune to survive long enough to become the grand old men of American genre fiction. John D. MacDonald, who died too soon in 1986, was of the same generation, and one of the very best. He will be remembered for a long time by fans of action-adventure crime fiction as the creator of one of the most attractive and durable series heroes of all time, Travis McGee.

The Deep Blue Good-By, published as a paperback original in 1964, marked the debut of Travis McGee and established him as a character strong enough to propel the series through twenty-one more books; the last was *The Lonely Silver Rain* (1985). The Travis McGee books are, individually and collectively, true classics of American popular fiction. An evening—or a day at the beach—in the company of Travis McGee is time well spent. The books are tremendous fun; they hold up well over time; and they offer a sense of escape from the mundane world. They are truly gripping; the reader is drawn to participate in a struggle between good and evil that is both more clear-cut and more dangerous than daily life normally provides. The sense of moral clarity that pervades these books defines the role of the crime novel in modern American literature; writers like MacDonald are the true heirs of such nineteenth-century novelists as Thackeray and Dickens.

Travis McGee is the archetypal reluctant hero, ostensibly out for himself but unable to refuse the call of justice for the oppressed or a damsel in distress. He comes across as a beach bum, a big, shambling guy who turns out to be stronger and quicker than he looks and smarter than he seems, a man whom people underestimate often, and at their own peril. He lives in a big houseboat moored at a marina at Fort Lauderdale and takes his retirement a chunk at a time, as long as his funds last between jobs. And the job? Salvage consultant, he calls it, operating on the fringes of the law, retrieving things of value for people who have no other recourse, and keeping half of the net recovery. He likes to think of himself as a hedonist and a cynic, except, of course, that he is really a hopeless romantic. If he sounds familiar, it is partly because so many later writers have modeled their own series heroes on Travis McGee.

In *The Deep Blue Good-By* one of McGee's many female friends asks him to help a friend of hers, Cathy Kerr, who has been swindled and jilted by a plausible but very nasty con man, Junior Allen. He turns out to have found and stolen some loot that Cathy's father had brought back from the Burma campaign in World War II. Cathy can't go to the police because she doesn't even know exactly what she's lost, and it was ill-gotten in the first place. Trav agrees to help, and soon finds out that Allen had also grievously mistreated another woman, Lois Atkinson; she is exactly the kind of wounded sparrow that McGee can't resist trying to nurse back to health with a good dose of fun and sun on his houseboat, *The Busted Flush*. He tracks and finds Allen, who turns out to be even more dangerous and ruthless than he seemed; after a deadly struggle, McGee prevails, but he winds up again alone, not much richer and only a little wiser than when he started.

Once MacDonald was sure he had the formula right, he wrote the McGee books, each with a color in its title, at an average of about one a year. The separate volumes (as with all successful series of genre fiction) add up in effect to one big, ongoing novel, and so it is very much worthwhile to read the whole series in order. Characters reappear, old episodes are recalled, the series builds continually on itself. In *Nightmare in Pink*, the second volume in the series, we meet Travis' friend Meyer, a successful, semiretired consulting economist living aboard *The John Maynard Keynes* just a few berths down from Travis' houseboat; he becomes McGee's frequent partner and confidant in the episodes to come. (Every Sherlock Holmes needs his Dr. Watson, and Meyer fills that role to perfection.) It is also very interesting, and a measure of MacDonald's skill as a writer, to see how McGee grows and changes over the years. He gets older and worries about his declining physical stamina and his accumulating scars and aches; he gives up smoking, drinks less, and learns more enlightened notions about women as time goes by. In each book he is a mirror of his times, but over time he has the capacity to grow. He is one of the most successful series characters ever created, and nearly forty years after he first made an appearance he continues to win new fans. You will be glad to join their number.

While he was writing the Travis McGee books, John D. MacDonald wrote other novels as well (maintaining the high productivity of his early days in the pulps), and like many Florida novelists, he used his literary talents to rail against the rampant corruption and greed that characterized the state's cancerous overdevelopment. One of his best nonseries novels is *Condominium*, the story of an ill-built coastal highrise in the path of a hurricane. It is a gripping read.

John D. MacDonald (1916–1986), *The Deep Blue Good-By* (New York: Fawcett, 1964). Reprinted many times. All of the Travis McGee books were published in Fawcett Gold Medal paperback editions by Ballantine; later volumes in the series were published in hardcover as well.

JERRE MANGIONE

Mount Allegro

~

This lightly fictionalized memoir of a Sicilian-American childhood in Rochester, New York, in the early years of the twentieth century is an enduring classic of American ethnic literature. It is a book that in some ways gains value with the passage of time, because the culture that it describes has nearly vanished from living memory and increasingly can be understood only from the documents that it left behind. (The Mount Allegro neighborhood of Rochester has already disappeared, flattened by an ill-conceived "urban renewal" scheme in the 1970s.)

Jerre Mangione, who appears in these pages as Gerlando Amoroso, writes as a man of two worlds, someone who lived the experiences he described but then gained perspective on them by leaving his old neighborhood for a life of education and a career as a journalist, administrator, and English professor. Much of his professional life was dedicated to preserving the experience of intense ethnic consciousness that was part of the so-called melting pot following upon the great waves of immigration from Europe at the end of the nineteenth century, and to encouraging others to reflect on the role of ethnicity in American life.

This is something that we were aware of in our own childhood. Our father was a man of Jerre Mangione's generation, and because we knew him to be an exceptionally broad-minded and unprejudiced democrat, we were surprised by the extent to which he identified his old friends (Americans all) as "Irish," "Italian," "Greek," and so on. In the world of his own youth, these categories conveyed information that he and his friends found important and useful, perhaps because they told in shorthand form where people were likely to live, what church they attended, and, of particular practical significance, who was allowed to marry whom. Although racial and ethnic consciousness has hardly vanished from contemporary American society, it still takes a deliberate effort to realize just how important ethnic identity and national origin seemed to Americans of a couple of generations ago.

Mount Allegro begins with the conversation of children, in the mixed Polish-Jewish-Sicilian neighborhood in which they lived, about what makes a person American. Some affirmed that they themselves were Americans, inasmuch as they had all been born in this country; others knew that they were Italians, or Jews, because that's what their parents were. Growing up involved learning to negotiate boundaries of "we" and "they." For members of Mangione's parents' generation, there was little doubt, and little conflict either, about who they were. The world in which they lived and felt comfortable was the world of Sicilians, and the larger world of Americans brought mainly intrusions and complications.

Mount Allegro was a community of working-class people: garment workers, bricklayers, pastry makers, and other skilled craftsmen. Money was not plentiful, but sharing made things easier. Books were viewed with suspicion, but Uncle Nino's knowledge of Dante was admired, and his storytelling ability made him popular. The author's parents "were on such intimate terms with God that they never felt compelled to attend church" (and Uncle Luigi had taken the extraordinary step of becoming a Baptist), but church feast days were celebrated with enthusiasm. And always in the background hovered the image of Sicily, a golden land reluctantly left behind for the opportunities of the New World. Much of the book is devoted to an affectionate and often very funny portrait of Mangione's family and their community, and it is clear that he inherited some of his Uncle Nino's ability to shape a tale.

The perspective of the book is a long one, and in it Mangione tells not only of his early years, but of his departure for college and gradual separation from the tight-knit community of his youth. He takes his first trip to Sicily and is surprised by its desperate poverty and the injustices of its semifeudal society, so different from the fantasy island that he had grown up with, glowing in the warm tones of memory. (He also finds, to his mortification, how corrupt and Americanized his native Sicilian had become after a generation or two in Rochester; his language is a source of much amusement to his old-country relations.)

This is not a resentful book. It tells of a mostly happy childhood in a mostly happy world dominated by firm ideas of honor, respect, and tradition. But Mangione writes with an awareness that the world of his childhood was inherently fragile; much of what made it special was destined to vanish, and so had to be transcended. We owe this extraordinary memoir to his growing sense of how special and ephemeral his parents' immigrant experience would be.

Mangione told one of us a few years ago that the publishers of the first edition of *Mount Allegro* worried that memoirs did not sell well; they wanted to present the book as a novel, and so insisted that he fictionalize it to some extent. But, he said, apart from giving the people in this book made-up names and changing a few other details, he wrote it as a memoir nevertheless. He followed the success of *Mount Allegro* with *An Ethnic at Large*, which considers ethnicity in American life from a broader perspective. In Mangione's long and interesting career, one highlight was his work as an administrator for the Federal Writers' Project. This was a Depression-era program to provide employment for professional writers who were otherwise unable to make a living; he later wrote a highly regarded book about the program, *The Dream and the Deal*.

Jerre Mangione (1909–1999), *Mount Allegro* (New York: Harper and Row, 1942, 1952). The 1989 Harper and Row paperback edition is out of print; the book is now available in a handsome paperback reprint (part of the New York Classics series) from Syracuse University Press (1998).

THOMAS MANN
Death in Venice

~

Thomas Mann is one of the towering figures of the twentieth century, awarded a well-deserved Nobel Prize for Literature in 1929. An opponent of the Nazi regime, Mann left his native Germany permanently in 1933, moving first to Switzerland and then to the United States, finally returning to Switzerland after World War II. A writer with an unusually incisive grasp of European intellectual and moral history, his achievement is exceptional. Of his works of short fiction, *Death in Venice* is the best known. It is a powerful evocation of artistic and personal compulsion, set in a city that has always fascinated northern Europe.

Death in Venice is a tragedy, one linked deeply to the meaning of art, intellect, and passion. It depicts the downfall of Gustave von Aschenbach, a great writer who has achieved fame throughout the European intellectual world. Aschenbach, a widower who is devoted to his work, becomes somewhat tired of it and decides one spring not to go to his summer cottage but rather to the south of Europe to revive his spirits. This is a choice that has more meaning than would at first appear. The idea of the south as different, more romantic, less ordered, than the gray north is an old one in German literature; Goethe prefaced his *Italian Journey* with the phrase "I too in Arcadia!"

Aschenbach first goes to an island in the Adriatic Sea, off the Istrian coast of what is now Croatia, but finds the weather too damp and the hotel full of Austrian provincials (a sly remark by the northerner Mann—could there be anything worse? he seems to ask). Aschenbach decides to go to Venice, then as now a fabled city for northerners. He immediately finds himself in "the south," with an odd encounter with the ticket seller on the ferry and a disturbing incident with an unlicensed gondolier. Then, safely at his hotel on the Lido, the seaside barrier island on the far side of the Venetian lagoon that protects the city proper, he prepares to relax and to revive his enthusiasm for work. He even, in the course of his stay, manages to write an essay on weighty questions of art and taste of current interest to the European intellectual world.

Early in the stay, however, the cause of Aschenbach's destruction appears: He sees a beautiful Polish boy, Tadzio, who is staying with friends and family at Aschenbach's hotel. When he is first fascinated by Tadzio, he considers the matter in highly intellectual terms, observing in his writer's way how Tadzio and his family interact and the qualities of the boy, and pondering intellectual issues of beauty and the senses. Seeing Tadzio on the beach and in the dining room is a matter of interest and amusement; Aschenbach thinks himself fully in control, but the truth is otherwise.

At the same time, Aschenbach begins to hear hints of Asiatic cholera in Venice, hushed up by the authorities, who are afraid of losing business. The matter is in the German-language papers but not in others, and so the German-speaking population begins to melt away. Aschenbach decides to leave, but a last-minute mixup with baggage gives him an excuse to stay, and his fate is sealed. He becomes hopelessly infatuated with Tadzio, following the lad and his family in the evenings through Venice, becoming unraveled intellectually and morally, descending into the squalid use of cosmetics and hair dye in a ludicrous attempt to impress the boy. On the last day of his life, when the Polish family is finally about to leave, Aschenbach sits in his beach chair, watching the boy, and dies of the sickness. It is in a way Aschenbach's intellect that kills him; his ratiocination fails to grasp the true situation at the start, and then it is too late—his controlled, northern habits of work and mind are not enough to deal with beauty, passion, and the senses. As Mann remarks of his protagonist, the whole cultural structure of a lifetime was destroyed by Aschenbach's Venetian holiday.

This is a distinguished work. Within its short compass, there are incredibly dense, rich layers of interrelationships, allusions to a wide range of literary works and cultural ideas, and profound insights into the creative process, all of which make *Death in Venice* a book that you will read and reread over the course of your life. Mann's fabled use of language is remarkable; as he says of his protagonist, he liberates from the "marble mass of language" the slender forms of his art.

Of Mann's extensive output, *The Magic Mountain,* a long, complex philosophical novel, is the most famous work; we think you will like *Buddenbrooks*, a story of change and decline in a commercial and civic family in northern Germany, published when Mann was still in his twenties. For young adults, especially those studying German, *Tonio Kröger* is a delightful and accessible novella. We like the fine English translations of Mann's work by H. T. Lowe-Porter.

Thomas Mann (1875–1955), *Death in Venice (Der Tod in Venedig,* Munich: Hyperion Verlag, 1912; English edition, trans. H. T. Lowe-Porter, London: Martin Secker, 1930). Widely available in various translations and in both hardcover and paperback editions; we like the Vintage Books paperback (1989) of the Lowe-Porter translation.

W. Somerset Maugham
The Razor's Edge

~

Maugham, read less often today than he should be, was one of the most popular and successful writers in the English-speaking world throughout the first half of the twentieth century. A hardworking, prolific author, he was equally at home writing for the stage and as a writer of short stories and novels. Born in 1874, he attended medical school, published his first novel at the age of twenty-three, and became a literary celebrity with his two best-known novels, *Of Human Bondage* (1915) and *The Moon and Sixpence* (1919). English by parentage, he spent most of his childhood in Paris, traveled widely in East and Southeast Asia as a young man, and, later in life, lived in comfortable elegance in a house on the Riviera. He lived long and well, and died in 1965.

The Razor's Edge is written as if in Maugham's own voice, with himself, as a famous and successful author, as a character in the book. He presents the story as a novelized version of events in his own life, real life, as it were, with only a few names and minor details changed to protect the identities of other people who appear in the book. But all of this is a literary conceit; the book is in fact a novel disguised as a disguised memoir. Its characters are invented (with clear elements of autobiography in the book's central character, Larry), and the events of the book are elements of a carefully constructed plot. But the literary conceit is a very effective one, and the reader quickly assents to it.

The story concerns several lives that repeatedly intersect over the years. Its two central characters are Isabel Bradley and Larry Darrell, whom we meet in Chicago at the home of Isabel's mother, a wealthy widow. Isabel's Uncle Elliott, visiting from Paris, deeply disapproves of Isabel's love for Larry, who comes from a poor family of no distinction and whose recent experiences as an aviator during World War I have left him restless and uninclined to hold a job. Gray Maturin, the hale-and-hearty son of a rich stockbroker, is openly in love with Isabel but stands aside because he's Larry's best friend.

Larry leaves for Paris to loaf, as he puts it, but actually to study and to think about his life. He declines to return to Chicago to marry Isabel, and she breaks off the engagement in despair, though she remains as much in love with him as ever. Isabel then marries Gray, who in a few years is bankrupted in the stock market crash of 1929; the Maturins move to Paris to live with the financial support of Uncle Elliott, who has managed to hold on to his wealth. Larry meanwhile has gone off to India to live for several years at an ashram; when he returns to Paris, he is a changed man. Other complications ensue; as the book's title suggests, a narrow margin of contingency is all it takes to make plans, and relationships, go awry. Maugham, in his guise as author-as-character, records these affairs with the air of a tolerant, observant friend of all of the participants; he points out to the reader that his book has near the end both a death and a marriage, which should satisfy readers of conventional fiction. The book ends with one of the cleverest wrapping-up paragraphs we know of.

There are a number of details in the book that give a modern reader pause. For example, because every generation imagines it invented the world anew, we tend to think of sexual liberation and an openly gay lifestyle as products of the sexual revolution of the 1960s; Maugham portrays Paris in the Twenties and Thirties as being totally unsurprised by some very unconventional sexual lifestyles. (In the novel, Isabel's Uncle Elliott, an effete, campy snob, is clearly gay, but Maugham leaves that conclusion to the reader's implicit understanding, just as he remained in the closet about his own homosexuality until very late in his life.) Similarly, many people today believe that going off to India to sit at the feet of a guru is something that was invented by hippies in the 1960s, and revived by New Age seekers in the 1990s; for Maugham, this was a perfectly plausible thing for a sensitive young man to do in the Thirties. *The Razor's Edge* is a pleasure to read not only because it is a beautifully contrived work of fiction, but because, like all literature that is in some way great, it invites us to share in aspects of the human experience that transcend our own lives.

W. Somerset Maugham (1874–1965), *The Razor's Edge* (London: Heinemann, 1944; Garden City, N.Y.: Doubleday, 1944). The Penguin paperback edition (1978) is widely available.

WILLIAM MAXWELL
They Came Like Swallows

~

This short and intense novel is set in the last weeks of 1918, in a small Midwestern town probably not too different from William Maxwell's own birthplace of Lincoln, Illinois. The protagonists are the Morisons, a conventional family whom we view through the perspective of Bunny, the shy, sensitive eight-year-old younger son. Bunny is indulged by his somewhat exasperated father and protected by his boisterous, extroverted brother, Robert (who is not much inconvenienced by his "affliction," a prosthetic leg), but all of Bunny's emotional life is centered on the transcendent figure of his mother. Mrs. Morison appears to us as an almost flawless figure whose intelligence, affection, and competence provide the glue that holds the family so securely together.

On the second Sunday of November, rumors are flying that the Great War is over; Bunny Morison is stunned to learn that his mother is going to have a baby a few weeks hence. Bunny has little time to get used to the idea of being displaced as the center of her attention. By the end of the next day, a splendid parade has been held to celebrate the Armistice, and Bunny has been confined to his bed, burning with fever from an attack of Spanish influenza. Events have been set in motion that will devastate the Morison family and alter Bunny's life forever.

William Maxwell's childhood was shaped by the values and life rhythms of small Midwestern towns. Life is perhaps never simple, but in that setting it seemed to many to be transparent, comprehensible, and solid—feelings that did not leave people well prepared for sudden misfortune. Maxwell's mother died in the great flu epidemic of 1918, and he wrote many years later that her death was the defining event of his life, one that colored everything that came afterward. It is probably true that Maxwell became a writer as a way of dealing with the incomprehensible tragedy that had befallen him as a child. *They Came Like Swallows* (which was Maxwell's second novel) is not a memoir, however, but a work of fiction. Bunny Morison is not Billy Maxwell, at least not exactly.

By reimagining the personalities and the actions of his family members, by creating characters that are composites or wholly made up—in short, by transforming his experience into a work of fiction—Maxwell turned his own experience into something that he could think about, write about, cope with, and share with his readers. The book is set against a background of national catastrophe—no one who lived through the flu epidemic of 1918 could forget its terrible aura of fear and helplessness—but it focuses entirely on the catastrophe that befalls one family and one child. The outcome of events in *They Came Like Swallows* is sad, but the book itself is not; Maxwell has used the detachment of fiction to create instead a work that transforms sadness into beauty.

In 1936, Maxwell joined the staff of *The New Yorker* and worked there for over forty years as an editor of fiction. In that capacity he was known as a patient, kind perfectionist; many of the magazine's most famous writers have testified to Maxwell's ability to bring out the best in their writing. At the same time Maxwell himself wrote steadily, producing short stories, novels, and memoirs that add up to a substantial life's work. He brought to his own writing the same formidable editorial skills that made him so appreciated by his colleagues. The defining characteristic of Maxwell's prose is its plainness, yet his controlled, understated, and spare declarative sentences add up to a magical reading experience. That they do so is because he is an exceptionally acute observer of details of fact and emotion, and he never allows a superfluous word or a dramatic exaggeration to interfere with his keen understanding of what is essential.

Maxwell (who died just as this book was going to press) was often described as a "writer's writer," which is a fair enough phrase for him if it means someone whose sheer craftsmanship is admired by his fellow professionals and who is better known among other writers than he is to the general public. The phrase can mislead, however, because it often is used to describe someone whose work is difficult, abstruse, be-yond the grasp of ordinary readers. None of that is true of William Maxwell's prose. His work is not hard to read, still less hard to grasp, but it does demand that you pay attention, that you be alert to nuances and subtle emotional currents beneath the calm surface of his narra-tives. Maxwell is a writer to be read seriously, and he offers serious pleasures in return.

Friends of ours, whose happy and durable marriage is based in part on a shared exquisite taste in literature, once confided that they knew they had found their perfect partner when, on a special occasion early in their relationship, each gave the other a present—in both cases, a rare first edition of *They Came Like Swallows*. Their sense of the value of Maxwell's work is well placed. This is a book to savor and to keep on one's shelves for future rereadings.

William Maxwell (1908–2000), *They Came Like Swallows* (New York: Harper and Brothers, 1937; revised edition, New York: Vintage, 1960). There is an attractive Modern Library edition (1997) with an introduction by the author.

CHARLES MCGLINCHEY
The Last of the Name

~

Charles McGlinchey was blessed with a long life in a traditional environment, and with a gift for remembering his life and the lives of his forefathers and transmitting those memories as stories. It is our good fortune that he also had an interested and sympathetic young neighbor who encouraged McGlinchey to tell his stories and wrote them down in longhand. For several decades, those stories remained in the form of an unedited, unpublished manuscript, before the playwright Brian Friel shaped them into the chapters of this memoir. That the book exists at all is a great piece of luck, for it holds up a wonderful mirror of memory to a time and place that might easily have been forgotten.

In recent years, the best-selling Irish-childhood memoir has become stereotyped almost to the point of self-parody: The writer grows up tough but sensitive in the bosom of a dysfunctional but nurturing family on the mean but life-affirming streets of Belfast or Dublin. *The Last of the Name* has nothing in common with books of that sort. There are no mean streets here, nor any egotistical posing, either; instead there are bandits and landlords, country priests and weavers and peat cutters, the sense of a life without luxuries that was simple rather than impoverished and enriched by the depth of its past.

McGlinchey (1861–1954) lived all his life in the Meentiagh Glen, near Clonmany, on the Inishowen Peninsula in County Donegal. Except once to work as a farm laborer in Scotland and another time to attend a church conference in Dublin, he never went more than a few miles from his native village. He never married, and he outlived all of the other members of his family, which gives the meaning to the book's title. McGlinchey's life might seem to modern eyes an impossibly narrow one, but what it might have lacked in spatial breadth it made up for in temporal depth. McGlinchey was more a man of the nineteenth century than of the twentieth; he grew up with the tales of his grand-father and his father in his ears, and remembered everything that he heard. For him, living memory goes back to the 1790s, and one reads in these pages tales of the early nineteenth century recounted as if they had happened a week or two ago. He begins an account of the fairs and markets that enlivened village life by saying,

> Long ago there was a great fair held on Pollan Green twice a year, the twenty-ninth of June and the tenth of October. The last fair was held there on St. Peter and Paul's Day in the year of 1812.

One has to make an effort to remember that he was not there person-ally on that occasion. Famous highwaymen, publicans, priests, and brawlers who lived two centuries ago come alive in these pages because to McGlinchey they were as much the companions of his youth through the stories of his forefathers as his own childhood friends were in the flesh.

Part of the effect of being transported by this memoir to a remote and unfamiliar land lies in the richness of McGlinchey's language, which is wonderfully fluent and shining with intelligence, but also filled with usages that force the reader to take notice. Part of women's work was to process lint; lint, we come to understand, means the flax plant from which linen is made. Weavers produce not a bolt or a length of cloth, but a web of cloth. Revenue men do their best to halt the pro-duction of poteen (bootleg whiskey), and people were terribly afraid that someone might blink them (put a curse on them). And everywhere were places known to be gentle—that is, enchanted by fairies. These pages are strewn also with old proverbs and songs that McGlinchey learned long ago, given here in the original Gaelic as well as translated into English. And some of them are true enough, too: "The ill-will of people could send a bullock to the pot or a man to the graveyard."

McGlinchey, though, is no stage Irishman with a rolling brogue and a line of blarney; his language is his own, and his recollections are plain and straightforward. The past was alive to him, but he was not oblivious to change. Indeed, he could not have been; his own trade as a hand-weaver, for example, had nearly vanished in the area around Clonmany by the time he was an old man. It was in part to share the experience of a vanishing world that he told his tales to his young listener. He knew that a time would come when no one would know how to keep witches from drinking the milk of cows with newborn calves (put a silver coin in the noggin when milking the cow for the first time) or how to prevent fairies from stealing a human baby (lay a protective bar of iron across its cradle), and he thought such knowledge should not be lost, though his own time was growing short:

> So, whenever I die, they will know where to bury me. And after my day the grave will not be opened again, for I'm the last of the name.

This is a life very much worth remembering.

Charles McGlinchey (1861–1954), *The Last of the Name,* ed. Brian Friel (Belfast: The Blackstaff Press, 1986; Nashville: J. S. Sanders, 1999).

PETER BRIAN MEDAWAR
Advice to a Young Scientist

~

Peter Brian Medawar was a brilliant biologist, the co-winner of the Nobel Prize in Physiology or Medicine in 1960, and a scientist with an extraordinary gift for clear exposition. Born in Rio de Janeiro of an English mother and a Lebanese father, he attended Magdalen College, Oxford, and began a long and distinguished scientific career in Britain. He is best known for his work on the immunological barriers to tissue transplants, which helped pave the way for modern transplant surgery.

This graceful book is organized and written in a deceptively simple way. It is at first glance just a series of linked essays directed to young scientists, starting with "How Can I Tell if I Am Cut Out to Be a Scientific Research Worker?" and continuing with essays of ever-widening applicability, including "What Shall I Do Research On?" "Sexism and Racism in Science," "Aspects of Scientific Life and Manners," "Prizes and Rewards," "The Scientific Process," and others. But the book is much more than these titles make it sound. We gradually come to see that what Medawar says in the introduction is exactly right: The book is for all those who are engaged in intellectual activities, and who is not? It is a humane assessment of our choices in life, whatever our careers may be, and for many of our readers it will become a book that is read again and again, each time with a more profound appreciation of its wisdom.

Medawar's overall description of science is that it is "an enormous potentiation of common sense," as indeed, we may think, must be true in some way of every worthwhile human activity. Medawar's view is that the nature of creativity is the same in many fields. His description of "The Scientific Process" is a wonderful introduction for the non-scientist: the centrality of hypothesis testing, the constant tension and interaction between conjecture and refutation, and the limitations of science. Nominally about the scientific process, this essay in fact describes what much of organized human endeavor is like if well done. For those of us who are nonscientists, it gives as a bonus the sense of how choices are made in a real laboratory.

The book also has some immediate practical virtues for the reader. For example, the chapter "Presentations" is as good a brief compilation of how one presents information in public, whatever the subject, that we know of. It is obviously the product of hard-won experience on Medawar's part. There is good advice on the personal qualities needed to work collaboratively, on how to choose topics for one's work (or avocation, we might also say), and on which models of good English prose will help one's own writing. Medawar likes the essays of the philosopher and mathematician Bertrand Russell and, among nonscientific writers, Dr. Samuel Johnson's *Lives of the Poets*. And there is advice that is challenging to each of us; for example, the penetrating observation that the intensity of belief with which we hold a hypothesis has nothing to do with whether or not it is true. Embracing this insight will save many a personal and professional blunder.

The book has a breadth of perspective that is very satisfying, encapsulated in elegant writing; Medawar's alertness, warm humor, and decency make it special. All of us read and see things worth noting, but Medawar actually does note them and use them in his work, scientific and literary. Few of us would think to quote, for example, apropos of a grasping careerist, from Francis Bacon (1561–1626): "He doth like the ape, that the higher he clymbes the more he shows his ars," yet all of us can immediately think of individuals of whom this could well be said. And Medawar's humor is gentle rather than hurtful, and as often as not directed to himself as much as to others. In one passage, he discusses the importance of being candid if there is a lapse in a public presentation. Following a serious illness, he found himself making a great muddle of a lecture. His wife came to the podium to help him get his notes organized, and he inadvertently said over the live microphone, "I see exactly . . . page 5 comes after page 4." The audience was on his side. In the chapter on "Sexism and Racism in Science," we read decent views to the effect that women and men have no special aptitudes for science different from each other, and that no nations have particular skills in science, although some have greater resources to devote to it. We would be satisfied if everyone demonstrated today the fairness and civility on such topics that Medawar had a quarter of a century or more ago.

We are all, or at least all have been, in need of advice, and there is an overflowing bowl of advice here. After reading this book, one might well feel, as we do, that if we had sat with Sir Peter at a dinner party and he had been willing to discourse on these subjects with his gracefulness and humor, we would leave thinking it the best dinner party that we had ever attended. This is a book that, in the best sense, is a companion to our own personal and intellectual lives. The book as a whole is one that each of us will read and say, "Why didn't I read this when I was just starting my career?" Perhaps after you have read the book, you will encourage some young person to do just that.

Peter Brian Medawar (1915–1987), *Advice to a Young Scientist* (New York: Harper and Row, 1979). Basic Books paperback reprint (1981).

WALTER MOSLEY

Devil in a Blue Dress

~

Walter Mosley's Easy Rawlins mysteries—six in the series to date, beginning with *Devil in a Blue Dress*—have been widely and justly praised for their realism as well as for their vivid plots, strong characters, and ironic humor. What makes the Easy Rawlins books stand out from the crowd of crime genre fiction is their feeling of place: a palpable evocation of the angry, violent, intensely masculine world of black Los Angeles in the 1940s. *Devil in a Blue Dress* tells how a hardworking man who wants nothing more than to mind his own business drifts into a career as a private investigator. As with all good series fiction, these books are habit-forming; once you have read this one, you will certainly want to read all of the other Easy Rawlins novels as well.

Ezekiel Rawlins, widely known as Easy, is a serious man. He is tough, and has to be. He is a smart, ambitious, upwardly mobile African-American World War II combat vet in the Watts section of Los Angeles in 1948, and that means he faces long odds. Life in Watts is hard, but it is interesting, too, and holds promise for the future; the very small house that Easy has purchased makes him a man of property and thus a person of substance in his own eyes. When he loses his job at an aircraft plant and the monthly mortgage payment is nearly due, he is determined to hold on to his house no matter what. And that is why he is willing to entertain the offer of a quite sinister-seeming white man, Mr. Albright, to be handsomely paid to find and report on the whereabouts of a young white woman who has been hanging out in the bars and after-hours clubs of Watts. Easy's conscience tells him that the job is not necessarily a good idea, but he doesn't see any other way of making money quickly.

Once he takes the assignment, he quickly gets caught up in events that are more complex, nastier, and more dangerous than he had bargained for. Several murders litter the trail of the missing young woman; there are hints of pedophilia and blackmail in high places; Easy himself is arrested, beaten up, and almost killed. Fortunately an old friend from his native city of Houston, Mouse, shows up to help. Easy is a tough man but has qualms about killing people; Mouse has no such compunctions, and his ruthlessness allows Easy to emerge from the tale in one piece. At story's end, he has completed his assignment and come into a substantial sum of money—not quite his, but not quite anyone else's, either—to fund the beginnings of his new career as a private investigator and further his ambitions as a man moving up in the world.

The story is told in Easy Rawlins' own voice, and from a considerable perspective of time—an unspecified time present from which Easy looks back to the time past of his young manhood, as if he were telling tales of the old days to an admiring young audience. This allows him to comment on how things were in those days, and specifically to note the parlous state of race relations at the time. He recalls the wariness with which blacks confronted the white world, white expectations of black passivity and fear, and black anger and resentment born of those expectations. Easy's refusal to be pushed around, his steadiness, and his determination not to deviate from the goal of making of himself someone he can admire place him firmly in a long tradition of tough-guy crime fiction, but on the other hand, they also turn him into a character who seems vividly real.

The most recent Easy Rawlins novel, *Gone Fishin'*, is actually a prequel to the first five and shows Easy and Mouse as young men in prewar Houston. Its title perhaps was also a suggestion that Mosley intended to take a rest from the series, and so far no more Easy Rawlins novels have appeared. Mosley meanwhile has written other novels and has been active as a literary figure and a champion of African-American writers. Mosley is sometimes described as an angry writer, but that seems to us to be not quite right; he is a black American justifiably angry about the legacy of discrimination against blacks, but he is also at the forefront of those who make effective use of art to combat the continuing effects of that legacy. On the page and in person, Walter Mosley is a figure to reckon with, and he seems to have put a great deal of himself into his marvelous character, Easy Rawlins.

Walter Mosley (1952–), *Devil in a Blue Dress* (New York: W. W. Norton, 1990). The Pocket Books paperback reprint (1991) is widely available.

JOHN MUIR

My First Summer in the Sierra

~

Next time you are in San Francisco, set aside part of a day to drive north over the Golden Gate Bridge and along Route 1 for a few miles. Turning off toward the southwest slope of Mount Tamalpais, you will soon enter what must surely be one of the most appropriate memorials anywhere: Muir Woods National Monument, a wonderful forest of towering redwoods, *Sequoia sempervirens*. The mysteries of these woods commemorate a man of enormous knowledge, courage, and foresight who played a vital role in the preservation of wilderness and the creation of state and national parks in the United States. Born in the little east coast Scottish town of Dunbar in 1838, John Muir was a person of quite extraordinary physical, mental, and moral stamina, reflected in his strenuous travels throughout his life, his deep interest in geological science, especially the effects of glaciers on the landscape, and his concern with the ethical aspects of nature.

In February 1849, Muir's hardworking father, Daniel, sold his prosperous grain and food supply business in Scotland and took John and two of his other children to the United States. They settled on a farm near the Fox River in Buffalo Township, Wisconsin, where John's mother joined them later with four other siblings. John's childhood was one of rigid religious discipline and oppressively hard work, a fact noted by several of his biographers. Yet if his upbringing was harsh by modern standards, it did at least force him to become proficient in a wide range of skills, and his own inquiring mind engendered an early and profound love of learning. A keen observer of his surroundings, he developed at a young age an awareness of the natural world and its fragility in the face of the onrushing civilization of the frontier. Having attained a local reputation for mechanical ingenuity as an inventor of improvements to clocks and other machines, he began his independent life as a young adult by exhibiting his machines at the State Agricultural Fair in Madison. He then attended the University of Wisconsin, founded only a decade earlier but already a considerable institution, for two and a half years, where he was a stellar student.

Following his studies at Wisconsin, Muir spent several years pursuing his interest in nature studies while working in machine shops and lumber mills, where his talent for improving machinery and production processes made him a highly valued employee. The shock of an accident that nearly deprived him of the sight in his right eye led Muir to rethink his goals and to recognize his true calling as a student of the natural world. After explorations that included a thousand-mile walk to the Gulf Coast, he traveled to California, arriving in San Francisco in 1868. In the summer of 1869, he took a job with a rancher acquaintance, overseeing the movement of flocks to mountain pastures.

As supervisor of the enterprise, Muir assembled a crew of two—a shepherd named Billy and a borrowed St. Bernard dog, Carlo—to go on the trip. Able to rely on their expert work in dealing with the sheep, Muir found himself with time to indulge his passion for explorations of nature. *My First Summer in the Sierra,* based on his contemporary journal (though not published until 1911), is the record of that extraordinary time. Although Muir was in the Sierra that summer for less than four months, we come away from the book feeling that his time there was much longer, and in some sense permanent.

The book follows the pattern of the summer: moving sheep to higher and higher elevations, as forage becomes available, from their winter ground up into the headwaters of the Tuolumne and Merced rivers, through what is now Yosemite National Park to the grazing area of the Tuolumne Meadows. This excursion reveals the author's intense reaction to the glories of the landscape and nature as a whole. What makes Muir's account so unusual is his ecstatic, exhilarated reactions coupled with his expert knowledge of the environment. This is not the work of an amateur. We see Muir's observations of the effects of glaciers on the rocks and his detailed knowledge of the flora and fauna of the area. There are lovely descriptions of flowers in upland meadows and detailed observations of everything from squirrels to bears. There is Muir, always the practical man, recounting proudly at the end of the summer that of the 2,050 lean and hungry sheep with which the expedition started, 2,025 were brought back strong and fat despite all of the hazards of the trip; we also read his observations on the destructive effects on nature of an enterprise such as the one he is supervising. We see Muir's readiness to take fearful risks to discover nature, including lowering himself to a tiny ledge on a sheer boulder face overlooking the falls of Yosemite Creek, the better to immerse himself in the beauty of the scene. (Even the intrepid Muir had a sleepless night after this harrowing adventure.)

Most striking, we sense the author's belief in the ethical and religious qualities of nature, and in the unity of humans and the natural world. No longer conventionally religious, Muir thanks God for his glimpse of Yosemite Creek. He spends a night alone on top of an eight-foot-tall flood boulder: ". . . the stars peering through the leaf-roof seemed to join in the white water's song. Precious night, precious day to abide in me forever." Thinking back on the mountains at the end of the summer, he sees that their beauties "are beyond all common reason, unexplainable and mysterious as life itself." In this short volume, we have our views of the natural world challenged and changed, probably for good. And it is Muir's sense of reverence for nature that makes a grove of redwoods such a fitting monument to his life and work; standing amidst the immense trees, it is easy to feel that something of Muir's soul remains in the forest he loved so well.

This is a classic of the environment, the American West, and the relationship of humans to nature. It is a wonderful book for a thoughtful young person. The text is little changed from the original journal of 1869 and reflects Muir before he became famous as a public advocate for natural preservation, friend of the great, and founder of the modern environmental movement. Of Muir's many other works, we like especially his last book, *Travels in Alaska*.

194 • 100 One-Night Reads

John Muir (1838–1914), *My First Summer in the Sierra* (Boston: Houghton Mifflin, 1911). An attractive edition is the Sierra Club Books paperback in the John Muir Library (1988). A fine biography of Muir is Linnie Marsh Wolfe's *Son of the Wilderness: The Life of John Muir* (New York: Alfred A. Knopf, 1945; reprinted, University of Wisconsin Press, 1973), based in substantial part on her interviews with those who knew and worked with Muir, including his daughters.

R. K. NARAYAN

The English Teacher

~

Rasipuram Krishnaswami Narayan is one of the most famous Indian authors writing in English, with a long and successful career. He was born in 1906 and received his education in Madras (now Chennai), the principal city of south India, and in Mysore. *The English Teacher* is the last of a trilogy, the others being *Swami and Friends*, Narayan's first novel, and *The Bachelor of Arts*. As with most of Narayan's work, the story takes place in the south Indian town of Malgudi. This is a fictional town that Narayan has constructed to give him freedom from literal reality in his stories. Yet for those who know Indian towns, it is intensely real. When someone goes to Malgudi Station, we have the feeling that it is as truly there as the station at, say, Saharanpur, in the north. Narayan, with impish humor, has located Malgudi variously, including the area in and around the Hotel Chelsea on 23rd Street in Manhattan, where he liked to stay when in New York.

The first pages of the novel focus on the protagonist, Krishna, who is a lecturer in English at Albert Mission College, the same school in which he was a student. He is living in the hostel (dormitory) of the school for the tenth year, although he has a wife and baby daughter, Susila and Leela, who live with his in-laws some distance away. When we first meet Krishna, he is a self-absorbed Brahmin (high-caste Hindu) academic, rather detached from daily life. Krishna enjoys the logic-chopping and arch humor of the faculty common room (familiar to anyone who has had exposure to British higher education and its colonial derivatives), but he is unhappy with the educational system, which is largely based on rote learning of English and European material. At the time of the novel, the British were still rulers of India, and the Raj and its servants come in for suitable whacks. Brown, the school

principal, is incensed that a boy has never learned that *honour* in British spelling includes a *u*. How can the purity of the English language
be neglected in this way by Indian boys? Krishna remarks to a colleague
that, be that as it may, Brown cannot after thirty years' residence say
"The cat chases the rat" in any of the hundreds of languages of India.

Soon enough, a letter comes from his father, reporting that he and
Susila's father are in agreement that Krishna should move out of the
hostel and have a house in town with his young family. (Like many
things in the novel and in traditional Indian real life, this change is set
in motion by the family rather than by the persons most directly af-
fected.) Krishna is in for a new life. There is an enormous amount of
nerve-wracking and pointless worry: Will Leela hit her head in the
process of debarking from the train? What is wrong with trains that the
doors are not more suitable for travel with children? How many children are injured each year? Krishna has a full measure of the useless
fussing that besets most of us from time to time. Despite imagined
dangers, Susila and Leela arrive safely, and the family embarks on a period of happiness in their new circumstances; this is a lovely time for
them. They have visits from parents (Krishna's mother-in-law is so tra-
ditionally trained to respect her son-in-law that she doesn't talk directly
to him); an old lady friend of the family arrives to help keep house. The
young pair are modern: They have promised each other to have just one
child. It is true that their marriage has been traditional in some ways
(Krishna recalls visiting, seeing, and approving the bride), but there
is genuine affection between them. Part of the quality of the novel
comes from the expert way in which Narayan interweaves the caring
and teasing with the petty arguments that seem to occur in nearly all
relationships.

Later, the older generation decides that the young family should not
continue to rent a house but should have their own, and disaster strikes.
On a visit to look at new houses, Susila sickens—perhaps in a restaurant, perhaps in the dirty lavatory of a house they inspect. At first it is
thought to be "only" malaria, but then it is clear that it is typhoid.
Susila dies, and her death and cremation are very moving. (The role of
illness in third-world countries, then as now, is one that we in the West
have largely forgotten. One of us remembers, in summer months in

India, sharing his malaria pills with local colleagues because the government had neglected to manufacture enough to meet the needs of the season.)

The story then subtly changes from one that seems firmly based in reality to one in which levels of reality shift. Deeply held beliefs in cycles of death and rebirth, in the closeness of life and death, and in the action of gods affect both perceptions and decisions, as does the constant presence of priests and holy men. The master of Leela's marvelous little school, which she begins attending after the death of Susila, has had the exact day of his death forecast by a wandering astrologer. The day arrives, with unexpected results. Krishna is contacted by a person who says that he is able to transmit to him Susila's thoughts from the other world in which she now dwells. Krishna believes this (although doubts surface sometimes), and he gradually feels himself to be communing ever more closely with his lost wife. We are truly touched by the conclusion of the story, although (and perhaps because) we are not sure what is and what is not reality as the novel ends.

This is a fine book, whose elements remain in the mind for a long time. Of Narayan's other work, we recommend the short stories, especially *Malgudi Days*. Narayan's career has been both long and very productive, and you may well find yourself reading a great many of his novels and becoming ever more immersed in the lives of the citizens of Malgudi.

R[asipuram] K[rishnaswami] Narayan (1906–), *The English Teacher* (London: Heinemann, 1945). The University of Chicago Press paperback (1980) is a handy edition.

ERIC NEWBY

A Short Walk in the Hindu Kush

~

In 1956, Eric Newby and his friend Hugh Carless set out to climb 20,000-foot Mount Samir, in the remote and wild Hindu Kush mountains of northeastern Afghanistan. They didn't make it to the summit, but the tale of how they failed to climb the mountain has become a classic of travel writing. Newby—a World War II hero who was clearly very good at taking care of himself—sometimes, one suspects, embroiders his tale for effect, portraying himself and his friend as more comically inept than was really the case. But Newby's self-deprecating charm is so seductive that the reader is perfectly willing to take his account at face value for the sake of a vicarious adventure.

Newby developed an early taste for strenuous pursuits. His English middle-class upbringing, in many respects conventional for its place and time, included some childhood years in India. On completing school in England in the 1930s, he abandoned a career with an advertising agency almost before it had begun, shipping out on a Finnish trading schooner. This was one of the last sail-powered cargo ships to carry grain from Australia to England, and Newby later chronicled his days as a merchant sailor in his first book, *The Last Grain Race*.

World War II found Newby signing up immediately. He became a commando in the Special Boat Squadron, which among other things conducted landings from submarines to operate behind enemy lines. On one such raid, aimed at an airfield in Sicily, he was captured, and he spent a year as a prisoner of war before escaping. Newby memorably described this adventure many years later in his book *Love and War in the Apennines*. As he made his way back to freedom he was helped by, and fell in love with, a woman whom he later returned to marry.

After the war, Newby tried to settle down to a career in the wholesale ladies' clothing trade. It took him some years to realize how un-suited he was for mundane commercial enterprise, but in the midst of preparations for the 1956 spring couture shows, and with *The Last Grain Race* just published, he had enough. He quit his job, cabled his friend Hugh to join him on a mountaineering expedition, and prepared to head off to Afghanistan.

A great deal of the charm of *A Short Walk in the Hindu Kush* de-rives from the way Newby portrays the adventure as a study in the quintessentially British qualities of courage, persistence, and muddling through despite all obstacles. The two friends, we are assured, knew nothing at all about mountain climbing, and what they learned in the weekend course they took in Wales to prepare for their trip wasn't of much use. Still, they managed to wangle a grant from the Everest Soci-ety to fund their trip, and set off with a carload of gear on the first leg of the journey—a drive from London to Afghanistan. (That trip alone would be adventure enough for most people.) Some distance up the Panjshir Valley beyond Kabul, with the car on its last legs, they reached the end of the road and started walking toward Mount Samir.

Once in the mountains, and beyond the more cosmopolitan parts of Afghanistan, where Carless' knowledge of Persian (he had been in the British colonial service) made communication with the locals pos-sible, they get out their 1901 *Notes on the Bashgali Language* and try out a few phrases. They are dismayed to find that the sample sentences given in the book include things like "If you have had diarrhea for many days you will surely die." But they do reach the mountain and begin the ascent—literally with their how-to-climb-mountains guidebook in one hand.

With more courage than good sense, they get to within seven hun-dred feet of the summit when at last they realize that going farther will probably be fatal, and wisely turn back. As a consolation for failing to climb the mountain, they decide to end their trip with a trek across the province of Nuristan, the most remote and mysterious place in Afghanistan, where the inhabitants, non-Moslems, are said to be de-scended from stragglers from Alexander the Great's army. After some days of this, dirty, weary, bedraggled, and ready to return home, they run into a fabled English trekker—Wilfred Thesiger, intrepid explorer of Arabia's Empty Quarter, legendary for his disdain of civilized conveniences (see p. 266). Newby, awed, describes him as "a great, long-striding crag of a man, with an outcrop for a nose and bushy eyebrows, forty-five years old and hard as nails." Thesiger invites them to join him in camping for the night. When Newby and Carless begin to inflate their air mattresses, the great explorer looks at the tyros with contempt. "God," he says, "you must be a couple of pansies."

It is notoriously difficult to describe humor or to explain why something is funny. Please take our word for it—this book will have you laughing out loud. A talent for writing about improbable and outrageous incidents with a perfectly straight face, and a charmingly open and guileless personality, make Newby a wonderful traveling companion, especially as, from the comfort of one's favorite chair, all of the hardships of the journey are his. In any case, *A Short Walk in the Hindu Kush* was a great success when it was published in 1958, and Newby went on to other adventures and a position as the travel editor of the London *Observer*. Of his other travel books we especially like *Slowly Down the Ganges*.

As funny as *A Short Walk* is, one finishes reading it today with a sense of loss. The land where Newby and Carless walked has been torn apart by decades of invasion, war, and civil strife and has been largely out of bounds for travelers. Around the world, the kinds of traditional societies that so interested writers like Newby and Thesiger have been shattered by change, and so this book has become a record of an era of unfettered travel, remote places, and cultural diversity such as we may not see again.

Eric Newby (1919–), *A Short Walk in the Hindu Kush* (London: Secker and Warburg, 1958; paperback, Arrow Books, 1961). After being out of print for many years, the book is once again available, in a paperback reprint from Lonely Planet Books (1998).

JOHN NICOL

The Life and Adventures of John Nicol, Mariner

~

John Nicol was a Scot, born in the village of Currie, near Edinburgh, in 1755. His father was a cooper, or barrel maker, and young Nicol received an education sufficient to fit him for that skilled trade. He early had a yen to go to sea but postponed this until his training was complete. When he was about fourteen, his father took him to stay for a year in London, where he had a job with a chemical works. Returning to Scotland, he completed his training as a journeyman cooper and then went to sea. Because of his skills, Nicol was valuable on ships of exploration, commerce, whaling, and war, and he served on all, being at sea for the greater part of twenty-five years, including two circumnavigations of the world.

As sturdy as he was to have survived the rigors of sea life for a quarter century, his stories would have disappeared with him were it not for John Howell, an Edinburgh bookbinder, inventor, and enthusiast of military and adventure stories. Howell met Nicol, who apparently had a reputation as a storyteller, and published his reminiscences. Nicol brings home to us a world that is entirely gone, one in which the oceans were filled with sailing vessels, the great transport and communications devices of their time. During his years at sea, Nicol was one of millions of people who found themselves on the oceans for war, commerce, exploration, emigration, or servitude. Nicol had the firm constitution, levelheaded attitude, and, of course, great good luck to survive as long as he did.

Nicol's first voyage was to Quebec on the *Proteus* at the start of the Revolutionary War. He enjoyed his time in Canada, and because the ship was laid up for six weeks while the crew recovered from dysentery, he was able to take work onshore (common at the time, especially for skilled craftsmen). He did not join the Frenchmen in eating snakes, although he helped to catch some, and reveals here as elsewhere his appreciation for the life of common people. He tells of the families floating down the river on log rafts, with their boats tied behind for the return journey after the wood is sold. He liked hearing the children singing on these rafts as they drifted past people on moored boats and onshore. Nicol, who in these pages consistently seems like a reasonable and decent man, reproaches himself, not for the last time, for falling away from his regular Bible-reading habits.

After several years of naval duty on convoy and fighting American privateers, Nicol returned to England and Scotland to find that his father had died. He then served on a whaler to Greenland and on a commercial ship to the West Indies. Here we find him sympathetically taking food to African slaves, who are treated with striking cruelty by their masters. He is invited in turn to an evening's celebration with makeshift drums and rattles, and "three bit maubi," or rum, bought especially for the visitor, and he records some of the slaves' songs.

In 1785, Nicol was taken on as cooper on the *King George*, at the insistence of an officer under whom he had earlier served, for a voyage of discovery and trade around the world. This was at the time an enormous undertaking; although long sea voyages were common by Nicol's day, any prolonged voyage away from routine trade routes was risky. The *King George* was the first ship to arrive in Hawaii (then called the Sandwich Islands) after the initial European encounter with those islands by Captain James Cook, and his murder there. (Nicol and his colleagues met Hawaiians who had bayonets obtained from Cook's party.) During their stay in Hawaii, each of the crew took a temporary wife from among the Hawaiians; of all the places Nicol visited, he thought Hawaii the best for climate, people, and provisions, terming it "a most endearing place." During this voyage, the *King George* headed north for furs, visiting Cook Inlet and Prince William Sound in Alaska. They met Russians, from whom they wisely concealed their fur-trading activities, and had difficult experiences with parties of Native Americans. The ship continued on to China, where Nicol was fascinated by Canton. As a foreigner, he could not enter the city itself, but he visited the quarter set aside for foreign trade, and he characteristically notes that the splendor of the place concealed vast misery for the many.

Nicol's most affecting trip is the one he undertook on returning from the round-the-world voyage of the *King George*. He signed on a ship transporting women convicts to Australia; during the voyage, he fell in love with Sarah Whitlam, one of the convicts, and had a child, John, with her. They had happy weeks by what is now Sydney harbor before Nicol left, hoping to bring Sarah and John to England later. But Sarah left Port Jackson, and despite years of effort, Nicol was never able to find out her whereabouts (he heard at one point that she had gone to Bombay). He never saw her or John again, to his great distress. Sarah was the love of his life. Her parents in Lincoln, whom he visited when he returned to Great Britain, had no more news than he.

After other voyages, including another circling of the globe, Nicol spent the last part of his sailing life, from 1794 to 1801, at war against the French, with many hair-raising adventures. Thereafter he returned to Edinburgh and married a cousin. He did not have a peaceful life, however, as during the Napoleonic Wars he had to live in small villages not far from Edinburgh to avoid the press gangs that seized sailors and by force put them into service on warships. When the fighting ended, he returned to Edinburgh; his wife died shortly thereafter, Nicol fell upon hard times, and it was then that he met Howell.

What is striking about this book is Nicol's humanity. He seems always to have had sympathy for those at the bottom of the ladder and to have maintained a certain innocence despite everything. His stories have a literary, almost musical quality. They were apparently little changed by Howell and have the finely honed character of sailors' stories, told many times and distilled to the essence. (We heard similar ones, from a later age, from our grandfather, who was an English sailor.) His stories do not, in this short book, include the details of sailing ship operation and maintenance found in the novels of O'Brian (p. 205); perhaps neither Nicol nor Howell thought these worth including for the audience of the time. Nor is there anything in the stories of the intellectual brilliance of the Edinburgh of Nicol's day; these are the stories of a working seaman who, always ready to turn to with a will, maintained his wonder at the wide world revealed by sailing ships despite incredible hardships. Perhaps most of all, this book reminds us how much there is in human experience that should be known, recorded, and remembered.

John Nicol (1755–1825), *The Life and Adventures of John Nicol, Mariner* (1822; ed. Tim Flannery, New York: Atlantic Monthly Press, 1999).

PATRICK O'BRIAN

The Unknown Shore

~

This rousing tale of shipwreck and rescue is a very lightly fictionalized account of a famous episode in British naval history, the wreck of His Majesty's Ship *Wager* off the wild southwestern coast of South America. Patrick O'Brian has stayed very close to the actual events of the *Wager* story but has turned it into a novel by adding plausible details, dialogue, and local color, and especially by fleshing out the personalities of the participants. One of the book's two central figures is closely modeled on real life; there actually was a midshipman named Jack Byron aboard the *Wager*. Jack's great friend Tobias Barrow is an inspired invention. The two are as unlike as chalk and cheese but inseparable companions nevertheless, each intuitively aware of the strengths and virtues of the other.

Jack is a rich, handsome, dashing, brave, and resourceful young gentleman, as happy climbing a topmast in a gale as he is sharing pranks with the other midshipmen. Toby, Jack's neighbor ashore, is a strange young man. A poverty-stricken lad who was apprenticed to an irascible and opinionated country surgeon, Toby has acquired a thorough if eccentric academic education but almost no preparation for life in the real world. When Jack leaves home to join his ship, Toby goes with him and is appointed surgeon's mate of the *Wager*. Toby hardly knows one end of a ship from another and never becomes more than an inept mariner, but he proves as tough, courageous, and resourceful as any man aboard. Together, Jack and Toby survive almost unimaginable hardships to return at last to England.

The actual *Wager* was part of a squadron of warships under the command of Commodore George Anson during the Anglo-Spanish War of 1739–41. Anson's assignment was to "annoy the King of Spain" by attacking ships and cities on the western coast of South America, and especially by capturing the Acapulco galleon that sailed once each year from Mexico to Manila, laden with silver to finance Spain's trans-Pacific trade. Anson's six undermanned and ill-supplied ships (the *Wager* was one of the smallest) carried munitions, trade goods, and a force of several hundred marines—most of them invalids conscripted from London's Chelsea military hospital. The squadron was delayed in sailing; its destination was an ill-kept secret, and a Spanish squadron lurked in the Atlantic to intercept Anson's ships. The odds against success seemed very long.

The late departure and an unusually slow Atlantic crossing (during which, however, they managed to evade the Spanish squadron) meant that Anson's ships reached the approaches to Cape Horn, at the southern tip of South America, just as the Antarctic winter was beginning. The crews were already seriously depleted by typhus, and during weeks of fruitless beating against western gales in an attempt to round the Horn, scurvy set in. (Scurvy is a vitamin C deficiency disease that was the scourge of long-distance voyages before the English navy discovered the virtues of citrus juice and its sailors became "limeys.") Sailors and marines began to die by the dozen, and few crewmen were well enough to man the ships adequately. Two of the squadron's ships became separated from the others and turned back. At last the ships turned northward, only to find to their horror that they had misjudged the current and were nowhere near as far around the Horn as they thought (at this time there was still no way to determine longitude with any accuracy; see Dava Sobel, p. 247). Narrowly missing a mass shipwreck, they clawed away from the land and tried to beat to westward again as the deaths from scurvy mounted still higher; by then nearly all of the marines were dead. In yet another storm, the *Wager* became separated from the squadron, made its way northward along the western coast of Chile, and finally was wrecked on a rocky, barren island.

On Wager Island (as it is still called), dissension broke out among the survivors, and Captain Cheap lost effective control of his crew. As starvation threatened, most of the sailors headed back south and around the Horn again in the ship's longboat; about half of them survived to return home after many hardships and adventures. The captain, along with Midshipman Byron and a few others, tried without success to go northward in a smaller boat. Near starvation, they were captured by Indians, who delivered them, after an appalling journey, to the Spanish authorities; they were treated well in captivity and eventually made it back to England at the end of the war.

Commodore Anson, meanwhile, pursued his mission, and in the end did succeed in capturing the Acapulco galleon and returning home with his one surviving ship laden with treasure—a brilliant triumph of seamanship and war, but achieved at a grotesque cost in human lives.

The tale of the *Wager* is brilliantly brought alive in this stirring, exciting novel. You will find this well worth your while even if it is the only Patrick O'Brian book you ever read. But we hope that it will whet your appetite to read all of the novels in O'Brian's masterpiece, his twenty-volume saga of Captain Jack Aubrey and the surgeon Stephen Maturin during the Napoleonic Wars. The series, from *Master and Commander* to *Blue at the Mizzen*, is in effect one single novel in twenty volumes, and one of the greatest works of historical fiction ever written. (You will need to budget time for this rather formidable reading project, because once you embark on reading these books you will find it almost impossible to stop.) What you probably will already have guessed is that *The Unknown Shore* was in effect a tryout for the personalities of Aubrey and Maturin, in the characters of Jack Byron and Toby Barrow. The experiment succeeded; Aubrey and Maturin are not actually depicted as survivors of the *Wager* (and, in any case, the timing wouldn't work), but in literary terms, they are grown-up reincarnations of the Byron and Barrow we have learned to like and enjoy so much in these pages.

In other ways, too, *The Unknown Shore* anticipates O'Brian's later novels: in its fanatical attention to the technical details and arcane terminology of sailing ships; in Barrow/Maturin's interest in ornithology as well as in medical science; in Byron/Aubrey's cheerful competence and careless bravery, and his equally cheerful devotion to good food and pretty ladies; and in O'Brian's distinctive narrative style, in which some events are minutely described, others elided in great narrative leaps in time without so much as a paragraph break.

Patrick O'Brian, who died while writing what was to have been the twenty-first and final volume of the Aubrey-Maturin novels, was in a sense as much a work of art of his own devising as any of the books that he wrote. Despite his name in later life, he was in fact not Irish but English, born Richard Patrick Russ and brought up near London in what appears to have been a very unhappy family. He abandoned his Welsh first wife in 1940, when he joined the British armed forces to fight in World War II; he is thought to have served as a British secret agent in France during the war, but the details of his wartime service died with him, along with many other secrets. After the war, he invented a new identity for himself as an Irish writer, and that is what he became. His first novel, *Testimonies,* set in a Welsh village, is a dark and tragic tale of passionate, illicit love. With his second wife, Countess Mary Tolstoy, O'Brian moved to a Catalan-speaking village in the hills of southwestern France, where they lived quietly, and indeed almost invisibly, for the rest of their lives. Except for a few carefully managed publicity trips for his Aubrey-Maturin novels in the 1990s, O'Brian seldom appeared in public. He preferred to present himself as he had invented himself, an author found most truly in the pages of his work; and that is how he will be remembered.

Patrick O'Brian (1914–2000), *The Unknown Shore* (London: Hart-Davis, 1959; New York: W. W. Norton, 1995). The Norton paperback edition (1997) is readily available. O'Brian's Aubrey/Maturin novels are also published by W. W. Norton. An excellent nonfiction account of the Anson expedition, including a detailed description of the shipwreck of the *Wager,* can be found in Glyn Williams, *The Prize of All the Oceans* (New York: Viking, 2000).

George Orwell

Animal Farm

~

George Orwell was born in Bengal, in British India, where his father was a civil servant. He went to England for schooling (he was a scholarship student at Eton, the most elite of English schools), and then went to Burma to serve as an officer in the Imperial Indian Police. He returned again to England to make an (at first marginally) successful career as a writer, served in the Spanish Civil War on the side of the Republic, was wounded, and went back to England for the rest of his life.

Perhaps Orwell's most distinguishing characteristic as a writer is his exceptional economy and power when dealing with moral questions; *Animal Farm* is a political satire truly worth reading. Orwell was a fierce opponent of political oppression and social injustice, and his moral sense was no doubt well grounded in his own life experiences: at Eton as a lowly scholarship student; in Burma with the realization that the local people hated him as a member of the constabulary; by his service in Spain, where he discovered the betrayal of the Republic by Moscow-led operatives and barely escaped with his life; and with the authoritarianism of Hitler and Stalin.

Animal Farm was published in 1945 (by coincidence in August, the month of the atomic attacks on Japan), when the war in Europe had just been won and the Soviet Union was officially the ally of the West. It is based on the specific historical circumstances of Stalinist absolutism, but its real significance is its general meaning for the just management of human affairs. *Animal Farm* is a fable—Orwell called it a fairy story—of revolution and its consequences, modeled closely on the evils of the Stalinist dictatorship that was the end product of the bright hopes of the 1917 revolution in Russia.

Manor Farm is in England, run by Farmer Jones, who drinks too much and mistreats his animals. An old pig ("old Major"—as it happens, not a relation of ours) is about to die, and he calls the other animals together for a night meeting in the barn (Jones is in a drunken stupor). He tells them of a dream he has had about revolution against the animals' human oppressors and how someday, after the revolution, the animals will own the farm in common, run it for their mutual benefit, and live in happiness. The revolution takes place sooner than expected, set off by greater-than-usual neglect by Jones and his hands. The farm is renamed Animal Farm, and at first the animals are truly happy. Some of the animals, especially the pigs, who are the smartest, learn to read and write; the seven commandments of Animalism are inscribed on the barn (#7: *All animals are equal*) and everything seems to go well. But practical problems, deceptions, and power-grabs creep in, and the consequences are inevitable.

The most active among the animals are the pigs Napoleon and Snowball, who are often at odds. Napoleon is the more taciturn of the two, and Snowball is the great orator and planner of projects. The first is modeled on Stalin, and the second on his defeated rival, Trotsky (who was exiled and later murdered). The animals, led by Snowball, bravely defeat an attack by humans to regain the property, and great plans are drawn up for the farm. In the midst of debate, however, Napoleon sics attack dogs he has secretly trained on Snowball, who barely escapes the farm with his life, and Napoleon is on his way to absolute power. Snowball is not seen again, but most of the evils that occur from then on are attributed to him. Gradually, Napoleon takes over with lies and terror, depriving the other animals of their freedoms and creating a new privileged class of pigs (and dogs), with himself as the unquestioned leader. Animals who err confess and are murdered on the spot (a reflection of the Moscow show trials of the 1930s), rations are short (except for the pigs and the dogs), and all are assured that their sacrifices are for the greater good (in the very long run, of course; no animals go out to contented retirements in pasture, as had originally been planned). The squalid ending, where the pigs get drunk at dinner with humans, discuss the happy problems of exploiting others (the lower animals for the pigs, the lower classes for the humans), and even begin to look like humans and walk on two legs, is lesson enough. After the optimism of the revolution, all is as it was, except that the other animals are exploited more by the new ruling class than by the old and, in a now famous phrase, the seventh commandment is altered: *All animals are equal, but some are more equal than others.*

The enduring power of *Animal Farm* lies in what is not said. Orwell simply recounts, in the style of fairy stories, what happens, but we draw our own powerful conclusions for our lives and societies. Orwell's vision may be bleaker than we think right in our own prosperous times, but we need always to be reminded of the dangers that may face civil societies (as Simon Leys demonstrates vividly in *Chinese Shadows*; see p. 158). The truths endure: Small lies turn into big lies; unjust persecution of one endangers all; people must not be oppressed because of class, race, or other distinctions; power corrupts. Orwell, with his brilliant writing, allows problems to insinuate themselves gradually into the story amidst the high hopes of the animals, making the inevitable fall from utopia more painful to animals and readers alike. Along the way we come to react strongly to some of the animal characters. For example, it's hard not to like Boxer, the horse who is the strongest worker. He isn't the brightest of the animals, and in fact has only been able to learn the first four letters of the alphabet, but if he ever gets to retirement, he intends to try to master the other twenty-two. He is a true believer in the revolution to the end, but when his strength gives out, he is sent by Napoleon to the glue factory. (Squealer, the odious pig who is spokesman for the revolutionary regime, reports that this is all lies and that Boxer died, grateful for Napoleon's rule, well cared for in a hospital; unfortunately his remains are not available for burial on the farm.)

Orwell's penetrating assessment of the particular historical context in which he wrote is breathtaking. At a time when making excuses for Stalinism was something of a cottage industry among intellectuals, he understood clearly the evils of that (and any other) authoritarian system. In fact, his insight appears greater now that the Soviet Union has collapsed. Orwell saw even during World War II that the vaunted capital projects were poorly constructed, the statistics were manipulated, visitors were deceived by outright fabrications about workers' welfare, and terror ruled. But if Orwell's work was brave in the context of his times, its larger significance is its meaning for the long-term future.

Orwell is known today to college students as the author of *Animal Farm* and his other famous novel of totalitarianism, *1984,* but he completed a much larger body of work that repays reading; we recommend especially *Burmese Days* and *Down and Out in Paris and London.* A distinguished essayist as well as novelist, he is one of relatively few authors almost all of whose work is worth revisiting.

George Orwell [Eric Blair] (1875–1955), *Animal Farm* (London: Secker and Warburg, 1945; New York: Harcourt, Brace, 1946). Widely available; the Plume fiftieth-anniversary edition (1996) has a worthwhile introduction by Russell Baker.

C. NORTHCOTE PARKINSON
Parkinson's Law

~

Parkinson's Law states that work expands to fill the time available for its completion. There really was a Parkinson, and he published this book to present his famous law and other ideas to the general public. Cyril Northcote Parkinson was born in Durham, England. An academic and a prolific writer, he served as a British army staff officer during World War II, and at the time of the publication of his best-known work was Raffles Professor of History at the University of Singapore. As a writer, Parkinson had an easy, witty style and an unusual ability to blend serious observation with spoofs of academic research.

Parkinson's Law is a series of essays reprinted from *The Economist* and other journals. The first is the enunciation of the famous law itself; the others propose other laws and principles relating to administration. In presenting his law, Parkinson first uses a down-home example: sending a postcard to a niece. This task would take a busy person, who has not much time, perhaps three minutes. It can easily expand to take an oldster at leisure an entire afternoon, as Parkinson shows by breaking up the tasks and suggesting some times for each (find the postcard, find the stamp, think of what to say, and the like; our favorite subtask is the twenty minutes it takes to decide whether to bring an umbrella while going to the postbox on the next street).

While the operation of the law is clear enough in everyday life, observing its effects can be complex in organizations. Parkinson therefore moves on to what he assures us, in his tongue-in-cheek style, is more scientific ground. The underlying reasons for his law in organizations, he says, based on his government experience, are that (1) officials like to multiply the number of their subordinates, and (2) officials make work for each other. (Anyone who has spent time in Washington will agree with this last point.) Thus whether the actual amount of work done increases, decreases, or even disappears entirely, there is an inexorable expansion of effort regardless of what (if anything) is accomplished.

To make his point, Parkinson provides employment figures from the British Admiralty showing that from 1914 to 1928, the number of large warships in commission declined from sixty-two to twenty (a decrease of almost 68 percent), whereas over the same period the number of Admiralty officials increased by more than 78 percent, a fact unexplainable except by Parkinson's Law. Lest his readers write this off as due to something like increasing technical complexity in the navy, Parkinson turns to the Colonial Office. In the peacetime years (excluding World War II) from 1935 to 1954, by which time it had begun to be clear that all of Britain's colonies would eventually be independent and the work of the Colonial Office would disappear entirely, the administrative staff of the office grew inexorably at about 6 percent per year. With this amazing observation, Parkinson regards (as may his readers) his law as established; we will perhaps be more careful in our time allocations in the future.

Another essay that we like relates to the quality of buildings in which institutions are housed. Parkinson slyly notes that, contrary to expectations, impressive, perfectly planned buildings are completed only for institutions on the point of collapse. To make his point, Parkinson provides a witty historical tour of buildings built for specific purposes. The magnificent structures at Versailles were completed when the decline of Louis XIV's powers had already set in. Across the Channel, Blenheim Palace was completed for the Duke of Marlborough, the victor in the famous Battle of Blenheim, after that gentleman was in disgrace and exile; he never lived in the palace. The Colonial Office— one of Parkinson's favorite targets—had a fine new building planned in London just as the last colonies were about to go away. Readers may feel that Parkinson's assessment can be applied to many technology firms today—perhaps the ones you genuinely want to deal with are those that are in the looniest and most unbusinesslike surroundings, as those in spacious glass buildings may be already over the hill. (We have some personal experience with the first type of firm. One of the very best consulting firms with which we have ever had occasion to deal was, in the early days of mainframe computers, housed in an utterly ramshackle old house on a street in Cambridge, Massachusetts, that was so out of the way that most MIT and Harvard faculty would have been unable to find it, although graduate students, of course, knew exactly where it was. Yet this small outfit had a brilliant staff and did path-breaking work.)

Other essays in this fine volume deal with how to find the most important people at a cocktail party, how to find the optimal date of retirement for an employee (tricky), why the amount of discussion time at budget hearings has no relation to the amounts involved, and how leaders of an organization beset by incompetence and jealousy take their organizations to ossification and failure. (Many readers will recognize some part of their employment history here, at the hands of such leaders.)

Parkinson's observations are incisive, and his witty writing helps us to remember his ideas much more easily than we would if we picked them up from a dry textbook. *Parkinson's Law* reminds us, too, of the physical nature of books and the memories they evoke. Our copy was given by one of us to the other as a going-away gift for the first trip either of us took overseas: to England, aboard the *Queen Mary*. Your own copy of this little book is one that will remain happily at home in your bookcase, to be read every few years both for sheer enjoyment and for learning.

C. Northcote Parkinson (1909–1993), *Parkinson's Law* (Cambridge, Mass.: The Riverside Press, 1957). Readily available in the Buccaneer Books hardcover reprint (1996).

KATHERINE ANNE PORTER
Pale Horse, Pale Rider

~

Katherine Anne Porter is probably most widely known today for her 1962 best-selling novel *Ship of Fools*. This is rather unfortunate, because that big, sprawling, melodramatic blockbuster, an allegorical story about a world sliding toward the disasters of Fascism and World War II, has none of the grace, subtlety, and delicate power of the short fiction on which her reputation rested for most of her lifetime. One can hardly begrudge the financial success that *Ship of Fools* brought her late in life, but to understand her position in American letters it is essential to go back to her short novels. (She disliked for people to call them novellas, though that is what they really are.) The best of these, *Pale Horse, Pale Rider*, has in the span of a few dozen pages a literary shapeliness and an emotional impact that few larger works can match. It has much to say about the two great problems of the human condition, love and death.

The novel is set in a small town in the Southwest and takes place during the final weeks of 1918. Miranda (a semiautobiographical stand-in for Porter herself, who appears in a number of the author's novels and stories) is working as the theater critic for the local newspaper. Hers is an independent life, if not an entirely fulfilling one. When she begins to be courted by Adam, a young soldier awaiting his orders to proceed overseas to fight in World War I, she is surprised by how happy she is, and cautiously wonders if it is wise to let herself fall in love with him.

Miranda and Adam are, in any case, quickly overtaken by larger events. The Spanish influenza epidemic has begun to rage across America, and Miranda falls ill. Adam nurses her through her first night of fever and then gets her to a hospital; she lapses into delirium, where the line between life and death blurs altogether, and the pale horse and pale rider of the Apocalypse seem ready to welcome her in death. She has, in fact, what is often now called a near-death experience, and perceives another existence beyond the grave that seems to her purer and more real than her own life. When she comes out of her delirium, bells are ringing to announce the Armistice that ends the war; Adam will not have to go abroad after all. But Miranda's road to recovery is still long, and in the end she may find that, having been recalled to life, she will long for what awaits her on the other side.

One of the pleasures of reading widely is to listen in on the ongoing conversation that books have with each other. In rereading the hundred books that we describe in these pages, we were often struck by the many ways in which they seem to reflect and play off each other, sometimes consciously on the part of their authors but more often not. This realization came to us with particular clarity when reading *Pale Horse, Pale Rider*, which takes place during exactly the same period of a few weeks as William Maxwell's novel of the influenza epidemic, *They Came Like Swallows* (p. 179). The two novels are congruent to a remarkable degree. Maxwell's achievement is to induce the reader to feel the shattering impact of the death of a mother on her young son. Porter conveys with vividness and sensitivity the disorientation and feeling of unreality that accompanies a life-threatening illness, and the sense of a world utterly changed that takes hold of a person who recovers from such an illness. Moreover, we happened to reread Thornton Wilder's *The Bridge of San Luis Rey* (p. 303) soon after finishing *Pale Horse, Pale Rider* and noticed that the final lines of Wilder's novel could easily serve as an epigram for Porter's: "There is a land of the living and a land of the dead and the bridge is love, the only survival, the only meaning."

Katherine Anne Porter was born and raised in Texas, and though she spent much of her life elsewhere, she kept returning to her Texas roots (both in person and in fiction as "Miranda"). The precision of her prose seems to contrast oddly with the untidiness of her own life. She lived through several marriages and numerous (and sometimes notorious) affairs; if others found her life scandalous, she herself relished living it with gusto. Her *Collected Short Stories* (1965) won both the National Book Award and the Pulitzer Prize for Letters; all of her short fiction is worth reading.

Katherine Anne Porter (1890–1980), *Pale Horse, Pale Rider* (New York: Harcourt, Brace, 1939). The attractive Modern Library hardcover reprint (1998) includes, as do several other hardcover and paperback reprint editions, two additional short novels, *Old Mortality* and *Noon Wine*. *Collected Short Stories* is available in a Harcourt Brace Harvest Edition paperback (1988).

CHARLES PORTIS

True Grit

~

True Grit was an instant and perhaps improbable success when it was published in 1968. Its hitherto little-known author (Portis, a journalist in his native Arkansas, had written one previous novel) found himself hailed as a new Mark Twain. Over the years more than two million copies of the book, in various editions, have been sold; one newspaper review proclaimed that *"True Grit* speaks to every American who can read; there are few books that can claim as much."

This success all stems from the book's extraordinary voice. Mattie Ross, of Yell County, Arkansas, is fourteen years old at the time of the events of the story but a cantankerous old lady as she tells them, and her narrative voice engages the reader's attention from the very first word of the book and never lets go. Comparisons to *Huckleberry Finn* are inevitable, and although on sober reflection it is true that Charles Portis is no Mark Twain, nor has his book anything like the enduring literary merit of Mark Twain's masterpiece, the temptation to see Mattie as a new incarnation of Huck is not entirely groundless. She, too, is stubborn, clever, willful, brave, foolhardy, good-hearted, and likely to drive adults around the bend in frustration and irritation. And like Huck, Mattie has the satisfaction of being able to look back upon her adventures with the knowledge that everything turned out just fine, as she knew it would all along.

The story tells of Mattie's quest to avenge the robbery and murder of her father, a prosperous farmer, at the hands of a low-life drifter named Tom Chaney. All of this takes place in 1870, in Arkansas and in the Indian Territory (later Oklahoma) across the river. By the time Mattie arrives in Fort Smith from her home in Dardanelle to enquire about her father, overdue home from a horse-selling trip, Chaney has fled to the Indian Territory, essentially beyond the reach of the law, and the authorities offer her little in the way of help or encouragement. Not to be put off, she hires a federal marshal to pursue Chaney on a private contract (such arrangements were possible in those laissez-faire times). Her hired hero is Rooster Cogburn, a man past his prime, overweight, given to drink, and in some difficulties with his superiors because of his habit of bringing more suspects in dead than alive. Mattie, a headstrong teenager with very definite ideas about propriety, does not at all approve of him but thinks he may be the man for the job anyway. To Rooster's utter astonishment, Mattie insists on coming with him in pursuit of Tom Chaney, and while he is adamant that she may not come along, nothing he does succeeds in making her turn back or shaking her off his trail.

It is quickly apparent that Rooster is profane, violent, and sometimes lazy; Mattie complains loudly to and about him, and Rooster makes no secret of his wish that she be elsewhere. But when they are ambushed by bandits, and even more when Mattie finds herself stuck in a crevasse, surrounded by rattlesnakes, and threatened by the villainous Chaney, we are not surprised to find that Rooster is also brave, resourceful, and honorable. Both he and Mattie, we find, are amply supplied with true grit, and despite enormous differences in age, temperament, and experience of life, they end their adventure as friends. One finishes this book with a smile of satisfaction.

The 1969 movie version of *True Grit* featured the best performance of John Wayne's later years, for which he won his only Oscar. The film is worth seeing for that performance alone, though it is otherwise forgettable and far inferior to the book.

There has been a revival of interest in the work of Charles Portis in recent years. His other novels—*The Dog of the South, Norwood,* and *Masters of Atlantis*—are now back in print, and appreciated for the same qualities of zany invention and understated humor that feature so prominently in *True Grit*. The man once called "the least-known great writer in America" may finally be receiving his due. You will enjoy seeing for yourself why Portis has such passionate fans.

Charles Portis (1933–), *True Grit* (New York: Simon & Schuster, 1968). Various reprints, including a Signet paperback (1995).

BARBARA PYM
Excellent Women

~

Barbara Pym has been called a Jane Austen for the mid-twentieth century, and the comparison is entirely apt. Like Austen, Pym tends in her novels to ignore entirely the great world of events to focus minutely on the lives and preoccupations of very ordinary people, finding in those lives material for social comedy of the highest and most refined sort. Pym's compass seldom extends farther than the boundaries of a parish, usually an urban parish in a respectable but unfashionable part of London. Her characters tend to be bachelor clergymen, marriageable young ladies, and the various "excellent women" who keep the parish running through their diligent attention to Christmas bazaars, jumble sales, feast-day decorations for the church sanctuary, the moral well-being of the vicar, and the responsibility of ensuring that, if possible, nothing should alter the self-satisfied, narrow-minded Victorian respectability of middle-class British life. Pym wrote about this world from the perspective of long, intimate familiarity and brought to it an understanding that is both sympathetic and ironic, amounting to a kind of literary perfect pitch.

Born in 1913, the daughter of a country lawyer, Pym earned an honors degree in English from St. Hilda's College, Oxford. Soon thereafter she went to work for the Censorship Board, an effort of the wartime British government to prevent leaks of military secrets. Later in the war, she joined the Women's Royal Naval Service and saw duty in England and in Italy. In 1950, she published her first novel, *Some Tame Gazelle*. *Excellent Women* followed two years later, and four more novels over the next decade. But none of her books sold very well or met with much critical success. Her publisher turned down *An Unsuitable Attachment* in 1963, claiming he could not project sufficient sales to justify publication. Another attempt to sell a new manuscript failed in 1968; deeply discouraged, the author stopped writing altogether.

Pym was saved from utter literary obscurity by what was not much more than a lucky accident. In 1977, the *Times Literary Supplement* published the result of a survey of leading literary figures who were asked to name "the most underrated novelist of the century." Barbara Pym's name was the only one to be mentioned twice, by Lord David Cecil and by the notoriously difficult-to-please poet and critic Philip Larkin. Suddenly Pym's novels were in demand, and her publisher had to scramble to bring them back into print in new editions. She had the belated but real satisfaction of becoming a famous author at last, and of publishing three more novels before her death in 1980. (*An Unsuitable Attachment* was published posthumously, as was *A Very Private Eye*, a fascinating collection drawn from her diaries, notebooks, and letters.)

In all of her literary work, she drew from the well of her own experience. Her father was a lawyer, not a clergyman, but she was familiar from earliest childhood with the minor privileges of the professional class in small-town society. When her characters venture abroad, it is to Italy; when we learn that the duties of the dashing Rockingham Napier as a staff officer in Naples included being "charming to a lot of dreary Wren officers in ill-fitting white uniforms," we can be sure that Pym remembered all too well being charmed, and condescended to, by just such an officer. Anthropologists populate her pages in unexpected numbers; for twenty years she was assistant editor of the academic journal *Africa*. Many of Pym's heroines are spinsters; she never married. This element of autobiography in her work is not a defect, but rather one of her greatest assets—it is clear that she spent her life observing minutely her world and the people in it, with an exceptionally keen awareness of the nuances of social and emotional life and an uncanny facility for turning her observations into stories. She viewed her world honestly and with a certain detachment, but she was very fond of it, too; she might laugh at her characters' foibles, but she was never mean to them.

Excellent Women is probably Pym's most famous novel, and it is a good place to begin your acquaintance with her work. The story is narrated in the voice of Mildred Lathbury, a somewhat dowdy thirtyish woman who already thinks of herself as a spinster. The daughter of a country clergyman, she lives in an obscure part of London, paying for her respectable but very modest flat from her small private income and her part-time work for a foundation for the aid of distressed gentlewomen. Her best friends are the vicar of her parish, Julian Malory, and his sister Winifred. The other women of the parish have long believed Mildred and Julian to be destined for each other, but Mildred herself has no interest in such a match, and the vicar seems quite content to let his sister keep house for him. Into Mildred's utterly uneventful life suddenly comes change, in the persons of flamboyant new neighbors in the downstairs flat, Helena and Rockingham Napier. She is an anthropologist (Mildred is not quite sure what that is), he a recently discharged naval officer, handsome, charming, and idle.

One change seems to beget another, and soon Mildred is having to navigate wholly unfamiliar seas: serving as mediator in the marital squabbles of the Napiers; being courted in a desultory way by Everard Bone, one of Helena's anthropological colleagues, a charmless man of no social graces who nevertheless brings a small element of adventure to Mildred's life; and, most upsetting, rescuing Julian Malory from the machinations of Allegra Gray, a vicar's widow intent on marrying Julian and persuading Winifred to move in with a most unwilling Mildred. These events take place over the course of a year, and it requires all of Mildred's self-respect and good sense to ride them out unscathed.

There is not a trace of melodrama or pathos here; on the contrary, the story is told with a sort of austere honesty that is part of the novel's charm. At the same time, this is a very funny book. Mildred is quite capable of recognizing when she is being fussy or slightly ridiculous (though she doesn't always know how to be otherwise) and of laughing at herself for it. And Pym knows how to write, and when to insert, an uproariously funny scene from time to time—witness here a dinner party with Everard Bone's batty old mother, whose worldview is deeply paranoid: " 'The Dominion of the Birds,' she went on. 'I very much fear it may come to that.' " But Mrs. Bone fights back: " 'I eat as many birds as possible. . . . I have them sent from Harrods or Fortnum's. . . . At least we can eat our enemies.' "

Barbara Pym's novels have much to say about the decency, and the comedy, of everyday life; they are delightful reading.

Barbara Pym (1913–1980), *Excellent Women* (London: Jonathan Cape, 1952). Paperback reprint editions include Harper Perennial (1980, 1987) and Plume Books (1988).

THOMAS PYNCHON
The Crying of Lot 49

~

Thomas Pynchon has a reputation for writing long, obscure, difficult books, the kinds of books that would appeal to fans of Marcel Proust or James Joyce but intimidate most readers. Indeed, most of Pynchon's books are long and obscure, and difficult, too; asked why he did not make his books easier to understand, Pynchon is said to have replied, "Life is not easy to understand." His books are dense with puns, inter-mingled real and made-up history, mathematical puzzles, in-jokes of various kinds, and plots that do not always seem to make sense. Read-ing a Pynchon novel is like peeling an onion, with always another layer beneath the surface.

Just as Proust and Joyce make serious demands on a reader but de-liver enjoyment and satisfaction in proportion to those demands, so with Pynchon, who deservedly is known as one of the great masters of modernist fiction. But—and this is crucial—he is also great fun. He lets himself cut loose as a writer, and it helps to read him in the same spirit. He fits solidly into a longer tradition of writing that rebels against conventionality. His immediate literary forebears were the writers of the Beat Generation, such as William Burroughs and Jack Kerouac, and he was a younger contemporary of the "merry prankster" Ken Kesey. Pynchon himself has clearly influenced such important younger writers as Don DeLillo and T. Coraghessan Boyle.

Fortunately, Pynchon has provided an easy wormhole through which to enter the alternative world of his fiction, and that is this short and very funny novel. *The Crying of Lot 49,* with its bizarre, disjointed story about an inheritance and an ancient conspiracy, characters with jokey names such as Oedipa Mass and Manny De Presso, and odd snatches of poetry, invites you down the rabbit hole, onto a roller coaster, into the funhouse—invites you, in other words, to step outside ordinary reality and into Pynchon's own world of the imagination. The book takes us through a year or so in the life of Oedipa Mass, an ordinary California housewife who unexpectedly finds herself named co-executor of the will of a stupendously rich former lover, Pierce Inverarity. She moves to Inverarity's hometown of San Narcisco and begins to work with her co-executor, a lawyer named Metzger. Very quickly things turn weird; in particular, an image of a muted trumpet keeps showing up in unexpected places, together with references to something called Tristero. This turns out to be a secret organization engaged in a centuries-long revolt against postal monopolies (don't ask); what we don't know is whether it is a "real" conspiracy, from which Oedipa barely escapes with her life and sanity, or an elaborate practical joke played on her by Inverarity for reasons of his own. From beginning to end, Oedipa makes her way through this madhouse world with an air of innocence that endears her to the reader.

It's hard to know exactly what to call this—science fiction? absurdist fantasy? However you classify it, you should approach it with an open mind and an expectation of having a good time. All Pynchon fans agree on this: If you are new to his work, the best way of getting into it is to just read on regardless, ignoring the parts that don't seem to make sense, not worrying about the occasional obscure word or convoluted (but never incorrect) grammar; soon, maybe before you quite realize it, you will sense how much fun you are having. Put yourself in the sort of frame of mind you'd adopt to watch an episode of *The X-Files* (or, from Pynchon's own time, *The Twilight Zone*) or to look at a painting by Dali. And remember that with *The Crying of Lot 49*, as with all Pynchon books, you will probably want to read it more than once; his books get better with each reading.

The Crying of Lot 49 is also powerfully evocative of its time. Readers who are old enough to remember the 1960s will find the atmosphere of the book almost startlingly familiar; others for whom that decade is history rather than memory will get a vivid sense from these pages of some of the spirit of that tumultuous time.

Thomas Pynchon is certainly the most reclusive, privacy-obsessed writer in America today (rivaled perhaps by J. D. Salinger, who has not, however, written anything for a long time). No clear modern photograph of Pynchon is known to exist. No one, outside a close and close-mouthed circle of friends, knows where he lives, or under what name. It is reliably reported that he delivers manuscripts for publication by putting them in coin lockers and sending the keys to his editor.

This much at least is known: He was born on Long Island, New York, in 1937, attended Oyster Bay High School, and, after a stint in the Navy, graduated from Cornell University, where he studied engineering but also became exposed to modernist literature under the tutelage of Vladimir Nabokov. In the early 1960s, he worked for the Boeing Corporation. He published his first novel, V, in 1963, and since then has evaded the public eye, preferring to be known entirely through his writing. (He was not so elusive, however, as to escape the notice of the MacArthur Foundation, which awarded him one of its prestigious five-year "genius fellowships" in 1989.) His most recent novel, *Mason and Dixon,* was published in 1997.

If *The Crying of Lot 49* appeals to you, the next step will be to read some of Pynchon's longer novels. The most challenging, and most rewarding, is his acknowledged masterpiece, *Gravity's Rainbow.* Not a one-night read by any stretch of the imagination, *Gravity's Rainbow* is nevertheless many people's favorite novel; you might want to find out why.

Thomas Pynchon (1937–), *The Crying of Lot 49* (New York: J. B. Lippincott, 1965; paperback reprint, HarperCollins Perennial, 1986, 1990, 1999). *A Companion to The Crying of Lot 49,* by J. Kerry Grant (Athens: University of Georgia Press, 1994) is useful for identifying topical references in the novel, such as to rock bands and popular dances, that have become obscure with the passage of time.

ERICH MARIA REMARQUE
All Quiet on the Western Front

~

Erich Maria Remarque was drafted into the German army at the age of eighteen, in the midst of World War I. In the course of the next two years, he was wounded five times, lost all of his friends, and managed to survive the war. After a variety of jobs, he became a sports journalist and writer. *All Quiet on the Western Front* is distilled from his experience. Its simple, direct writing style, unusual at a time when public information was heavily restricted, permitted the reader no doubt of the horror of warfare. In its bitter honesty it remains a stunning book more than seventy years, and several wars, after its completion.

The novel was published in German in 1928 and sold hundreds of thousands of copies in a short time. It was immediately translated into English and made into a film, which was banned in several countries as offensive to authority in various ways. Remarque left Germany in the early Thirties for Switzerland; his German citizenship was revoked by the Nazis, who had earlier publicly burned his books. He later settled in the United States and finally returned to Switzerland. *All Quiet on the Western Front* captures, perhaps better than any other novel, the soldier's experience of World War I.

The narrator of the book is Paul Bäumer, who has enlisted early in the war with his classmates through the encouragement of his schoolmaster, Kantorek. (One of our college professors was a boy in Germany at this time, and he remembered the troops in their new uniforms, the festive atmosphere of bands playing, and the high hopes of immediate victory.) Paul and his friends begin to realize quickly the differences between the patriotic fervor that encouraged them to join up and the reality of military life. During basic training they are bullied mercilessly by their noncom, Himmelstoss, a lowly functionary in civil life. The schoolboys lose their innocence rapidly: On the evening before they are to be shipped out, they waylay Himmelstoss and beat him senseless.

The soldiers arrive at the front and experience very quickly the madness of trench warfare in World War I, when millions were slaughtered in the process of moving a front line a few hundred yards back and forth. Paul tells of explosives, machine guns, wounds, the horror of gas attacks, killing another man with his knife in a watery foxhole, and the occasional access to good food and to women other than in military brothels.

Life at the front revolves about such delicate issues as whether, before a battle, it is better to eat one's soup, since if one is killed, one will miss out on the soup entirely, or whether it is best not to eat, since if one is wounded in the abdomen, the wound could be treated more effectively with the stomach empty. The troops are in a back-to-basics life in which, as Paul says, three-quarters of the soldier's vocabulary is based on the stomach and intestines. They understand that they will never be the same after the war and that if they are to survive, they must depend on their comrades. They realize, too, that as ordinary people, they have little cause to fight the French or the English—a highly subversive thought to the politicians of the time—but they are in a situation in which they nevertheless have to fight as well as they can for their own survival. Their bitterness and resignation is summed up by Paul's older colleague, Katczinsky, who has perhaps the best-known lines from the book: "[L]et all the Kaisers, Presidents, Generals and diplomats go into a big field and fight it out. . . . That will satisfy us and keep us home."

Paul's visit on leave with his family is agonizing to read about: the misunderstandings of those at home, with learned discussions of which parts of France and Belgium should be annexed to Germany and a complete unawareness of life at the front; his mostly silent communion with his mother, desperately ill with cancer; his inability to talk with his father. These passages tell us more about the importance and meaning of family than we can easily stand to hear. The only saving grace of Paul's leave is his encounter with a friend who by chance is now the superior officer of Kantorek, who has been called up into the territorial guard. Kantorek is reminded of the early death of a student who had not wanted to enlist but did under pressure from the schoolmaster, and he is tormented in every available way by Paul's schoolmate. In one touch peculiar to Germany, Kantorek is sent on bread detail, when he has to cross the town working, in full view of the citizenry, on equal terms with the school porter, a situation of incredible misery for a schoolmaster in a hierarchical society.

Paul is wounded, goes to a hospital, and of course is sent back to the front; the Germans are desperate for troops. The fresh troops are killed like rabbits; it is the more experienced ones that have a chance, although as Paul says earlier, no soldier can survive a thousand chances. The influx of American troops and weapons and the lack of supplies for the Germans make the outcome hopeless. (The role of the Americans comes home to us each time we read this novel: One of our uncles, an American marine faced by the real-life contemporaries of Paul, was gassed, wounded, and won a high French military decoration, matters of which he never spoke.) As rumors of an armistice circulate, Paul and his friends allow themselves to think of surviving, although each knows that he can never return to the life he had led, even if he outlives the war. But, in the end, all of his gang are gone, dead or badly wounded. Paul's own fate is delivered quickly in October 1918, just before the armistice, on a day in which the front is so still that the German military report is one sentence: "All quiet on the western front."

Remarque wrote many other books dealing with political upheaval in Europe, several of which were made into popular movies; of these volumes, we like *Three Comrades* and *Arch of Triumph*. None of his later books, however, married directness of style and subject matter so well, made contact with the experiences of millions of ordinary readers so directly, or so profoundly disturbed officialdom as did *All Quiet on the Western Front*.

Erich Maria Remarque [Erich Paul Remark] (1898–1970), *All Quiet on the Western Front* (*Im Westen nichts Neues;* Berlin: Propyläen Verlag, 1928. English trans., Boston: Little, Brown, 1929). Various editions available in both hardcover and paperback; a convenient edition is the Ballantine paperback (1996).

ADELE CROCKETT ROBERTSON

The Orchard

~

Adele (Kitty) Crockett Robertson was born in Ipswich, Massachusetts, northeast of Boston, in 1901. She enjoyed a privileged childhood in Ipswich, attended Radcliffe College, and used her earnings from her jobs for a fine yawl and trips to Europe. In 1932, in the midst of the Great Depression, her doctor father died, leaving the family with his uncollected accounts and many debts. Most of the family wanted to sell the family farm in Ipswich, on which all of Dr. and Mrs. Crockett's children had been born, to cover the heavy mortgages and unpaid bills. Robertson, on the other hand, decided to return to the farm, to preserve it and her family's history by raising and selling apples. This book is a manuscript happily discovered by her daughter and published after Robertson's death; it tells of her amazing energy and dedication to the farm and to the apple orchard that was to have saved it.

The farm was located at the edge of a salt marsh, near the present Crane Beach at Ipswich. There was history aplenty on the property: The original owners had built the house in 1760, before the Revolutionary War, and some of the trees on the property when the Crockett children were young had been planted at that time. One of many happy memories for them was the apple harvest. Robertson's childhood was a fortunate one: From a young age, for example, she always had a sailboat. But she was also used to hard work. Unlike her playmates, during the summer she had to work four hours each day around the property before going off sailing or to participate in other young people's activities. Dr. Crockett wanted his daughter to be "ready for whatever happens." The fate of the farm involved everyone in the family financially; its loss would implicate them all. Moreover, as her younger brothers reminded her, the property was subject to larger forces: in the short run, the economic conditions of the Depression, and in the more distant future, the likelihood that Ipswich would not remain an area of commercial farming but rather would become a residential community accessible to Boston.

After quitting her good museum job in Hartford to return to the farm, Robertson faced problems beyond the rocky soils and harsh weather that have always been part of New England farming. The farm machinery was out of condition, and to get it running cost her money and enormous effort. Moreover, Robertson had no family with her to help with the work (for company, she mainly had Freya, the family Great Dane). She therefore had to do most of the backbreaking work herself and hired farmhands to help with the rest. In this respect, she made one of her best decisions: She would pay her help, all of whom were struggling desperately during the Depression, more than the going wage. She was rewarded, in turn, with steadfast loyalty. Among her friends and helpers many readers will like best Joe LaPlante, a "Frenchman" (in fact, of French Canadian stock) who was her most reliable colleague. A description of Christmas dinner at the LaPlantes' house in Frenchville, a part of Ipswich, is unforgettable. Robertson does not neglect to include in her narrative a suitably negative portrait of the bank man who drove around in his Cadillac to inspect "the Bank's property." There are things that are hard for us to remember: The sprays that were used to control the different types of pests that threatened the apples were lethal, and it is a wonder that Robertson managed to survive the stuff. Something that will surprise many readers is the prevalence of thievery, both by strangers and by those who were supposed to help.

In addition to learning to work harder than she had ever imagined, she learned more about her family. One day, old Mr. Patch and his wife arrived to buy some of the famous Spy and Russet apples from the Crockett farm. Mr. Patch regaled Robertson with tales of playing on the property with his cousins, one of whom died at Missionary Ridge in the Civil War; Robertson remarks that the events recalled seemed as if they were yesterday. Mr. Patch also solved the mystery of the three sunken granite blocks that Robertson had often noticed in her youth while sailing. On the way from the West Gloucester granite quarries (in whose abandoned dark waters one of us used to swim), a sled had gone through the ice and took with it the granite, Amasa Brown, and four span of oxen.

Against all expectations, Robertson had a bright first year. She staved off the bank and other creditors with a bumper apple crop sold to Boston institutions through a lucky meeting with a college purchasing officer whose son her father had treated. The second year looked good, but a cold spell rotted many of the stored apples, and she had to give up; there was no money to cover the mortgage payments and costs of operation. The property was put up for sale as a whole, but there were no takers. It was deeded by Mrs. Crockett to the more business-like of her sons, and pieces were sold to Robertson's other brother, to neighbors, and to Robertson and her husband, a Scot whom she married in 1936. They built a small house on part of the orchard land near the salt marsh, and she lived there to the end of her life. The big house still stands.

After her struggles with the orchard, marriage, and the birth of her daughter, Robertson continued a life of hard work, serving as a union shop steward on an assembly line, picking apples, and fishing with her husband on their boat after World War II. She later became an Ipswich town selectwoman, a well-known citizen, and an award-winning regional journalist; she also bore the burden of her husband's later illnesses.

This beautiful manuscript is the kind that everyone might wish that their parents or other relatives had left for them: a story of who we were and are. It is wonderfully literate but not overdrawn, telling the story just right. Although in some ways the story might seem slight (just another farm machine to fix), it is in fact deeply meaningful, a moving human struggle against larger forces. That Robertson's cause, in the end, didn't work out exactly as she had dreamed doesn't seem to matter: Her striving was admirable, and we are glad that, through the instrument of her daughter, her hopes and her courage are shared with us.

Adele Crockett Robertson (1901–1979), *The Orchard* (New York: Henry Holt, 1995).

PHILIP ROTH
Portnoy's Complaint

~

Philip Roth achieved success at an early age with his celebrated story "Goodbye Columbus" (1959) and quickly became recognized as an important new voice in the chorus of Jewish-American writers who were such a vital part of the American cultural and literary world in the second half of the twentieth century. But where I. B. Singer (p. 244), himself an immigrant, remained rooted in the vanished Jewish culture of the Polish *shtetl*, and Saul Bellow was concerned in his fiction principally with urban Jewish intellectuals, Roth drew from a seemingly inexhaustible well of anger and resentment to portray a vulgar, materialistic world of Jewish suburban life. He knew that world intimately; he was born in 1933 in Newark, New Jersey, and raised in the kind of middle-class Jewish neighborhoods that have formed the setting for almost all of his fiction.

Portnoy's Complaint is the story of a rebellious young man who has a great deal to be rebellious about. Alexander Portnoy grows up in a superficially supportive and loving but really quite dreadful family. His father is overworked and ineffectual; his older sister is unsupportive and unattractive; and his overwhelming mother is a genius at inducing guilt. Alex learns from an early age that, on the one hand, there never has been in the entire history of the world a child as intelligent, beautiful, and talented as he, and that, on the other hand, it is shamefully wicked of him not to develop his gifts to the fullest extent and, no matter how long he lives, he will never deserve all of the sacrifices and love his mother has given him. The entire novel is, in effect, a book-length elaboration on every Jewish-mother joke you've ever heard. Like those jokes, the book is often extremely funny, but the humor masks a great deal of pain.

The whole book is told in the form of a monologue delivered by Alex, now thirty-three years old, to his psychoanalyst, Dr. Spielvogel. The setting of the book, by the way, accounts for the double meaning in its title. Portnoy has a lot to complain about, and he complains throughout the book; but Dr. Spielvogel also identifies Portnoy's problem as a "complaint" in the medical sense of that term. Thus Portnoy's Complaint: "A disorder in which strongly-felt ethical and altruistic impulses are perpetually warring with extreme sexual longings, often of a perverse nature." Alex channels his unhappiness into obsessive sexual acting out—masturbation from an early age, supplemented in adulthood by a relentless promiscuity. What makes his life a torment is that sex, for him, invariably carries a heavy load of guilt, an unshakable legacy from his childhood. Alex has a wonderfully developed sense of irony and sees how funny his predicament is, but he is its prisoner nevertheless.

The book is explicit sexually, with a great variety of sexual acts described in sometimes lurid (and often extremely funny) detail. In our own time, such sexual forthrightness has become routine and unremarkable, but when Portnoy's Complaint was first published, in 1969, its daring language caused a sensation. American government censorship of sexual language had ended only a few years earlier—the last, unsuccessful U.S. legal action against Lady Chatterley's Lover was abandoned in 1959—and writers in the 1960s were still testing the boundaries of sexual free speech. Roth, for better or worse, was a key force in toppling the barriers altogether. And his choice of pathologically obsessive sex as a vehicle for conveying the image of a personality deranged by parental pressure is wickedly effective.

In Roth's depiction of middle-class Jewish family life he obviously exaggerates for effect, and yet it is clear that he has struck a chord with many people whose response derives from personal experience. Roth raises questions that are relevant to people regardless of ethnic or communal identity. Notions of personal and ethnic identity—religion, intermarriage, assimilation, tradition versus change, and tradition versus choice—loom large for Roth. To what extent is a person a creation of his parents and environment, and to what extent must one accept responsibility for being oneself? These things give Portnoy's Complaint its enduring value, and the provocative questions it poses remain quite relevant to American life today.

Not only is *Portnoy's Complaint* a Jewish-mother joke writ large, it is a novel with a punch line. Because you may be coming to the book for the first time, we will not risk spoiling the joke, but you will find that Roth brings his book to a truly inspired conclusion.

Philip Roth (1933–), *Portnoy's Complaint* (New York: Random House, 1969). Vintage International paperback reprint, 1994.

W. C. Sellar and R. J. Yeatman
1066 and All That

~

Every one of us from time to time has to play the role of teacher—if not necessarily in the profession of that name, then at least by training a new employee at work, by teaching one's own children, by making a business presentation. This wonderfully amusing book is fundamentally about teaching: How students (that is, all of us) apprehend and integrate facts and ideas. It is subversively put in terms of history taught to youngsters in British schools, written to show how what the history teacher is saying (or droning on about) is actually grasped in the mind of a young scholar scribbling desperately to get everything down. The great success of *1066 and All That* is that it manages to be both hilarious and deeply insightful. The book originated partly in articles in *Punch*, the humor journal that for decades was enjoyed by educated readers in Great Britain and throughout the English-speaking world for its insight and wit.

The book is organized as a rapid tour through British history. We have, of course, the famous Two Genuine Dates, 55 B.C. for the invasion of Britain by Julius Caesar and A.D. 1066 for the invasion of Britain by William the Conqueror. These are the only two dates in all of history that need to be remembered. (The authors report that two other dates were considered for the book but were discarded at the last moment on the grounds that they were *not memorable*.) There is also a full menu of Good Things and Bad Things. For example, Magna Charter (*sic*) was a Good Thing, being the chief cause of democracy in England (leaving aside the common folk). St. Paul's Cathedral in London is a Good Thing, inasmuch as it caused Sir Christopher Wren. On the other hand, Edward III's manipulation of the wool trade during the Hundred Years' War was a Bad Thing, being the cause of Political Economy (many will agree here).

The authors are devilishly clever in the way in which they manipulate and present facts, or what pass for facts. The simplest items are misspellings or misapprehensions. Joan of Ark, it seems, is a French descendant of Noah. Perkin Warbeck and Lambert Simnel, two fifteenth-century pretenders to the throne, have names that are sufficiently alike that they go through permutations (Perkin Warmel) in the mind of the young scholar. These gentlemen finally show up on one of the quizzes scattered through the book as Lamnel Simkin and Percy Warmneck.

There are more complicated confusions of ideas as well. In the discussion of Caesar's invasions, we learn that 54 B.C. comes after 55 B.C., owing entirely to the peculiar Roman method of counting. William of Orange and his queen, Mary, are conflated as Williamanmary and referred to as either *they* or *it*, with great confusion as to why an orange should sit on the throne. And, of course, no amount of earnest schoolmasterly instruction about Ethelred the Unready (from the Anglo-Saxon for "without counsel") will convince a youngster that Ethelred was anyone other than a king who forgot to grab his sword before running off to battle.

There is also the schoolchild's fascination with which country is Top Nation. The Romans were, of course, and then Britain. The Dutch rather treacherously attempted to be Top Nation in the seventeenth century but failed because they were too small; other claimants failed as well. On the other hand, America finally becomes Top Nation, and this is a great historical event from the standpoint of a young British scholar. With the ascent of America, history comes to an end (at least in the British classroom), and there are no more troublesome facts to learn. This is a wonderful spoof of the book itself. It rises above its Britishness both because of its universal insights into ways of learning and because almost every country's teaching can be satirized by its own brand of chauvinism.

What is so insightful about the volume is that all learning shares some of the characteristics that we observe in the mind of the schoolchild. All of us learn in pieces, and we put the pieces together in sometimes odd (and in this book, very funny) ways. Becoming mature means learning to get the pieces more in the right order. But who among us does not have tucked away somewhere something utterly wacky that we heard (and confused) as youngsters from a great-uncle, mixed with advice from Dad? By the end of the book, one is left with a (perhaps) salutary caution about how much or little one knows about anything.

Aside from this, there is the pleasure of rereading the book and trying to track down all of the confusions and errors perpetrated by our clever authors. This provides some of the fun of a scavenger hunt, and we are reminded that a good rule is never to repeat as true anything that you read in *1066 and All That* (aside, of course, from the Two Genuine Dates) unless you've checked it in an encyclopedia.

Finally, there is a note of caution in this book for those of us who have been teachers. Did we really ask examination questions such as "Write not more than three lines on the advantages and disadvantages of the inductive historical method with special relation to ecclesiastical litigation in the earlier Lancastrian epochs"? Yes, we probably did, and so retrospective apologies all around to former students.

W[illiam] C[arruthers] Sellar (1898–1951) and R[obert] J[ulian] Yeatman (1897–1968), *1066 and All That* (London: Methuen, 1930; first American book edition, New York: Dutton, 1947). Readily available in the Sutton paperback reprint (1993); we like the old-fashioned Methuen Humour Classic paperback, now unfortunately out of print.

VIKRAM SETH
The Golden Gate

~

This is something quite unusual in contemporary literature: a novel written entirely in verse. And not, as one might expect, in a kind of free-form blank verse, but as a series of six hundred linked sonnets, each a perfectly rhymed and metrical example of that very demanding form. What makes the book remarkable as well as unusual is that it does not seem at all like a trick or an oddity, but rather reads smoothly and beautifully. The compressed, controlled medium of verse narrative also is surprisingly effective as a means of focusing the novel's emotional impact. One might pick up this book out of curiosity, but one reads it straight through because of the beauty of its language, the interest of the story it tells, and one's emotional involvement in the lives of the novel's characters.

In its bare outlines, the story is ordinary enough, simply one variant on the theme of boy meets girl, boy loses girl; as usual, fate deals out happiness and sorrow in unequal measures. The author's ingenuity and skill in telling the tale is what makes it all seem fresh and new. The time is around 1980, the setting San Francisco and the Bay Area, the players affluent young professionals—yuppies in the early years of Silicon Valley. The novel's central figure is John, a hardworking, serious, politically conservative technical worker for a defense firm, whose love life is seriously deficient—in fact, it hardly exists, after the breakup some time earlier of a long-standing affair with Janet, a sculptor and rock-band drummer. Janet still thinks kindly of him and manages (by placing a personal ad on his behalf) to fix him up with Liz, a beautiful, levelheaded associate in a law firm. Love blossoms quickly, but there are many pitfalls on the road to fulfillment, as John and Liz learn. (Among them, as we learn in hilarious detail, is Liz's malevolent old cat, Charlemagne, who hates John and does everything he can to drive the interloper out of his and Liz's life.) Others who play important roles in the story are Liz's religiously conflicted gay younger brother, Ed, John's bisexual best friend, Phil, and (once again) Janet, as she and John learn that their bonds are stronger than either of them had realized. We follow this engaging group of very disparate people through a period of about two years, as their lives go through many twists and turns, before the author ties up all of the loose ends for us. Once launched into this book, the reader will find it very hard to put down. John may be a twit, Liz can be ungenerous, Phil is sometimes insensitive and overbearing, but these are people that one comes to care about.

Seth is also very adept at grounding this romantic tale in its particular time and place. We get a vividly real picture here of the affluent, hedonistic Bay Area lifestyle, of the genuine terrors of the Cold War (a long and very effective scene depicts a demonstration against nuclear weapons), of the characteristically late-twentieth-century conflicts of work and personal time in the lives of the upwardly mobile. Along the way, too, Seth holds our attention with excursions into, among other things, the foibles of cats, the delights of olive preserving and wine making, and the fickle meanness of art critics. All of this is conveyed in dramatic fashion through the verse form in which the author has chosen to write his novel.

Why, after all, write a novel in verse? And why in sonnets? One can venture at least some answers to these questions. The sonnet is indeed a demanding form: Each one must be precisely fourteen lines long, divided by rhyme scheme into two groups of four and two groups of three lines, and with each line following a prescribed metrical pattern. What comes as a surprise, but what English poets have known from the Renaissance onward, is how naturally conformable English speech is to the rhythm and length of the sonnet. This is evident from any one of Shakespeare's sonnets; for example, here is the opening quatrain of Sonnet LVII:

Being your slave, what should I do but tend
Upon the hours and times of your desire?
I have no precious time at all to spend,
Nor services to do, till you require.

One says those lines in natural English speech, with no awkwardness or artificiality. And the full fourteen lines of the sonnet turn out to be just about right for conveying a complete thought. What Seth has done is to take this marriage of verse form and natural speech to create a narrative that in its compression and liveliness continually urges the reader forward, and he does so in a way that seems effortless on the part of both author and reader. One can't guess at the effort that went into the creation of the six hundred stanzas of this verse novel, but the outward impression they convey is that Vikram Seth writes sonnets as easily as he breathes.

But this apparent ease comes as no surprise, for Seth is a writer of truly prodigious talent. Indian by birth and upbringing, resident at various times in Europe and America, he crosses cultural frontiers as easily as he switches from one form of writing to another. His works include a skillful volume of translations of Chinese poems from the Tang dynasty; a volume of his own verse; a huge, deliberately old-fashioned novel, *A Suitable Boy* (about the dilemmas created when the son and daughter of two Indian families, one Hindu and the other Moslem, fall in love with each other); and his most recent novel, *An Equal Music*, set in the rarified world of professional music in England and France. *The Golden Gate* shows him at the peak of his inventive power and his ability to engage and entertain his readers.

Vikram Seth (1952–), *The Golden Gate* (New York: Random House, 1986). Vintage paperback edition, 1991.

ISAAC BASHEVIS SINGER
The Magician of Lublin

~

The Magician of Lublin is set in Poland around 1885. Like most of Isaac Bashevis Singer's works, it builds on his own childhood experiences and on stories told by his parents and grandparents to create a sense of the thriving and diverse Jewish communities of that time and place. By the time Singer matured as a writer, those communities had all been obliterated by the Holocaust; his entire career, one might say, was devoted to reconstructing them in fictional form. Yet Singer's novels and stories are not works of history, but works of the imagination; they evoke the past but do not chronicle it. They are, in that way, similar in spirit (but usually much darker in mood) to the paintings of Marc Chagall or the retold folktales of Sholem Aleichem.

When we first meet Yasha, the magician of the book's title, he is resting at home in Lublin between performance tours. He is a prosperous entertainer, well thought of in Warsaw and other major cities, and he has been able to provide a comfortable home for his devoted wife, Esther; their only regret is that they have never been able to have children. Yasha, in the book's early chapters, is relaxing and having a good time, and we get a sense of him as a charming rogue, a man who lives too close to the edge of physical and moral danger for his own good but so far has gotten away with it. The mood of the book at first is lighthearted, as we learn (often as he drinks with his old friends) of Yasha's travels, his many love affairs, his card tricks, and his skeptical, agnostic religious views.

As Yasha journeys toward Warsaw for another season onstage, we see that he has been pushing his luck too far. He stops in Piask to pick up Magda, his stage assistant, with whom he lives as man and wife in Warsaw. In the same town he visits Zeftel, an old flame whose brother and family associates are thieves; she promises, to Yasha's dismay, to follow him to Warsaw as well. Worst of all, in the big city Yasha has another mistress, Emilia, the beautiful Christian widow of a professor, with whom he has fallen deeply in love. He has rashly promised to convert to her faith and immigrate with her to Italy to start a new life, although he does not have the money needed to do so and although, too, he agonizes about the unfairness of deserting the faithful Esther back in Lublin. Yasha has always been able to rationalize his many love affairs as having no significance for his marriage; the new experience of being in love with one of his mistresses, however, sets in train events that cause his whole life to unravel.

The mood of the book darkens as Yasha proves unable to cope with the moral dilemma he has created for himself. As he lies and temporizes and improvises on every hand, he begins not only to destroy his own life (for instance, by not beginning to rehearse for his new show, to his manager's despair), but also to make life increasingly miserable for the very people he cares about. Yasha's life becomes a purgatory of evasiveness and guilt from which he finally emerges a changed man, convinced that only a lifetime of penance and self-discipline can make up for the damage he has done.

In fact, as the reader begins to realize, this novel is not at all the carefree shaggy-dog story that it at first appears to be, but is rather a serious and sometimes tormented story of guilt and expiation, of religious faith spurned and recovered, and of the need to be ever vigilant if one is to live a truly devout life. And, this being a novel by I. B. Singer, Yasha's fate involves a hefty dose of irony as well; if in conventional morality no bad deed goes unpunished, in the author's wry universe no good deed goes unpunished, either.

Isaac Bashevis Singer was born in a small town in Poland in 1904, the son of a Hasidic (ultra-Orthodox) rabbi. He had an appropriately studious childhood, moved to Warsaw to become a writer, and in 1935 immigrated to the United States (in the footsteps of his brother, the writer I. J. Singer). There, as a freelance writer for the *Jewish Daily Forward*, he quickly became a well-known figure in New York's intensely politicized and faction-ridden Jewish intelligentsia. He wrote exclusively in Yiddish, a language that he found much more expressive than

English, and he often collaborated in the translation of his own work into English.

As was true of many other Jewish emigrés from Poland, all of the relatives that Singer had left back home perished in the Holocaust. His writing then became an act of remembrance for a vanished world; but he was criticized by some religious readers for filling his tales with thieves, prostitutes, goblins, witches, and other figures and themes that were offensive to an Orthodox sensibility. Why, these critics asked, could he not write about good Jews? Singer, however, rejected such criticism out of hand and responded that he had no interest in prettifying a culture that had owed its vibrancy as much to its rogues as to its saints. He was awarded the Nobel Prize for Literature in 1978; friends described him in his great old age, still living a simple life on New York's Upper West Side, as being gratified by his fame and success but baffled by it as well.

Among Singer's many other novels and collections of short stories we like especially *Gimpel the Fool and Other Stories* (1957).

Isaac Bashevis Singer (1904–1991), *The Magician of Lublin* (New York: Farrar, Straus and Giroux, 1960). Paperback reprint, Bantam Books, 1965.

DAVA SOBEL
Longitude

~

This remarkable book tells the story of how a stubborn, self-taught eighteenth-century British eccentric solved one of history's great intellectual and practical problems, the determination of longitude (position on an east-west axis) at sea. This may seem to be an abstruse matter, but it was in fact a crucial issue in the development of safe and reliable navigation. Only with the solution of the longitude problem could a long-distance sailor have any more than a vague notion of where he might be. This was brought home in dire terms to the British government and public on a foggy night in 1707, when the unfortunate Admiral Sir Clowdisley Shovell, who was much farther east than he thought he was, sailed a small fleet onto the Scilly Islands in the English Channel, with the loss of four warships and the deaths of over two thousand men.

But if the need for a solution was clear, a usable one continued to elude the best thinkers of the day. In 1714, in an attempt to shed fresh light on the problem, the British Parliament passed the Longitude Act, establishing a Longitude Commission and offering a prize of £20,000 (a very considerable fortune at the time) for a workable solution. The prize went unclaimed for decades.

The problem of determining where in the world you are (in the absence of landmarks) has two components, latitude and longitude. Latitude—the distance, in degrees, north or south of the equator—is easy; all you need is a fairly simple instrument for observing the height of the sun above the horizon at noon, and some straightforward mathematical calculations. Longitude is not easy at all. For a start, whereas the equator (an imaginary line around the earth, midway between the poles and perpendicular to the earth's axis of rotation) is a consequence of the geometry of the planet itself, there is no natural baseline from which to calculate the values of "east" and "west." One is forced to rely on a purely arbitrary zero value: 0° longitude is now defined by the location of the Royal Observatory in Greenwich, England. More important, there is no easy celestial marker (such as the height of the sun at noon) from which one can calculate distances in degrees east or west of the zero line once it has been chosen. Longitude can be derived from the observed position of the moon, or of the moons of Jupiter, but it is extremely difficult to make sufficiently accurate observations of those positions from the heaving deck of a ship at sea. It is also difficult to calculate by hand appropriate tables, extending several years in advance, for translating the observations into actual positional terms, as would be necessary to make such a system useful on long voyages.

By the seventeenth century, it had already been widely recognized that the longitude problem could be reduced to a trivial calculation if it were possible to make an extremely accurate and reliable clock. In theory, the clock would always show the time at the arbitrary baseline one had chosen (for the British, and later the world, the Greenwich Meridian); clock time could then be compared to local noontime (wherever one happened to be) by direct observation of the sun. Because a complete circle around the globe is equivalent to twenty-four hours of clock time (that is, an hour equals 15° of east-west distance), the difference between baseline time and local time would quickly convert into an exact distance in degrees east or west of the baseline. Translating this theory into a practical solution to the longitude problem would, however, require the construction of a clock of unprecedented accuracy. The technical demands on the instrument would be extreme; it would have to remain accurate to within a few seconds over a period of months, or perhaps years, and it would have to remain accurate despite the constant and erratic motion of a ship at sea, variations in temperature from arctic cold to equatorial heat, and the effects of salt air on delicate gearwork. The consensus was that it could not be done.

Then John Harrison entered the scene. Born in 1693, the son of a Lincolnshire woodworker, Harrison was a self-educated mechanical genius obsessed with clocks. With no formal training as a clockmaker, he had made a wooden clock of his own design while still a teenager; in his early twenties he designed and built two long-case (grandfather) clocks that were impervious to variations in temperature and accurate to one second per month. Around the same time, he decided to compete for the Longitude Prize. For the next fifty years, he would create, with increasing success, a series of motion-proof, heat-proof, low-friction, noncorroding clocks that even today remain marvels of mechanical ingenuity. (One can see them at the museum at the Royal Observatory in Greenwich, England, still ticking away.) Throughout those fifty years, he was opposed and thwarted by professionals on the Longitude Commission and at the Royal Observatory, who for their own professional reasons wanted very much for the solution to the longitude problem to be an astronomical rather than a mechanical one.

Harrison, it must be said, was a difficult individual, stiff-necked and aloof; he was not adept at cultivating patrons or at expressing himself clearly in writing so that others could evaluate his ideas. Nevertheless, he was treated shabbily by the British authorities, who delayed certifying his claims and ultimately paid him only a fraction of the prize money he had legitimately won. Harrison had, however, the satisfaction of hearing his best clock praised by no less an authority than Captain James Cook, explorer of the South Seas; Harrison's son William would live long enough to see the marine chronometer become standard equipment on oceangoing ships. But while the story of John Harrison's achievements makes a stirring tale, his personal story is a poignant one.

Dava Sobel, a former science writer for *The New York Times*, tells the story with verve, economy, and clarity. The book became a huge bestseller and brought riches both to its author and to the small publishing house that published it. It has spawned a host of imitators; every writer, editor, and publishing executive since 1995 who hoped that a quirky, short book of nonfiction on an obscure subject would become a surprise bestseller has resorted to describing the new contender as being "like *Longitude*." But in fact nothing is like *Longitude*; this is an exceptionally interesting and rewarding book to read, and truly one of a kind; it is a book from which we are sure you will get a great deal of pleasure.

Dava Sobel (1947–), *Longitude* (New York: Walker, 1995). Widely available in both the original Walker hardcover and in the 1996 Penguin paperback reprint.

ALEXANDER SOLZHENITSYN
One Day in the Life of Ivan Denisovich

~

More than any other writer, Alexander Solzhenitsyn brings the disasters of twentieth-century totalitarianism to the fore; he is one of the very few writers whose work truly must be read in order to comprehend our era. Solzhenitsyn grew up in southern Russia, in Rostov-on-Don; his parents were a former World War I artillery officer, who died in an accident before his son was born, and the daughter of Ukrainian landowners. After his graduation from Rostov University, he served as a Soviet artillery captain fighting against the Germans in World War II, with decorations for personal bravery. For the careless mistake of mocking Stalin, the Soviet dictator, in a letter to a friend, he was arrested at the front and sentenced to eight years in forced labor camps. He survived both the camps and subsequent exile to emerge as a prolific writer.

Solzhenitsyn began his writing in the prison camps, secretly composing and memorizing vast quantities of verse. It was in the camps that he conceived the idea of representing the prison camp system by writing about a single day in the life of a typical inmate. In the novel, this is the peasant Ivan Denisovich. (In the Russian style, these are his first name and patronymic; his last name is Shukhov.) The year is 1951 and the camp is one of those set up for political prisoners serving long sentences based on largely specious charges of anti-Soviet activities. In the realistic tradition of nineteenth-century Russian literature, the characters in the book are based on actual people. For example, the name Shukhov is that of a soldier commanded by Solzhenitsyn in World War II, and Ivan Denisovich's personality and experiences are a composite of those of the real Shukhov (who did not serve in the camps), of Solzhenitsyn himself, and of his fellow inmates.

The story of the day is told from Shukhov's point of view. The narrative employs his peasant idiom and describes his ways of looking at camp life, but it is told in the third rather than the first person, a device that lends generality to the novel. The day of the novel begins and ends in the wretched hut in which Shukhov, hardened after years in the camps, lives with other inmates. We read about the elements of an ordinary day in a forced-labor camp: meager food, bad clothing, work assignments in murderously cold weather, brutality and repression by the camp administration, guards with itchy trigger fingers, inmate resentments, and, on this day, Shukhov's luck in getting some extra food by doing a favor for another inmate. The day is unremarkable by the standards of the camps, but it is actually a good one for Ivan Denisovich. This insightful literary device is what gives the novel its tremendous impact: What is for Ivan Denisovich a good day would be for most people unbearably harsh and possibly fatal. This is a work of outstanding historical significance as well as literary excellence, with Solzhenitsyn giving us the essence of artistic truth about a corrupt, inhumane, and unsustainable regime. He is an exceptional writer, a person in whom outrage has fueled the creative process.

One Day in the Life of Ivan Denisovich was the first (and, for a long time, the only one) of Solzhenitsyn's longer works to appear in his homeland. It created a sensation when it was published in the Russian journal *Novy Mir* in 1962, at a time when de-Stalinization was under way under Nikita Khrushchev. However, official acclaim for the work was short-lived, and after Khrushchev was replaced by Leonid Brezhnev, in 1964, Solzhenitsyn suffered renewed repression, including an assassination attempt by the Soviet secret police. He was deported to West Germany in 1974, lived in Switzerland and in Cavendish, Vermont, and returned to Russia in 1994 after the dissolution of the Soviet Union. He won the Nobel Prize for Literature in 1970.

Solzhenitsyn is often thought of primarily as a novelist (*The First Circle*, *The Cancer Ward*), but you might also wish to look into *The Gulag Archipelago*. This intense study of the Soviet prison camp system is one of the great documents of our times, and it provides the framework within which *One Day in the Life of Ivan Denisovich* was conceived.

Aleksandr [Alexander] Isaevich Solzhenitsyn (1918–), *One Day in the Life of Ivan Denisovich* (*Odin den' Ivana Denisovicha;* Moscow: *Novy Mir,* 1962; English trans., New York: Noonday Press/Farrar, Straus and Giroux, 1991). This authorized edition restores some elements censored in the Russian text published in the journal *Novy Mir* in 1962. Available as a Signet Classic paperback reprint (1998). *The Gulag Archipelago* was published in English by Harper and Row (3 vols., 1973–78); it is available from the same publisher in a one-volume abridgment.

WALLACE STEGNER
Remembering Laughter

~

Wallace Stegner was born in Lake Mills, Iowa, and spent his childhood being hauled about a series of U.S. and Canadian towns in the West by his father, always hopeful for a break. Stegner attended the University of Utah and had a long career as a novelist, essayist, and short-story writer dealing with the West, its people, and the conservation of its land and water. *Remembering Laughter* made his name as a writer, providing a prize-winning entry into public esteem. Stegner was a teacher as well as a writer: He founded the Creative Writing Program at Stanford and directed it until his retirement, in 1971.

Western Iowa is full of gently rolling land with tree-bordered streams flowing to the Missouri and the Mississippi. It is beautiful as well as fertile country, and it is here that this powerful novella takes place. *Remembering Laughter* is a finely written story of people trapped in their own beliefs, loves, and icy correctness. Sac County, where the story takes place, is northwest of Des Moines. At the time of the novella, it is a society in transition. It is no longer the pioneering frontier of Wilder (p. 301), but it is still a long way from our era of computerized irrigation. There are horse-drawn carriages and cars; the population includes the poor and the unlucky in addition to the well-to-do. It was a society in which the skill and energy of the farmer were (together with luck) all-important, inasmuch as it was necessary to utilize on a daily basis knowledge of soil, weather, animals, and crops. One of us remembers standing with an Iowa friend at his farmhouse early one morning, watching him examine his property and listening to an explanation of where a fog bank on a distant field would be later in the same morning, and exactly how its presence would affect operations that day. This is what the farmers of Sac County needed to know.

Margaret and Alec Stuart, who have no children, are among the leaders of Sac County farming and society. Margaret keeps a fine home on their prosperous farm and shops on occasion in Omaha and Chicago. Later in the story, Alec will be a much-respected state senator representing Sac County in Des Moines. Margaret is a correct woman and rather beautiful; her husband is handsome, confident, successful, and given to very tall stories. He also likes to share a bottle with his friends as occasion permits, without the approval of his wife. While the Sac County in which they live is partly a settled American society, it is still also an immigrant society. Minnie, a young Scandinavian woman, helps in the kitchen of the Stuarts' house, and Ahlquist, a Norwegian sailor, works for them for a time so that he can pay off his debts and rejoin his family in Norway. Later in the book, there is a poignant memory of the Glasgow kitchen of Margaret's mother, and of a song that she sang there.

Although the novella does not open in this way, the principal action of the story starts with Margaret and Alec inviting her sister, Elspeth MacLeod, to join them from her home in Scotland, where Margaret and Elspeth's mother has recently died. On the trip back to their farm from the station, Alec regales the wondering Elspeth with the tallest of tall tales, she hardly knowing what to believe. In the winter, Alec says, snow piles thirty feet above the houses, it takes smoke forty-eight hours to melt through, and when it does it is tired and freezes—Alec promises to show Elspeth a stick of frozen smoke he's saved in the icehouse.

Elspeth is introduced to the life of the farm and of Sac County. Margaret gives a party so that Elspeth can meet the eligible bachelors in town, but these prove not to be a tremendously attractive lot, ranging from the prissy minister (descended from an old New England family) to ill-behaved locals. While Elspeth at first is happy on the farm, Alec's good humor, drink, and great confidence combine to cause events that stun all three adults. As a result, the household, despite its outer correctness, becomes for many years devoid of inner life amidst a Calvinist sense of retribution. Although Alec's good spirits are not entirely submerged and play a role later in the story, the two sisters appear locked in a sterile lifetime of silent recrimination. At the end of

Remembering Laughter, there is a sense of new life, of possibilities, of truth, and of acceptance, but we cannot be entirely sure. We are left to wonder how it is that disastrously mistaken family events occur so readily and appear to be beyond the touch of any healing, and whether it is possible that some things should not heal, or whether the unforgivable should be forgiven.

This novella is exceptional for its power within a very short compass—Stegner provides a sense of foreboding almost from the first page, but we are not entirely certain what is coming and whether what happens is worse in the end than we expected. And his sense of the landscape within which the events take place is fine—western Iowa can still be the way it is described here, with the brutal sow in the pen, the calves, the fine little streams, the changing seasons. Stegner is not now as widely read as he was, perhaps because of his traditional style, but we think that after reading *Remembering Laughter* you will want to explore further. Among Stegner's many works of fiction, we like especially *Angle of Repose*; his last book of essays, *Where the Bluebird Sings to the Lemonade Springs: Living and Writing the West*, provides an introduction to the man and his ideas.

Wallace Stegner (1909–1993), *Remembering Laughter* (Boston: Little, Brown, 1937). The Penguin paperback reprint (1996) is readily available.

ROBERT LOUIS STEVENSON
Treasure Island

~

One hundred years ago, it would hardly have been necessary for us to recommend this book; everyone would have read it, some (especially teenage boys) several times. Even fifty years ago, Robert Louis Stevenson's works were widely read. In recent decades, his novels have gradually slipped from the consciousness of most readers, though they continue to be held in very high esteem by writers (who admire Stevenson's economical plots and his skill at depicting settings and characters). If you have never read it before, *Treasure Island* is a great treat waiting to be discovered; if you read it only in your youth, you will be surprised by how rich it is when reread with adult understanding.

Robert Louis Stevenson was born into a famous Scottish family of civil engineers, and his father clearly intended that Robert should follow in the family business. He was a delicate child, however, and it soon became apparent that his constitution would not be up to the demands of building lighthouses and railway bridges. He was allowed to study law, rather than engineering, at Edinburgh University. By the time he had completed his studies, he was already becoming known as an author of essays and stories, and he never pursued any profession other than that of a writer. Writing gained him a slender livelihood, however, until the publication of *Treasure Island* brought him both fame and fortune.

Meanwhile, Stevenson had married an American woman, Fanny Osbourne, in 1879, and moved with her to California. By then he was seriously ill with tuberculosis and had begun a long search for a climate that would help to improve his health. This led eventually to his travels with his family in the South Pacific; they settled in Samoa, where he died at the age of forty-four. Despite his poor health he was an energetic and productive writer; his books, to name only the most famous, include *Treasure Island, Kidnapped, Dr. Jekyll and Mr. Hyde, The Master of Ballantrae,* and *A Child's Garden of Verses.*

The plot of *Treasure Island* is famous and does not need much retelling here. It is an account of how a young boy, Jim Hawkins, came into possession of a treasure map and with his friends Squire Trelawney and Dr. Livesey went off in search of the buried pirate gold. The squire buys a schooner, the *Hispaniola,* and hires the excellent Captain Smollett to sail her; but the squire also talks too much and lets out the secret of the treasure. Unwittingly he engages a crew composed mainly of pirates (led by the amiable one-legged cook, Long John Silver), who are happy to get free passage to Treasure Island. There, according to their mutinous plan, they would recover the treasure and murder their employers. Jim, by a combination of luck, intelligence, and nerve (and a certain amount of naughtiness), plays a key role in thwarting the pirates' plot, and the adventure ends happily.

Most of Stevenson's novels fall into the genre of "boy books" that were extremely popular throughout the nineteenth century. Stevenson was particularly influenced by the historical romances of Sir Walter Scott and by James Fenimore Cooper's tales of wild American woodlands and prairies. Stevenson's novels are rather more sophisticated in vocabulary and style than most books written for young readers today, and they now work better for an adult audience than for a juvenile one. (You don't have to be male to enjoy them, either.) They hold up well, in part because Stevenson was a highly accomplished writer (as can be seen in his nonfiction also; his *In the South Seas* is a masterpiece of travel writing) and in part because of his ability to invent colorful characters and portray them vividly. Both of us remember, for example, being terrified by the malevolent figure of Blind Pew when we read *Treasure Island* for the first time.

One aspect of the book that seems aimed at young readers, and which certainly would be both intriguing and instructive to them, is its demonstration that evil can lurk behind a friendly facade. The genial figure of Long John Silver is a wonderful fictional creation: Who would believe that a man so kindly, so knowledgeable, and so possessed of a natural grace of bearing would at bottom be a pirate, a cutthroat, and a mutineer? An adult reader might be a bit suspicious of him from the start, but for a child, his treachery is a rude surprise. That things may not be as they seem is something that everyone needs to learn, and Long John illustrates the lesson well. (Stevenson softens this harsh lesson by tempering Silver's villainy at the end of the tale; there's no point in frightening his young readers too badly.)

We also think that part of the tremendous appeal of *Treasure Island* for the reading audience of Stevenson's own time—it was a huge bestseller—lies in its particular relevance to the great era of emigration and world travel during which it was written. Throughout the final decades of the nineteenth century, hundreds of thousands of people a year sailed from Europe to America, Australia, Argentina, and other far-flung places to begin new lives; it was, to an extent now largely forgotten, an era attuned to a sense of adventure. This is an idea with personal resonance for us; our grandfather ran away to sea from his home in Manchester, England, at the age of twelve, just about the time this book was published. Whether he was inspired by the example of Jim Hawkins we do not know.

Robert Louis Stevenson (1850–1894), *Treasure Island* (Edinburgh and London: Cassell, 1883; Boston: Roberts Brothers, 1884). Widely available; the Penguin Classics paperback edition (1999) has a useful introduction by John Seelye.

FRANK SULLIVAN

Frank Sullivan Through the Looking Glass

~

Greetings, Friends! This is a lovely selection of the humorous pieces and letters of Frank Sullivan, who was a *New Yorker* writer during the magazine's great years under the editorship of Harold Ross. You may have read a descendant of one of Sullivan's old standbys, if not one of the originals: He wrote forty-two of *The New Yorker's* annual Christmas poems (each titled with the first two words of this paragraph), from 1932, the first, through 1974, and the tradition continues in *The New Yorker* to this day. Sullivan's humor is still a joy to read because of the gentle way in which he focuses on the foibles of the human condition and the skill with which he depicts his times. His work is festooned, where appropriate, with matchless wordplay. *Frank Sullivan Through the Looking Glass* contains pieces written for *The New Yorker* and other papers and magazines, letters to his friends, and several poems, including the 1968 Christmas poem.

The pieces look easy and offhanded (they are not), which is part of their charm, and they are all fun to read. Of the pieces in this book, we like especially an examination of the supposedly tone-deaf branch of the Bach family; this is carefully crafted humor that allows you to guess the general lines of what is to come but renders you unable to stop nonetheless. We also like "Proust and the Life Sentence," a two-page work of literary criticism focusing on the length of the great writer's sentences, which is as good a bit of humorous literary insight, word for word, as one can find. There is also a piece on Aunt Sarah Gallop, of Holcombe Landing in the Adirondacks, a figure Sullivan invented to fill an empty space in an article about the 1924 Democratic convention in New York for the old *New York World*. Aunt Sarah was, at the time, 102 years old, and had traveled to New York to root for Al Smith. There are also several of Sullivan's pieces on Dr. Arbuthnot, the Cliché Expert. Once you've read these, you will find yourself listening much more carefully than usual to your own words, and with good effect.

It is the letters that bring out Sullivan's personality best. Sullivan had a galaxy of friends, ranging from school and college chums to glittering New York literary types, and his letters to all of them reveal the special, familial quality of his friendships. In an age when nearly everything seems packaged for sale, it is amazing to us that Sullivan would, in a letter, send to someone simply out of love and friendship a beautifully crafted small work of literature—nowadays one would expect writers to try to offer such gems instead to a magazine, newspaper, or Web site.

The letters come in various types. In his letters to Ross (more or less on business), Sullivan referred to the editor as Hal, Ross, or Harold, depending on his mood. (Sullivan was inventive in his salutations and the form of his correspondents' names in his letters, and signed off with whatever variant of his own name—or, indeed, others' names—that struck his fancy.) In one letter to Ross, Sullivan commented in a mild but humorous huff about one of his books being left out of *The New Yorker*'s annual Christmas list of books by *New Yorker* authors; it didn't meet Ross' firm rule of having at least one-third of the content by *The New Yorker* writer. Sullivan signs off with "One third of a Merry Christmas to you." His letters to others on the death of friends bring out the meaning of human friendship and relationships in ways that make our own small efforts at such times seem woefully inadequate. His letter to Edna Ferber ("Dearest Ferb") on the death of Russel Crouse (the writer of, among much else, *Life with Father,* with Harold Lindsay) is astonishingly moving.

Of the letters here, most are catchings-up, humorous riffs on something that caught Sullivan's eye, and arrangements for get-togethers. In one of the latter, giving directions to his home in Saratoga Springs, he helpfully notes that a cemetery is placed at the entrance to the town to remind visitors that the town is a health resort. His short letter of appreciation to Helen Hayes on one of her performances is unbeatable. Sullivan knew how hard good writing is, and was free with his praise and admiration of other writers. His letter to Groucho Marx thanking him for the inscribed copy of *The Groucho Letters* is delightful, as is his letter to James Thurber about the party at the Algonquin Hotel in New York for James Thurber's *The Years with Ross*, which was dedicated to Sullivan. Sullivan signed off on this one as "The 1st Dedicatee of his Generation."

Sullivan was a lifelong bachelor, happy to emphasize his Irish heritage, fond of brew and racing, and (most writers will be on board here) constantly wondering about productivity and how hard it is to work. In middle life, he moved from New York City back to Saratoga Springs, New York, whence many of these letters issue. If you have occasion to visit Saratoga Springs, you will note with pleasure that the atmosphere in which Sullivan worked for much of his mature career remains largely unchanged. Each August, during the races at Saratoga, something occurred that hardly seems conceivable in our own hurried times: Friends from all over would come to the town, ostensibly to visit the track but really to join their friend Sullivan on his front porch for a drink and talk.

There are books that we cherish not only for themselves but because of the people with whom we have shared them, perhaps many years ago. One of us loaned our copy of *Frank Sullivan Through the Looking Glass* toward the end of Sullivan's life to the distinguished American classical sculptor Walker Hancock, who knew Sullivan and enjoyed the book mightily. In reading a book, we often remember old friendships.

Frank Sullivan (1892–1976), *Frank Sullivan Through the Looking Glass,* ed. George Oppenheimer (Garden City, N.Y.: Doubleday, 1970). Out of print, but not hard to find in used-book stores or online. As you search, you may also find other collections of Sullivan's work; he published several throughout his career.

Malba Tahan
The Man Who Counted

∽

This delightful book is by a Brazilian mathematician and writer, Júlio César de Mello e Souza, who used the pseudonym Malba Tahan. It is a graceful work that combines storytelling and mathematics in an unusually comfortable way. The tale of *The Man Who Counted* is set in the Arab world during the great medieval flowering of mathematics there, and it captures the tradition of the traveler: meeting persons along the way, and visiting markets, inns, and the courts of dignitaries. The hero of the story is Beremiz Samir and the narrator is Hanak Tade Maia, who meets Beremiz by chance on the road to Baghdad.

It seems that Beremiz began counting as a young shepherd in Persia; he counted sheep for practical reasons, and other animals and plants for the sheer pleasure of doing so. Gradually he became a brilliant mathematical reasoner. The two companions set off on the road to Baghdad together and have many adventures. Beremiz becomes famous for his skills, and people bring him problems to solve, often wrapped up in stories both lifelike and fabulous. The two men are soon invited to meet the Vizier (government minister) Ibrahim Maluf, who, after observing Beremiz's skills, takes him on as secretary and the narrator as scribe. Later, they are invited to the Caliph's (ruler's) palace, and there Beremiz solves some of his most interesting problems.

Beremiz is capable of rapid counting (for example, the number of butterflies in a swarm), and he also has a facility for rapid logical analysis and knows the properties of numbers and the history of mathematics. The first problem that Beremiz encounters on the road to Baghdad in the company of the narrator shows his style. Three brothers are observed quarreling violently about the division of thirty-five camels. Of these, their father has willed half to the oldest brother, one-third to the next oldest, and one-ninth to the youngest. Unfortunately, all possible solutions appear to involve cutting up several of the camels to achieve the terms of the father's will. One-half of thirty-five camels, for example, is seventeen-and-a-half camels, obviously an unsatisfactory approach in a society in which camels are among the most valued of possessions. Beremiz quickly sees the solution, and winds up with a camel for himself to boot. He grasps immediately that the three fractions do not add up to one; this provides the necessary latitude to satisfy everyone in an elegant way without cutting up any camels. Most of the stories have the endearing quality of this one: They are so interesting that they cloak, at first sight, the underlying logic, and it is this that Beremiz unfailingly finds.

Many fascinating mathematical matters emerge in the course of the stories and puzzles. Although all are so neatly explained that they are accessible to the reader and do not require any specialized mathematical knowledge or ability, we often need Beremiz to guide us at first. There is a fine figure explaining Pythagoras' theorem (for a right triangle, the sum of the squares of the two sides is equal to the square of the hypotenuse). Beremiz talks about mathematical curiosities such as perfect numbers. These are numbers (such as twenty-eight) that are equal to the sum of all the numbers (except themselves) by which they can be divided. Magic squares, which some people at times have taken to be really magical, have different numbers arranged so as to yield the same sum along any line, column, or diagonal. There is also a neat example of the principle of false induction, whereby correct observations can be used to generate an incorrect rule. All of these things, which may seem dry in themselves, are so cleverly illustrated in the context of stories plain and fantastic that they give a true feeling of the relevance of mathematics to all things. (Among the stories is a fine one about the origin of chess.) The book concludes with a grueling challenge at the Caliph's palace, where seven wise men propound problems for Beremiz, all of which he solves.

The setting of these tales in medieval Arabia reminds us of the vital role that the Islamic world played in the development of Greek mathematical (and other) knowledge during the centuries of the European Dark Ages. Malba Tahan's evocation of the Arab world is clear-eyed and just; he describes its palaces, poetry, calligraphy, and other lovely aspects of high culture, but he also notes some of its violence. And there are reminders of the breadth of contact of that cosmopolitan area: a prince comes from India; a poem is recited that is actually from the New Testament (and is attributed to a "Nazarene poet"); a wise man who lived in Córdoba in Spain encounters political difficulties and thereby comes to Baghdad.

Beremiz himself is a somewhat dreamy fellow who is protected by his ability, his fine beliefs, and his friends and employers. For Beremiz, mathematics aids all of our arts and sciences; a quality we like about him is that in solving mathematical problems, he is concerned not only with rigor but with justice. He stoutly defends the ability of women to do mathematics, and this advocacy turns out in the end to his great personal satisfaction.

The Man Who Counted captures the interrelationships of mathematics to real life, the relation of the abstract to the real, in a remarkably immediate way. Few books seem to be one of a kind, but this one is. We know of nothing else like it. It is a convincing demonstration, even to the math-shy, of the beauty and relevance in our lives of number and calculation, and it is a delight to share with a bright and imaginative young teenager.

Malba Tahan [Júlio César de Mello e Souza] (1895–1974), *The Man Who Counted (O homem que calculava),* trans. Leslie Clark and Alastair Reid, illus. Patricia Reid Baquero (New York: W. W. Norton, 1993).

WILFRED THESIGER
Arabian Sands

❦

One day in the summer of 1946, Wilfred Thesiger stood on a mountain ridge in southern Arabia, surrounded by green forest and streams of fresh cold water, and realized that he wanted only to return to the heat and sand of the desert he could see in the distance. This scene, with which he opens his classic travel narrative *Arabian Sands*, captured for him the hold that the desert had on him; he felt drawn to it as to nowhere else, and felt nowhere else so fully at home. He was in the early stages of a five-year stay in Arabia, ostensibly doing research but in fact simply following his own mad pursuit of living with the desert Bedu and riding with them wherever they would accompany him. His feats included two crossings of the truly hellish Empty Quarter of southeastern Arabia, a region of mountainous dunes, no water, and extreme temperatures; he endured hunger, thirst, gunfights, scorpion stings, and much else, and couldn't get enough of it.

This straightforward, unpretentious account of Thesiger's five years in Arabia is justly famous as one of the most amazing travel books ever written. And yet reading *Arabian Sands* today raises questions that would not have occurred to most readers when it was first published some forty years ago, a period when explorers were nearly unambiguously admired—celebrated in the media, lionized on the lecture circuit, viewed as heroes. That time, like the age of exploration itself, is gone, and it seems clear in hindsight that every explorer, regardless of his motives, was a precursor in some way of the expansion of European and other powers and of the conquest and exploitation of societies and territories around the globe. Even an explorer as disinterested as Thesiger could not really escape the consequences of his actions.

Where he might go on camelback with a few Bedu companions, traveling for no reason but the freedom he felt in his beloved desert, less intrepid travelers would soon follow with trucks and surveying gear, oil rigs, and mineral leases. He knew that, and he also knew that there was nothing he could do about it; the conquest of the world by modern Western civilization was going to continue with or without his help, and all he wanted was to experience as much of the unspoiled world as he could while it still existed.

Thesiger spent his childhood in an Africa already substantially controlled by the governments of Europe. His father was British minister in Addis Ababa, Ethiopia, where Thesiger was born in 1910. In the world in which he grew up, it was simply assumed that Europe bestrode the globe; he writes quite straightforwardly of the Nuer of the Sudan, for example, that "the district had only been administered since 1925, and there had been some fierce fighting before they had submitted." The basic assumption was that the district would be administered and that the natives would submit; that is simply the way things were going to be. Yet Thesiger himself hated the trappings of imperialism; of the great center of British administration in northern Africa, he writes that "Khartoum seemed like the suburbs of north Oxford dumped down in the middle of the Sudan." And he understood that he himself was unsuited to the life of a district commissioner in the colonial service: "I had no faith in the changes which we were bringing about. I craved for the past, resented the present, and dreaded the future."

Many young men raised in colonial environments grew up with a firm belief in the correctness of Europe's domination of the world. Thesiger's response was quite different. Sent "home" to England for schooling at the age of ten, he felt himself an alien in what was supposed to be his own country; bullied by schoolmates who found him strange, he craved the colorful disorder and ancient pageantry of the Ethiopian capital. A royal summons to attend, at age twenty, the coronation of Haile Selassie, King of Kings of Ethiopia, brought him joyfully back to Africa. No sooner were the ceremonies concluded than he organized an expedition to trace the lower Afar River through Danakil country, a region where every previous European expedition had been wiped out. He received the local sultan's blessing and made it through unscathed. From then on, his goal was to spend as much time on the back of a camel, away from anything resembling civilization, as he possibly could. His wartime service in Ethiopia, Syria, and Libya gets little more than a page in this book; what must have been hair-raising combat duty with the Special Air Service, raiding behind enemy lines, is dismissed as of scant interest because "I was in the desert, but insulated from it by the jeep in which I traveled."

A postwar assignment to do research on outbreaks of desert locusts in Arabia proved the key to the defining experience of his life. That research led directly to the five years' travel in Arabia's Empty Quarter described in this book and to what Thesiger calls the happiest years of his life. Part of what makes this book so powerful is the sense of a man perfectly matched to his destiny. Thesiger, it would seem, was born to challenge himself in the toughest environments he could find, and to feel the joy of being where "time and space were one. Round us was a silence in which only the winds played, and a cleanness which was infinitely remote from the world of men."

By the end of 1949, the political situation in Arabia had made it nearly impossible for Thesiger to continue to pursue his unfettered travels; his presence in the desert had become too awkward for too many people. With his life in immediate danger, he reluctantly parted from his friends and returned to an England that he could not call home. In later years he sought out other untraveled places, in the marshes of Iraq, in the mountains of Afghanistan (see Eric Newby's meeting with him, p. 199), and elsewhere. But while he has been regarded with almost reverential awe by fellow writers and adventurers, he has spent the rest of his life feeling like a man without a country.

The traditional age of bold exploration of the land is over, both because there are hardly any places left to explore and because it may be harder in the modern world than it was in Thesiger's day to summon up the unwavering self-reliance that the explorer needs to stay alive. We may understand, on reading this book, that Thesiger helped— however unwillingly—to change the very lands and peoples that he cherished. Nevertheless, it is as stunning a record of dauntless courage, stubborn endurance, grandeur of vision, and nobility of soul as one could hope to read. This is a dazzling book.

Wilfred Thesiger (1910–), *Arabian Sands* (London: Longmans, Green, 1959). Paperback reprint, Viking, 1985.

DYLAN THOMAS
Under Milk Wood

~

The "sloeblack, slow, black, crowblack, fishingboat-bobbing sea" (say this out loud) laps the fictional little Welsh town of Llaregyb. Once you have encountered this sea on the first page of Thomas' play for voices, you will be enchanted for life, and the whole strange orchestra of Welsh personalities that Thomas summons up in his masterpiece will be part of your world.

Thomas was born in Swansea, on the south coast of Wales, in 1914, the first year of World War I. He moved to Laugharne, the model for Llaregyb, in 1938, where he lived for years and where he is buried in St. Martin's Churchyard. Laugharne (rhymes with *darn*) is a seaside village on Carmarthen Bay, twenty-five miles west of Swansea. By all accounts the village was filled at the time of Thomas' residency with hardworking, brawling fishermen, their families, and a few artists and writers.

The play depicts one twenty-four-hour period, from midnight to midnight, in Llaregyb. The characters in the play—Captain Cat, the blind sea captain, and his cronies; Polly Garter; Willy Nilly, the postman; Mrs. Waldo; Organ Morgan; and many others—engage both in conversations and in internal soliloquies, ranging over the entire gamut of small-town emotions and gossip, the whole infused with a wonderfully raucous sexuality. We peep in on the romances of Mr. Mog Edwards and Myfanwy Price, and of Sinbad Sailors and schoolmistress Gwendolyn B.; we overhear Mrs. Ogmore-Pritchard, twice widowed, still laying down the household law of chores in excruciating detail to each of her dead husbands; and we meet up with the Reverend Eli Jenkins, Nogood Boyo, and many another stalwart of Llaregyb. Thomas' genius in this work is to give his cockeyed, marvelously enjoyable fictional characters dreams, desires, and complaints that we can relate both to ourselves and to people we know. Thomas, though Welsh, was not Welsh-speaking, so he saw his Welsh villagers from the double standpoint of both an insider and an outsider; this circumstance, together with his poetic gifts, is what makes *Under Milk Wood* so effective.

In the early 1950s, Thomas expressed a desire to turn from poetry (his *Collected Poems* was published in 1952) to larger forms; *Under Milk Wood* is the only one of these we have. In fact, the existence of this work is a matter of remarkable good luck, because Thomas completed it only a month before his unfortunate death in New York, apparently from overdrinking. The Hotel Chelsea on West 23rd Street in New York, where he lived and where a plaque commemorates his stay, is a suitably offbeat reminder of the poet; you may want to visit it when in New York. Of Thomas' other work, the illustrated version of *A Child's Christmas in Wales*, widely available in bookshops in December, is a favorite of many. Thomas' *Collected Poems* repays a visit; it includes, among others, "Do Not Go Gentle Into That Good Night."

Dylan Thomas (1914–1953), *Under Milk Wood* (London: J. M. Dent, 1954). Reprinted many times and widely available in various editions; we like the original J. M. Dent small hardcover edition, which remains in print after almost half a century.

J. R. R. TOLKIEN
The Hobbit

~

J. R. R. Tolkien, born in South Africa and raised in England, was a distinguished professor of medieval literature and language at the University of Oxford. This quiet teacher and scholar, who each December wrote Father Christmas letters to his children filled with imaginative tales about the North Pole, became unexpectedly famous through *The Hobbit* (first published in 1937) and its sequel, *The Lord of the Rings*.

The Hobbit is one of the very few books that can be read with immense enjoyment by both adults and children. Hobbits, it seems, are somewhat plump, handy with tools, a bit smaller than dwarfs, and above all fond of creature comforts. *The Hobbit* is a quest story that revolves around one innocent, bumbly hobbit, Bilbo Baggins. Unbeknownst to him, the anxious but finally heroic Bilbo has been chosen to accompany a group of likeable, quarrelsome dwarfs, chaperoned by Gandalf the wizard, on a mission that is of great importance to the dwarfs. This is to restore their ownership of a mountain and its treasures, which are now in the power of an enormous and avaricious dragon.

Tolkien is a master storyteller, and you will find yourself enthralled by the adventures of his characters, who include elves, humans, and goblins as well as hobbits and dwarfs, and whose interactions are depicted in a deeply believable way. Tolkien has the gift of putting matters so that you will always remember them; after reading *The Hobbit*, you will find yourself thinking of many life situations and characters in terms of this story. Bilbo's frightening and ultimately successful mission, entrancing in itself, has consequences that go beyond the quest and lead to *The Lord of the Rings* trilogy.

Tolkien's work stays with us because of his storytelling ability, but also (and perhaps surprisingly) because of his scholarship, which provides an unobtrusively satisfying element for his adult readers. For example, Tolkien's linguistic skills enable him to give subtlety and coherence to the invented languages of dwarfs and elves and other creatures used throughout his works; these languages are based on real languages, including Welsh and Finnish. And many of the names in his stories derive from early heroic works. Gandalf ("sorcerer elf") and the names of the dwarfs in *The Hobbit*, for example, come from an Icelandic saga. Tolkien also thought through carefully what it means to create a separate world, a process that he refers to as subcreation and which he described in a famous essay reprinted in *The Tolkien Reader*.

When you finish *The Hobbit* and find yourself hooked, you can embark on the three volumes of *The Lord of the Rings: The Fellowship of the Ring*, *The Two Towers*, and *The Return of the King*. These are not one-night reads, but together they form a truly fine work. Despite Tolkien's denial of any connection, it is difficult to read the larger work, with its epic battles between forces of good and evil, without thinking of the tragedies of World War II. If you like Tolkien's work, you will enjoy the many essays and papers dealing with various elements of Middle Earth, his "subcreated" world, that he left when he died, in 1973. A substantial number of these have been ably collected and edited by his son, Christopher, and are available in paperback editions. You might even learn to speak Elvish!

J[ohn] R[onald] R[euel] Tolkien (1892–1973), *The Hobbit, or There and Back Again* (London: George Allen and Unwin, 1937; new edition, Boston: Houghton Mifflin, 1982). The authorized paperback edition is published by Ballantine (1990). Fine copies of the 1937 first edition now sell for upward of $40,000.

RICHARD TREGASKIS
Guadalcanal Diary

~

On August 7, 1942, a twenty-five-year-old Boston newspaper reporter and recent Harvard graduate went ashore on a landing craft with troops from the 1st Marine Division on Guadalcanal. From this experience and the battles that followed, Richard Tregaskis produced a classic of battlefield reporting, publishing the original version a few months after his experience on Guadalcanal, even before the island was fully secured. What makes this book so special is that Tregaskis, although a seasoned writer, was young enough to share both physically and emotionally the experience of the Marine troops he accompanied. Over the years, the book has also come to be recognized as a historically significant document because it is an eyewitness report on the first decisive Allied ground victory in the Pacific theater of World War II.

Guadalcanal is the largest island in the (now independent) Solomon Islands. It is about a thousand miles northeast of Australia and has a central mountain range with peaks up to eight thousand feet. Its strategic importance for both sides in the Pacific war was due to the fact that the Japanese, following up on their initial successes, were constructing an airstrip on the northern part of the island. If completed and put into service, this airstrip would have permitted the Japanese to sever links between the United States and Australia. For this reason, the Guadalcanal amphibious landing was pushed through only eight months to the day after Pearl Harbor. Because of the rapid buildup time, the landing troops had little in the way of practice (an earlier landing exercise on Fiji was termed by the commanding general "a complete bust").

The book closely follows Tregaskis' combat diary. He had requested permission to accompany the Marines on a rumored landing at an unrevealed destination; the book itself begins one day in late July 1942 aboard a troop ship, goes through the initial unopposed landing on Guadalcanal, and chronicles the weeks of desperate fighting that ensued. Tregaskis stayed until after the key Battle of the Ridge in September. The success of this book, and what makes it such a gripping narrative so many years later, lies in Tregaskis' simple, real-time reporting style, with himself almost always out of sight. We follow the details of battle plans, equipment, and resupply, expertly interleaved with point-of-battle descriptions of the fighting; we see, in other words, with the eyes of the young Marines as they encounter boredom, battlefield humor, intense effort, and death.

Tregaskis writes with youthfulness and wonder in the face of danger: He sees Japanese bombers overhead and, looking at them through his binoculars, ponders their silvery beauty even as they threaten to destroy him within a few moments. He writes plainly of brutish combat, including the annihilation of a large Marine patrol, and of racial stereotypes on both sides of the lines. The writing is fast paced in the good sense of that term, and the narrative is the more compelling because it is written from the perspective of a time when no one knew what the outcome of the fighting for Guadalcanal would be. The Marines, holding a small area around the airstrip, Henderson Field, were constantly faced with Japanese attacks. These were the result of continued Japanese achievements in supporting their own forces on Guadalcanal, landing fresh supplies and reinforcements at many points on the large island beyond the Marine perimeter.

Part of the appeal of this book is that we only gradually and subtly realize how much of its success derives from Tregaskis' own unassuming courage. His accomplishment is the result of continued participation in extremely hazardous missions, during which he is always armed. This element of the book is made clear in a laconic way at the end, when Tregaskis recounts his departure from the island late in September. He hitches a ride on a B-17 bomber flying from Henderson Field to the American base at Espiritu Santo. During reconnaissance over the Japanese base on Bougainville, Tregaskis uses a .50 caliber machine gun in the nose of the plane to lead the other gunners in shooting down an attacking Zero float plane. This is true combat reporting.

Tregaskis, who drowned in the sea off the coast of Hawaii near his home in 1973, had a long career as a writer and war correspondent, but it is *Guadalcanal Diary* by which he is remembered; it is the combination of his youth, freshness, stamina, and the fact, unknown at the time of writing, that Guadalcanal would be a turning point in the Pacific war that make the volume unforgettable. As we read it and react to the immediacy of the writing, we might pause to remember that it is because of battles such as this one that we are able to read in peace in our own homes.

Richard Tregaskis (1916–1973), *Guadalcanal Diary* (New York: Random House, 1943). Most modern versions, such as the Modern Library edition (2000), include Tregaskis' additional perspectives and background, and restore cuts originally made during wartime by Navy censors. Inexpensive copies of the 1943 first edition can often be found in used-book stores.

ROBERT H. VAN GULIK

The Chinese Gold Murders

~

Robert H. van Gulik was born in the Netherlands East Indies (now Indonesia), the son of a Dutch army medical officer. He was raised in an atmosphere that would have seemed very exotic to most Europeans but which in his case fostered a lifelong sense of being at ease in Asian cultures. He showed a remarkable talent for languages as a young man and attended the famous school of Asian studies at the University of Leiden in Holland, where he added expertise in Sanskrit, Chinese, and Japanese to his near-native ability in Indonesian.

Trained as a scholar, van Gulik rejected the academic world in favor of a career in the Dutch diplomatic service, working with distinction in a variety of posts throughout Asia. At his death, he was ambassador of the Netherlands to Japan.

Throughout his diplomatic career, van Gulik saw himself as being also an amateur scholar—amateur in status, that is, but not in qualifications. Leaving weighty issues of politics, philosophy, and society to professional academics, he explored the fringes of scholarly research; over the years he produced treatises on, among other things, the history of the Chinese lute, Chinese erotica, and the furnishings of scholars' libraries in traditional China. One of his enthusiasms was for traditional Chinese detective novels. In 1949, he translated one of them, *Celebrated Cases of Judge Dee,* and had it published in a small private edition to give to his friends. The book was greeted with acclaim, and van Gulik was urged by his readers to produce more stories of Judge Dee. He made the switch from translator to novelist with ease, and for the rest of his life wrote Judge

Dee novels as a way of relaxing from the demands of his diplomatic career.

There really was a Judge Dee. Di Renjie (to use the more conventional spelling of his name, surname first in the Chinese fashion; his dates are 630–700) was an official of one of China's most glorious imperial regimes, the Tang dynasty. Di was a district magistrate—a powerful local officer who combined the functions of police chief, prosecutor, judge, tax collector, and chief of public works, among others. In this work, he acquired a reputation as a tenacious and highly successful criminal investigator. His reputation survived him, and Judge Di became the hero of many Chinese detective stories and ghost stories, often as a sort of magistrate-wizard, able to enlist occult forces in the detection of wrongdoers. Van Gulik's genius was to turn these tales into novels that satisfy the expectations of modern readers of crime fiction while still preserving much of the flavor of the original sources. Van Gulik's deep understanding of traditional Chinese culture was crucial in this respect; the details in his novels are not made-up exotica, but thoroughly authentic.

The Chinese Gold Murders was not the first Judge Dee mystery that van Gulik wrote, but it is a good choice as the place to begin one's reading of the series, because it shows Dee at the beginning of his career, heading off to take his first magistrate's post at the coastal city of Peng-lai. We meet Sergeant Hoong, Dee's trusty confidential secretary, and his two muscular constables, Ma Joong and Chiao Tai, who remain with him for the fifteen or so novels in the series. Here, too, we encounter dissolute Buddhist monks, crafty smugglers, a charming prostitute, grasping merchants, a devious retired scholar—all stock figures from traditional Chinese popular fiction, brought to new life in these pages. The mystery itself, which concerns a murderous gang of gold smugglers, is close in spirit to the classic English fictions of Agatha Christie and Ngaio Marsh; the Judge Dee books are entertainments pure and simple, without the heavy overtones of much modern crime fiction. They are delightful, and one night spent reading *The Chinese Gold Murders* will lead to others devoted to reading the remaining books in the series. Like other readers, you will lament that van Gulik died young; we wish there were dozens more Judge Dee mysteries.

Robert H[ans] van Gulik (1910–1967), *The Chinese Gold Murders* (New York: Harper and Brothers, 1959). Paperback reprint, University of Chicago Press, 1977, 1979; several other Judge Dee novels are available from the same publisher.

JULES VERNE

Around the World in Eighty Days

∼

This is a book that you are more likely to have heard of than to have read. If that is the case, we think you will be in for a pleasant surprise when you spend an evening racing around the world with Mr. Phileas Fogg and his servant Passepartout.

Around the World in Eighty Days has been continuously in print for more than 125 years, and its plot is well known. The hero, Phileas Fogg, is an English gentleman of considerable wealth and no discernable occupation, a man of fixed and invariable habits who spends every day dining and playing whist at the Reform Club. (One of us has had the pleasure of staying at the Reform Club on several occasions and is pleased to report that it is still much as Jules Verne described it.) One day, Fogg remarks to his whist partners that it has become possible to travel around the world in eighty days. They dispute this; he bets them £20,000 not only that it can be done, but that he will do it, leaving that very evening. Fogg tells his valet, an energetic but slightly foolish young Frenchman known as Passepartout (French for "master key," here understood to mean something like "jack-of-all-trades"), to pack a small valise with cash and a few clean shirts, and they're off.

Complications arise. Fogg is mistakenly identified as the mysterious well-dressed man who had lately robbed the Bank of England. (Where else would he get all that cash?) A detective, Fix, sets out on his trail, and follows him around the entire world trying to arrest him. Along the way, the party is enlarged through the rescue of Mrs. Aouda, an Indian princess whom they discover about to be cremated alive on her late husband's funeral pyre. Fogg and Passepartout certainly will not permit this; they rescue her from the flames, and she accompanies them for the rest of the trip. The trip seemingly falls just short of its goal; the wager is rescued through a final twist that will appeal to the scientifically inclined.

This is above all a work of entertainment, and Verne takes a rather facetious attitude toward his characters. Fogg is the stereotypical Victorian Englishman—humorless, methodical, unemotional. Passepartout is a slapstick French servant—talkative, slightly bumbling, more than slightly ridiculous in his pretensions, but also brave and resourceful in a pinch. Fix is a parody of Javert, the relentless and malevolent policeman of Victor Hugo's *Les Misérables*. One running joke here is that Fogg is utterly indifferent to the interests and charms of the places through which he passes; he has made a bet and intends to win it, and is unconcerned with distractions. Another is that whenever an obstacle arises, Fogg simply hands out enough money to overcome it. A break in the railway line in India? Buy an elephant, at extravagant cost. Running out of coal for the steam engines on the Atlantic crossing? Buy the ship and burn every scrap of wood aboard. Here perhaps Verne is catering particularly to his French readership, resentful of English commercial success in the era of high imperialism. The humor lends the adventure a lighthearted air, making this an easy, enjoyable read.

Some readers may feel offended by Verne's consistent assumption of the cultural, technological, and (for want of a better word) racial superiority of Europeans to everyone else on the earth. For example, it is implicitly understood that the budding romance and eventual marriage between the lovely Aouda and Phileas Fogg is in a sense permissible only because she is already, by virtue of her light complexion and Western-style education, an honorary European. It is worth remembering, however, that Verne's attitudes in this respect were shared by virtually all educated Europeans of his time. Verne does not advance his Eurocentric views with any ill intent or obnoxious insistence. They are part of the landscape of the nineteenth century, noticeable but fairly easy to ignore.

Other aspects of Verne's work show him in a light that is both more favorable and more consistent with the source of his enduring reputation—that is, as a prophet of technology. He was particularly fascinated by innovations in transportation; in his various books he explored the possibilities of submarines, spacecraft, aircraft both lighter and heavier than air, motor-powered land vehicles, and much more. It seems to us that *Around the World in Eighty Days* is not only an exuberant celebration of various modes of transportation (from the modern to the ingenious to the exotic, including steamships, railroads, an iceboat, and that elephant), but also, and more fundamentally, is about the modern conquest of time. Fogg is constantly consulting his railroad and shipping timetables; he makes his wager that he can circle the globe in eighty days because he already knows that published schedules make such a trip possible with a reasonable margin of error. We today are completely used to that idea, but in Verne's day it was still quite remarkable to think that one could plan a trip around the world with such safety and predictability. A century earlier, a voyage around the world would have taken a year or more and would have been fraught with danger and uncertainty.

Jules Verne was born into a middle-class French family and showed talent as a writer early in his youth. Nevertheless, he pursued a conventional education in the law, and for many years he worked as a stockbroker while turning out plays, stories, and musical librettos in his spare time. He found his true calling in the 1860s, when he began to write science-fiction adventure novels—a genre that, in effect, he helped to invent. His books were extremely popular in his native France and were translated into numerous languages; he became one of the most famous writers of his time. A number of his works hold up nicely today and are well worth reading; we would recommend particularly *Twenty Thousand Leagues Under the Sea*, an astute exploration of both submarine technology and of the psychology of egotism run amok.

Jules Verne (1828–1905), *Around the World in Eighty Days* (Paris: J. Hetzel, 1873; London, 1874). The Scholastic paperback, widely available, is cheaply printed and ugly. It is often possible to find attractive and inexpensive hardcover editions of the book in used-book stores, and you might prefer that option.

JAMES D. WATSON
The Double Helix

~

A helix is a continuous curve in three-dimensional space, such as the figure formed by the outside support of a spiral staircase; two such figures winding about the same core yield a double helix. This elegant configuration is the shape of deoxyribonucleic acid, or DNA, the molecule that encodes the genetic rules that pass life on from generation to generation. James D. Watson and Francis Crick won the Nobel Prize in Physiology or Medicine in 1962 for their discovery of the helical structure of DNA; the implications of that discovery make their research one of the most significant scientific advances of the twentieth century. Watson and Crick's work lives on in this sparkling classic of scientific writing. From its irresistible opening sentence—"I have never seen Francis Crick in a modest mood" (many would say the same of Watson himself)—the book charges on in a vivid account of world-class science in action.

Watson, at the time of the discovery, was a young American scientist abroad in Europe, where he had gone in search of exciting areas in which to work. Trained at the University of Chicago and at the University of Indiana in zoology, he began postdoctoral work in Copenhagen and then migrated to Cambridge, England (not entirely with the approval of those providing his fellowship). He was attracted both by the unparalleled opportunities at that great center of science and by the noted charm of the Cambridge environment. The work on the DNA molecule was done at the university's famous Cavendish Laboratory, where Watson and Crick recognized in each other the extremes of brilliance, ambition, and energy that would make them such a remarkable team.

Over a period of several years, through moments of intense

inspiration, dogged work, and depressing failure, Watson and Crick tested ideas, looked for clues, talked to the right people, misled themselves with dreadful errors of fact and reasoning, and finally succeeded in a classic scientific race for success. Their work was informed by the X-ray crystallography of Maurice Wilkins (who shared the Nobel prize with them) and Rosalind Franklin of Kings College, London. Crick and Watson were energized by the knowledge that other formidable scientists, notably Linus Pauling of Caltech, were on the track of DNA, and they knew that those who succeeded would establish a permanent place for themselves in the history of science.

Watson, in writing this book, made a conscious effort to present his perspectives at the time of the work, with all of the accompanying highs, lows, and nagging uncertainties. His willingness to forgo the wisdom of hindsight is one of the things that make the book so vivid. The text is accessible, and any momentary complications can be skipped over in pursuing the narrative. The excitement of the book derives from its palpable air of involvement in a high-stakes race.

The scientific problem was to fit all of the then-known information about DNA into a structure that could be chemically and physically stable and would demonstrate a suitable method of replication. At the start there were many uncertainties, including substantial doubt about the appropriateness of a helical model and about whether the supporting "backbone" of the molecule, helical or not, was internal or external.

In reading the book, it comes as almost a shock to realize how cumbersome scientific work was in the 1950s, before the widespread use of computers. This is, in part, a story of old-fashioned lab-bench science as well as of great theoretical insight. There is a comical quality to the image of Crick and Watson, on the verge of success, struggling with an assortment of metal shapes and connectors fabricated by the lab's technicians, trying to construct what we would now think of, in our age of computer-aided three-dimensional design, as an utterly ramshackle model.

This book is a description of doing real science, characterized by a constant process of conjecture and testing, reliance on others' work and on new technology, and periods of optimism and moments of seeming failure. Perhaps the key to Watson and Crick's success was their ability to see what was important, and what irrelevant, to framing their approach. The volume shows also the scientific interest in aesthetic qualities—Watson comments in the book that the structure they proposed was "too pretty not to exist." Watson's book has sometimes been misunderstood to say that science is just another arena for human ego and competitiveness, but read carefully, it is clearly a description of something much more than that.

Watson is perhaps as famous for his outsized personality as is Crick (Crick weighs in on the DNA story and other matters in his own 1988 book, *What Mad Pursuit*). However, one of us who was acquainted with him during graduate school days found him helpful and insightful in conversation, even with someone not in the hard sciences, and perhaps a little more modest than his reputation. He once said, apropos of how one could rank original scientific concepts, that it might have taken ten years for someone else to do Einstein's work on relativity, but it probably would have taken just six months for someone else to catch up to Watson and Crick. No wonder they felt the pressure of being in a race.

Some of Watson's personal attitudes at the time of the work now strike us as, at best, sophomoric, and even rather discordant in terms of the level of science being done, but Watson's gift here is to tell it like it was, and that element of honesty is what makes this book so attractive. There is an affecting epilogue that adopts a longer perspective and offsets to some extent the youthful tone of the book. In this, Watson gives full credit to Rosalind Franklin, Wilkins' colleague, who is sometimes thought to have gotten less than her share of the glory.

An interesting footnote to the DNA story is that although everything pointed to the correctness of the double helix structure, the first X ray with atomic-level resolution showing the crystallographic structure of a double helix was made only in 1973, by Alexander Rich of MIT. Watson telephoned Rich after this final detailed confirmation of his discovery and said, "I've just had the first good night's sleep in twenty years."

Following his DNA work, Watson moved on to a professorship at Harvard and then to the leadership of the distinguished Cold Spring Harbor Laboratory on the North Shore of Long Island, New York.

James D. Watson (1928–), *The Double Helix* (New York: Atheneum, 1968). Widely available in several paperback editions; the Norton Critical Edition (1980) includes helpful notes.

EVELYN WAUGH
The Loved One

❧

The Loved One is the only one of Evelyn Waugh's books to be set in America, but it is largely about Englishmen—in this case, the English expatriates (and there were many of them) who, in Waugh's view, sold out as serious writers to move to Hollywood in search of money, sunshine, and creature comforts. It is perhaps not possible for modern readers to feel what would have been the full impact of this book on Waugh's English audience at midcentury, because few people today will feel viscerally the contempt that Waugh and his circle entertained for what they saw as the shallow provincialism of American culture. Even so, this can be read today as an exceptionally funny dark comedy about, among other things, death, poetry, advice columnists, and the excesses of Los Angeles, and that is plenty for a great evening's entertainment. (It is interesting to read *The Loved One* in close conjunction with Nathanael West's *The Day of the Locust* [see p. 293] for two very different takes on the same subject.)

The book's principal character is Dennis Barlow, a young English writer who has come to Hollywood to seek his fortune but so far has not had much luck in finding it. He is advised by his older countrymen Sir Francis Hinsley (once successful, now a failing alcoholic has-been) and the fashionable Sir Ambrose Abercrombie to hold out for suitably dignified opportunities. In their view, the British expat community must unfailingly uphold its reputation for upper-class manners and occupational snobbery. But Dennis doesn't care much about such things, and he has to eat; in fact, he already has a job, in deepest secrecy, as an assistant mortician at a pet cemetery, the Happier Hunting Grounds. The services offered by Dennis' establishment are modeled, more modestly, on those of Los Angeles' most socially desirable human cemetery,

Whispering Glades, a place of staggeringly pretentious and expensive vulgarity, where the deceased are invariably referred to as "Loved Ones."

Dennis' easy routine of sliding pet coffins smoothly into the crematory furnace and filling out memorial cards is interrupted by the untimely death of Sir Francis and by Sir Ambrose's insistence that Dennis take over the funeral arrangements. This brings Dennis to Whispering Glades and into contact with the spookily beautiful and unworldly cosmetician Miss Aimée Thanatogenos (whose made-up Greek name means something like "death-bringer"), with whom he falls instantly in love. She, however, adores and idolizes Mr. Joyboy, the head embalmer at Whispering Glades, who is her ideal of an artist and a gentleman. The two vie for Aimée's affections; she, alas, finds out all too soon that both of her suitors are only human in their imperfections. Her understanding that to love means to be disappointed leads to the book's shockingly funny conclusion, involving the combined resources of Whispering Glades and the Happier Hunting Grounds.

Evelyn Waugh was a writer whose entire sensibility was tied to the circumstances of Great Britain between the 1920s and the 1950s. The British Empire was in the last stages of dissolution, with colonial peoples no longer looking to the "mother country" and the doctrine of imperialism itself increasingly called into question at home. The British ruling class had been decimated on the battlefields of World War I; many surviving members of the upper class felt that a divinely instituted social hierarchy was crumbling and that the whole country was going to the dogs. Deeply conservative in his social views, Waugh used his great talents as a writer to celebrate the fading world of British gentility (in serious works such as *Brideshead Revisited*) and to satirize scathingly the failings of less worthy countrymen, including military men (*Put Out More Flags*), colonials (*Black Mischief*), and many others. He is still read, not because many people will sympathize with his political and social views (indeed, much of what would now be called his aggressive political incorrectness is enough to make one cringe), but because like his eighteenth-century model, Jonathan Swift, his satire was backed by a fierce comic genius. His sense of what pretensions needed puncturing was so acute that his works remain hilariously funny even (or perhaps especially) at their most outrageous.

Waugh, according to the testimony of his contemporaries, was not a very nice person; he was often bitterly critical of others, a snob, a bigot, and a social and intellectual bully. We are fortunate to be able to enjoy the white heat of his humor at a remove, through the medium of the printed page, where it can entertain without (usually) singeing too much. *The Loved One* still hits home because there continues to be plenty about the shallowness, pretentiousness, and excess of Hollywood culture to serve as targets for its arrows. We laugh, but it makes us squirm a little, too.

Evelyn Waugh (1903–1966), *The Loved One* (New York: Little, Brown, 1948). The Dell paperback reprint (1962) is widely available.

GLENWAY WESCOTT
The Pilgrim Hawk

~

This delicate, psychologically subtle, and beautifully written novella takes the form of a reminiscence. The narrator, of whom we learn little except that he is an American at home in Europe and a person of taste and independent means, tells us of an episode from about twelve years earlier—that is, around 1928—that has stayed in his mind ever since. The story is a deceptively simple one.

The narrator, Alwyn Tower, is the houseguest of Alexandra Henry (his sister-in-law by the time he tells us the tale, but earlier simply his "great friend") at her country place not far from Paris. The household is a quiet one. Alex generally lives alone, attended by her cook and maid, Jean and Eva, a young Moroccan-French couple whose romantic, tempestuous relationship Alex finds amusing. The routine is broken one day by the unexpected arrival of guests, old friends of Alex's named Madeleine and Larry Cullen. They are Anglo-Irish gentry unable to keep up the expense of their grand country seat in Ireland, and they are on their way (in a splendid Daimler automobile driven by their handsome, sullen chauffeur, Ricketts) to spend the summer in Hungary. As Mrs. Cullen emerges from the car, the narrator sees that she has on her gloved wrist a magnificent peregrine falcon.

Mrs. Cullen is an avid sportswoman, in the tradition of the British country gentry, and Lucy, the hawk, is her obsession; she speaks of little else and devotes most of her attention to taking care of it. Jean, the cook, is unprepared for visitors; when he goes off to buy pigeons from a neighbor to roast for dinner, he is instructed to get an extra one that can be fed, raw, to the falcon. In contrast to Mrs. Cullen's focused intensity (which is mirrored in the fierce demeanor of her pet), Larry

Cullen is a big, blustery, ineffectual man, a heavy drinker. His wife, it seems clear, loves him deeply, but perhaps she does not respect him much at all. As the day wears on, Larry Cullen gets quietly drunk, and it becomes apparent that he both hates and is pathologically jealous of his wife's precious hawk; at one point, he even makes a clumsy attempt to get rid of it. As the visit degenerates further, Eva, who had been flirting with Ricketts, worries that Jean might try to kill her in a jealous rage. Dinner is served but never eaten as the Cullens depart in haste amidst events of high drama.

What intrigues the narrator about all of this, and what intrigues us in turn as we read his account, is how the banality of the events themselves becomes infused with psychological tension. Tower is a bystander, an observer; he plays little active role in these events except to give Larry too much to drink (a bit of malicious mischief that he later regrets). He observes how beautiful and detached from her surroundings Mrs. Cullen is, how good Alex is at coping with noisy and unwanted visitors, how little substance lies behind Larry's bluster, how dangerously Eva plays with her husband's jealousy. He tries to figure out, as the day wears on, the shifting ripples of emotion that play among these people, and is frustrated by his inability to see where things will lead. Standing wholly aside from these events is Lucy, a superbly beautiful killing machine, a bird that can be tamed but not domesticated, immune to love, jealousy, and every other emotion. Does Tower envy Lucy her complete detachment? Perhaps, but perhaps, too, he envies Larry's passion, Alex's competence, even Jean and Eva's untidy romanticism; his own inability to become engaged is not something he remembers with any pride or pleasure.

But he does remember the day itself, in intricate detail, and as he shares it with us we realize that his story is essentially about how unknowable other people's relationships are to even the closest observer. Will the Cullens' love hold their marriage together in spite of all strains? And if so, will those strains nevertheless one day explode in a spasm of deadly violence? Will Eva tempt fate once too often? And for that matter, why are Alex and Tower not themselves lovers? In Tower's cool, controlled account of these matters, we find a subtle dissection of the inexplicable vagaries of human emotion. The novel is brief and its plot tenuous and insubstantial, but the book nevertheless packs an unexpectedly intense psychological charge.

Glenway Wescott was handsome, rich, and artistically gifted, a prominent member of the New York homosexual literary subculture of pre–Gay Liberation days. He and his friends were out of the closet, but only to their peers; the gay subculture was real enough, but to outsiders it was hard to distinguish from the more broadly unconventional bohemian culture of Greenwich Village and Fire Island. A posthumous collection of Wescott's journals, *Continual Lessons,* provides a candid window into the lives of the author and his friends, who included Christopher Isherwood, W. H. Auden, and a number of other important literary figures. *The Pilgrim Hawk* is Wescott's best-known novel; of his other works, we recommend *Apartment in Athens.*

Glenway Wescott (1901–1987), *The Pilgrim Hawk* (New York: Harper and Brothers, 1940). The Noonday Press paperback edition (1990) includes a helpful critical essay by Howard Moss.

NATHANAEL WEST
The Day of the Locust

~

Nathanael West had a checkered career and regarded himself as largely a failure in his own lifetime. A friend of the noted humorist S. J. Perelman (who later married West's sister) when they were both undergraduates at Brown, he came to share Perelman's dim view of Hollywood. West managed small hotels in New York City to support his writing, and first went to Hollywood in 1933. In 1940, he married Eileen McKenney (the real-life heroine of a classic memoir of life in New York, *My Sister Eileen*); they died later that year in an automobile accident just after the death of West's friend Scott Fitzgerald.

The Day of the Locust is one of the very best literary depictions of the film industry, and West himself has over the years gained the esteem as a writer that eluded him in life. The book was written at a time when Hollywood occupied an enormous place in the national consciousness and the Los Angeles area was a beacon for migrants from the rest of the United States. The book is set in a city that is physically much different from the Los Angeles of today. The streetcar system was still in place, not yet demolished in favor of the automobile, and the city had not spread beyond all reasonable bounds. A backdrop to the book is the substantial unemployment of the time, which added to the turmoil and deracination of southern California communities.

What is special about the book is the exceptionally effective way that West makes his characters stand for different elements of a situation in which human hopes and dreams are rendered successfully on celluloid but are almost inevitably dashed in the reality of Hollywood. The book does not have a conventional plot, yet the characters, although not drawn in detail in this short novel, remain with you. You will like, among much else, West's marvelous opening passage, in which the fantasy and petty tyranny of the motion picture industry present themselves right up front, and his descriptions of faux-everything Hollywood houses. There is also a reproduction of the Battle of Waterloo in which the scenery is not quite ready for the troops, with disastrous results.

The Day of the Locust, comic and bleak by turns, relates the adventures of Tod Hackett, a Yale graduate in fine arts who has been hired sight unseen as a designer of sets and costumes. The book is written in the third person, but it is through Tod's eyes that we see Hollywood. Tod, who lives in a nondescript apartment house called the San Bernardino Arms, falls in with a variety of odd but typical types in the Hollywood of the day. These are from the lower strata of Hollywood, not the stars and producers who are usually the subject of Hollywood novels. The characters include Tod's neighbor Faye Greener, whom he pursues without success, and her father, Harry, a failed vaudeville artist and current purveyor of homemade silver polish ("used by all the movie stars"). Faye is an aspiring but untalented actress with constant and unrealistic dreams who wittingly takes advantage of her suitors. One is Earle Stroop, an unsuccessful cowboy actor, who shares a camp in a canyon with Miguel, a Mexican breeder of fighting cocks. There are also Abe Kusich, a dwarf horse player and roustabout, and the sad Homer Simpson (much less resilient than the TV cartoon character of the same name), from Waynesville, Iowa. All of these people are hurt in one way or another by the motion picture industry.

Two threads throughout the book are the presence of those who come to California to die (the retirees) and who are disappointed by the California dream, and Tod's vision of a painting that he calls "The Burning of Los Angeles," an apocalyptic end to the tinsely city. He works on sketches of this throughout the book and thinks of the painters through whose eyes he might see Hollywood. The painters he likes at the start of his time in Hollywood (others are added) are Goya, the famous illustrator of the horrors of war, and Daumier, the matchless satirist of nineteenth-century France. The famous end to the novel is a mindless riot by fans waiting to see celebrities at a theater, the Persian Palace, at which a film is to have its premiere. Tod (whose apocalypse thereby becomes true) barely emerges safely from the riot, which, we are led to believe, has terrible consequences for Homer. It embodies the title of the book, which refers to a passage in Revelations about a horde of dreadful locusts. We are left feeling that none of the characters will come to a good end, except perhaps Tod.

The book is easy to read, yet it is a deep meditation on the interrelationship of communication, industry, and human hopes that comes out on the side of bleakness. Hollywood is a much smaller part of our world than it was, but the meaning of this novel continues to resonate in other parts of the economy in which technology, greed, and dreams intersect—day trading comes to mind. Of West's other works, you will certainly want to read *Miss Lonelyhearts*, a remarkable and tragic novella of a newspaper advice columnist, usually bound with *The Day of the Locust*.

Nathanael West (1903–1940), *The Day of the Locust* (New York: Random House, 1939). Available in a New Directions paperback (1950, still in print); a hardcover collection of West's work is published by the Library of America (1997).

EDITH WHARTON

Madame de Treymes

~

During her lifetime, Edith Wharton was one of the most famous writers in the world, known for her brilliant storytelling ability, keen powers of observation and description, and emotional subtlety. *Madame de Treymes* was published in 1906, relatively early in her long career, after her reputation had been established by the early masterpiece *The House of Mirth* but before she had settled down to the life of a permanent American expatriate in France. In this short novella of gossamer delicacy, Wharton explores two of her favorite themes: the cultural divide between Europe and America, and how a lifetime's worth of happiness or unhappiness can flow from decisions constrained by the manners and customs of society.

John Durham is in Paris with a second chance to marry his beloved Fanny Frisbee. In earlier days he had not pressed his courtship ardently enough; rather than wait for him to declare himself, she had married into an ancient, aristocratic French family and is now Madame de Malrive. But several years have passed; her husband is a beast, and if John will assist her in obtaining a divorce so she can return to America with her young son, she will be delighted to become Mrs. Durham. Looking for a way to overcome the implacable coldness of the de Malrive family, Durham tries to enlist the sympathy and aid of Fanny's sister-in-law, the alluring, worldly Madame de Treymes. But he finds her manner and behavior nearly incomprehensible; there seems to be no common ground between his blunt American openness and her French pride and indirection. In the end, Madame de Treymes helps Durham obtain what he wants, but under circumstances that make it impossible to act on his success.

Edith Wharton, née Jones, was the daughter of a well-to-do and very respectable old New York family. Shy and bookish, she hated the elaborate rituals of high society but learned to observe those rituals with minute care from the sidelines. Her marriage to the wealthy and socially prominent but vapid Bostonian Teddy Wharton proved an emotional disaster, but her budding career as a writer convinced her that she could rely on her own resources to create a fulfilling life. Soon she began spending more and more time in Europe, leaving behind her beloved country house in Lenox, Massachusetts, and the life of the American gentry that it represented. *Madame de Treymes* reflects two personal issues that concerned its author deeply in the early years of the new century: divorce and permanent residence in Europe. Mrs. Wharton decided in favor of both divorce and exile and, settling down in France, became a rich and famous American author without ever returning to America.

Edith Wharton's most famous short novel, *Ethan Frome,* has, like many other good books, been spoiled for some readers by being assigned as required reading in high school and then analyzed to death in the classroom; it is well worth revisiting. Wharton was a very prolific author, and if these shorter works recommended here whet your appetite for her longer fiction, try *The House of Mirth, The Custom of the Country, The Age of Innocence*, and *Hudson River Bracketed*.

Edith Wharton (1862–1937), *Madame de Treymes* (New York: Charles Scribner's Sons, 1906). Paperback reprint in *Madame de Treymes and Three Novellas* (New York: Scribner, 1995).

E. B. WHITE
Charlotte's Web

~

E. B. White (known to his friends as Andy) was born in Mount Vernon, New York, just north of New York City, to a comfortable family (his father was a piano manufacturer). He knew early on that he wanted to write, and among other things he was an editor of his high school newspaper. He served as a private in the U.S. Army in 1918, went to Cornell, was editor in chief of the college paper, and graduated in 1921. He did miscellaneous writing, and with a friend crossed the country in a Model T Ford named Hotspur, surviving on journeyman writing and other work.

When White returned to New York City, he was asked by Harold Ross to join the staff of *The New Yorker*. White (together with James Thurber) became central to the magazine, editing, writing, and rewriting pieces. He wrote many of its "Notes and Comment" pieces; he also edited the famous "Newsbreaks." These were inane and inarticulate quotes, often from newspapers, that filled up column space when an article ran a few lines short; White's comments on these quotes were among the week's funniest events. White married Kathryn Sargeant Angell, the magazine's fiction editor, and in 1939 they bought a farm in North Brooklin, Maine, where they moved and from which Angell and White continued to work as editors and writers. White enjoyed widespread esteem throughout his career.

Charlotte's Web is the second of White's three classic children's books; the others are *Stuart Little* and *The Trumpet of the Swan*. *Charlotte's Web* is the story of Wilbur the pig, his friend Charlotte the spider, the other animals on the Zuckerman farm, and assorted humans. Wilbur is born a runt, and Mr. Arable, the farmer, is therefore inclined to do away with him immediately. He is saved by the pleas of Fern, Mr.

Arable's daughter, who nurses little Wilbur from a bottle. He is then sold to her uncle, Mr. Zuckerman.

Things go along swimmingly for Wilbur, although he gets some bad advice from the silly geese and escapes, to his great confusion, from his pen for a brief time. Charlotte, the spider up in the eaves, befriends him. Fern visits and gets to listen to the animals talk (Dr. Dorian assures her mother that this is all right—perhaps animals really do talk, but humans just don't listen carefully enough). Wilbur's happiness is shattered, however, when he is told by the wise old sheep that at Christmas, when he is fat, his life will end. Charlotte takes pity on her friend and promises to figure out a way to save him. With some careful thinking and some help from the other animals, most notably the odious rat Templeton, she figures out how to use her web for an imaginative and impressive rescue campaign. Wilbur is saved, although Charlotte herself must die after producing her autumnal egg sac. Wilbur lives a long and contented life, each year with the company of some of Charlotte's descendants.

The animals in the story, on the whole, are good folks; it is the humans who are fussy, credulous, angry, and silly. Even Fern begins to drift away from the animals as she becomes interested in boys. Charlotte points out to Wilbur that humans, who think they know a lot, are not even very good at making webs. One that they did build, the Queensboro Bridge, took eight years, and even then they never seem to catch anything in it. White's writing represents well how children really are. When Wilbur has something of importance to announce, for example, he uses the wonderfully sententious language of a child who has just learned that it is possible to be formal in speech. And there is much in the book for adults as well. When the crickets announced that summer was over, a little maple tree in the swamp heard their song and turned bright red with anxiety. No one traveling in New England in the autumn can forget that little maple tree and the crickets.

Charlotte's Web is especially good for children who are still young enough to have their sense of wonder in blossom. Adults are superior to children in only a few ways; one is that they may read *Charlotte's Web* with pleasure at any grown-up age. White's other children's books are also fine. The 1979 Hanna-Barbera cartoon film version of *Charlotte's*

Web is very popular with young children, but White is said to have hated it; he was displeased by how prettied-up the animals were and how childish everything seemed. (The book's illustrations, by Garth Williams, are much more realistic.)

You may have encountered White in yet another guise in high school or college, where the short, accurate, and inimitable *Elements of Style*, White's revision of the classic writing guide of his Cornell professor, William Strunk, is often assigned. There also are collections of White's essays and *New Yorker* pieces available; of his essays, we like best "Here Is New York" (in *Essays of E. B. White*), which still captures well the city that he loved.

E[lwyn] B[rooks] White (1899–1985), *Charlotte's Web* (New York: Harper and Brothers, 1952). The Harper Trophy paperback is widely available.

LAURA INGALLS WILDER

On the Way Home and *West From Home*

~

These two short books exhibit the informal yet careful writing of Laura Ingalls Wilder before she became famous for her stories based on the experiences of her family as pioneers on the prairie. They add richness and dimensionality to the image one has of Wilder from the *Little House on the Prairie* series. It is worth remembering that the first book of the series, *Little House in the Big Woods,* was published in 1932, when Wilder was sixty-five years old. The volumes in the *Little House* series, written with the editorial guidance of Wilder's daughter, Rose, followed Wilder's lack of success in selling the original autobiographical manuscript on which they are based, *Pioneer Girl*. Wilder's books were shaped in the course of family storytelling, and their entrancing immediacy puts a child listening to the books to sleep feeling that he or she is really on the prairie and is perhaps Laura's sibling or friend. *On the Way Home* and *West From Home*, by showing us something of the real Wilder, add to the magic of her stories, because they make it clear how special she and her family were, and that her transformation in the minds of millions into the Laura of the stories was a remarkable artistic feat, preserving historical truth but presenting it in the form of novels seemingly seen through the eyes and sensibility of a little girl.

On the Way Home is Wilder's daily record of her and her husband's move from De Smet, South Dakota, to Mansfield, Missouri, with their daughter, Rose, in 1894. The book shows both Wilder's sense of narrative and her passion for accuracy. She notes carefully when each county is entered, the cost of a bushel of tomatoes, and the quality of crops and water. The book reflects the historical era in which Wilder lived, and her family's story encompassed the transition from the frontier to the modern world. The trip to Missouri was made in a horse-drawn wagon covered with black oilcloth, but when the Wilder family passed through Lincoln, Nebraska, they encountered trams that frightened their traveling companions' horses, and they could admire new streets and the grand State Capitol (a predecessor to the modern building by Bertram Goodhue, which was completed in 1932). Arriving in Mansfield after a journey of a month and a half, they found and purchased the farm on which they spent the rest of their lives together.

West From Home, like *On the Way Home,* was published after Wilder's death. It is a collection of Wilder's letters to her husband, Almanzo, when she visited Rose in San Francisco for two months during the Panama-Pacific International Exposition of 1915. By then, Laura had a writing and civic career, serving as the home editor of and columnist for the *Missouri Ruralist,* a farm magazine, and in civic capacities including secretary-treasurer of a farm loan association. Rose was a successful author and journalist in San Francisco and was able to show her mother about in style. Wilder's letters to Almanzo are a lovely, well-written mix of her travel impressions and her concerns for her husband and the farm.

The enjoyment of these books will be enhanced for many readers by visits to the sites where they and the *Little House on the Prairie* series took place. These include the farm in Mansfield, Missouri, Almanzo's boyhood home in upstate New York, and the homesteads in De Smet.

Laura Ingalls Wilder (1867–1957), *On the Way Home: The Diary of a Trip from South Dakota to Mansfield, Missouri, in 1894,* with a setting by Rose Wilder Lane (New York: Harper and Row, 1962), and *West from Home: Letters of Laura Ingalls Wilder, San Francisco, 1915,* ed. Roger Lea MacBride (New York: Harper and Row, 1974). There are Harper Trophy paperback reprints of both books (1994); the two volumes can usually be found alongside the *Little House on the Prairie* series in bookstores.

THORNTON WILDER
The Bridge of San Luis Rey

∼

Thornton Wilder was born in Wisconsin but spent most of his childhood and youth in China, where his father was in the American consular service. He was an undergraduate at Yale and attended graduate school at Princeton. After finishing his master's degree, he spent some time studying archaeology in Rome (the setting for his first novel, *The Cabala*, 1926). His second novel, *The Bridge of San Luis Rey,* won the Pulitzer Prize for Letters in 1928, solidifying his reputation as an accomplished young writer. For most of his career he was both a professor of literature (he taught at several universities, including Harvard) and a highly successful writer. He wrote a number of other novels but eventually became best known as a playwright. His play *Our Town* (1938), winner of another Pulitzer Prize, for many years was—and still is—a staple of high school drama society productions, with the result that a great many people have seen the play performed but few have seen it performed with the sophistication it deserves.

Much of Wilder's work asks the question "What is real?" and challenges his readers (or viewers of his plays) to work toward their own answers to that question. He does not make it an easy task, for his work often toys with time and mingles fact and fiction, leaving readers unsure of the boundary between the real and the imagined. His great virtue as a writer is to be engrossingly thought provoking and at the same time very entertaining; he is serious without being heavy.

The Bridge of San Luis Rey takes as its starting point the collapse of a suspension footbridge over a deep gorge in Peru one day in 1714, a mishap that threw five people to their deaths. Wilder is not interested in what made the bridge's cable snap, but rather in why those five people happened to be on the bridge at the time. The novel is supposedly based on the research of a witness to the accident, Brother Juniper, who wondered if the victims had been singled out by God for punishment for their sins. He therefore, we are told, did exhaustive research into their lives, seeking some answer to the riddle of their fate.

Three linked stories recount the lives of the victims. The first is the story of the Marquesa de Montemayor and her little maid, Pepita. The Marquesa is a gross and comical figure, socially awkward, ignorant, and superstitious, but a formidable member of Lima society because of her wealth and the advantageous marriage made by her daughter to a Spanish nobleman. (We are told, too, that however ridiculous the Marquesa may have appeared to her contemporaries, her letters to her daughter later became recognized as a landmark of Baroque Spanish literature; Wilder here shows his extraordinarily convincing ability to present fiction as history.) Pepita, temporarily in service to the Marquesa as a maid, is a bright and personable young orphan girl for whom the abbess of the convent where she was raised has high hopes. The two have just begun a homeward journey from visiting an important shrine when they begin to cross the bridge.

The second story is that of another orphan, Esteban, who with his twin brother, Manuel, was raised by the sisters of the convent. After pursuing a variety of trades, Manuel and Esteban become scribes; Manuel works confidentially as the writer of love letters for a famous actress, with whom he falls hopelessly in love. When Manuel dies from an infected injury, Esteban is devastated; he travels inland, where he meets a famous adventurer and signs on with him to undertake a long voyage of exploration. He has just begun his journey back to the coast when he steps onto the bridge.

By the time we begin the third story, we understand that the lives of all of the victims were intertwined in ways of which they themselves were unaware. The fourth victim is Uncle Pio, a jack-of-all-trades freebooter who long ago settled down to become the famous actress's manager. He has just visited her in the inland town where she has retired, to escort her young son back to Lima to attend school; on their way back they have to cross the bridge of San Luis Rey.

In each case, we begin to feel a sense of an inexorable destiny at work; by the novel's end, it seems to us entirely convincing that these five people, and only these five, should have been on the bridge when it fell. But was some divine force (of retribution or otherwise) at work, or were these deaths all consequences of a meaningless accident? Brother Juniper, for all his research, could come to no clear conclusion. Moreover, his labors were soon ruled heretical by the Inquisition, and both he and his books were burned in the public square of Lima. But an unknown copy of his book survived, on which, the anonymous narrator tells us, the account that we are reading has been based. And so the matter is posed to us once again: perhaps an accident, perhaps an intention.

If Wilder gives us no answer, he asks the question very well. By the end of his life he perhaps began to feel that there were no answers to be had. His last novel, *Theophilus North,* published two years before his death, is an account of a young man's adventures in Newport in the summer of 1929—the last summer of untroubled wealth before the stock market crash and the Depression. It is funnier and more cynical than most of his work, and we recommend it to you after you have read *The Bridge of San Luis Rey.*

Thornton Wilder (1897–1975), *The Bridge of San Luis Rey* (New York: Albert and Charles Boni, 1927). Harper Perennial paperback reprint, 1998.

P. G. WODEHOUSE

Something Fresh

⌢

P. G. Wodehouse was born in Surrey, England, spent his early years in Hong Kong, where his father was a judge, and returned to England for schooling. He had a remarkably successful career as a writer of stories, novels, librettos for musicals, and song lyrics (including "Bill," from *Show Boat*, with Oscar Hammerstein II, music by Jerome Kern). He was also widely regarded by fellow writers as a master literary craftsman. He spent much of his time in the United States and became a U.S. citizen in 1955. (His name is pronounced, in the English fashion, "Woodhouse.")

Something Fresh has a notable place in Wodehouse's professional history. It is the first of a series, the Blandings novels (the perhaps more famous novels featuring the inimitable Jeeves, butler extraordinaire, and his master, Bertie Wooster, came a bit later), and it was the first story sold by Wodehouse to the *Saturday Evening Post* for serialization. Early in the twentieth century, sales to the *Post*, a magazine of great influence and popularity at the time, marked the difference between being an ink-stained wretch and a comfortable man of letters, a distinction that mattered a great deal to Wodehouse at that stage in his career.

The Blandings novels are named after Blandings Castle, a vast Tudor pile that dominates its landscape somewhere west of London, reached via Market Blandings Station on the train from Paddington Station. Blandings Castle, Wodehouse tells us, is the seat of the present Lord Emsworth, a man whose outstanding quality is absentmindedness. Fortunately this is not usually a problem, as he is completely content with his privileges and excels at puttering about and leaving everything in the hands of the Efficient Baxter, his secretary.

Blandings Castle has an immense establishment of staff, who behave according to prescribed customs and precedents that would do credit to a make-believe court in a Viennese operetta. The main point of *Something Fresh* (insofar as Wodehouse stories have any point other than to be wonderfully entertaining) is that Lord Emsworth seems finally to have solved the problem of what to do with his Younger Son, the Honorable Frederick Threepwood. The Hon. Freddie is engaged in a rather languorous manner to Aline Peters, the daughter of Mr. Peters, an American millionaire who has bought an estate near Blandings Castle.

The other characters include the gorgeous Joan Valentine, a down-on-her-luck former school chum of Aline; Ashe Marson, an Oxford track-and-field man who is, indeed, an ink-stained wretch (he grinds out the utterly dreadful Gridley Quayle mystery stories); George Emerson, a Hong Kong police officer; and assorted relatives and hangers-on. There is a complex subplot about scarabs (the beetle talismans of ancient Egypt), of which Mr. Peters is an avid collector, and there are extremely funny after-midnight encounters in the main hall of Blandings Castle having to do with a (possibly stolen) scarab and certain other matters. Just when you think that you've got it all figured out, the old master puts one over on you, and the outcome is far more elegantly plotted than you could have imagined.

Wodehouse's books are known for their outstanding humor, beautifully crafted sentences, and well-structured plots (his best books make one think that a finely honed play is taking place in one's own living room). But their fundamental appeal has to do with Wodehouse's ability to exaggerate his characters' traits for humorous effect, while grounding their actions in the feelings and motives of real life. His novels are set in a never-ending Edwardian (pre–World War I) world, but in fact they have a continued relevance to our everyday behavior. The awkwardness and misunderstandings of his couples seem universal— only the very fortunate among our readers will have escaped entirely the romantic embarrassments chronicled in Wodehouse's books. And Lord Emsworth's forgetfulness, in a milder form, is a part of many families' lives, as are, it may be, young men and women who are not quite working hard enough to suit their parents. Wodehouse was prodigiously productive—he wrote almost one hundred books—so if you like Blandings Castle and the loony mob contained therein, as we think you will, you have what amounts to a lifetime of enjoyment ahead of you.

P[elham] G[renville] Wodehouse (1881–1975), *Something Fresh* (London: Herbert Jenkins, 1915). Paperback reprint, Viking, 1986; there is also a Penguin paperback, *Life at Blandings* (1988), that includes *Something Fresh* and two other Blandings novels in a single convenient volume.

ANN WROE

A Fool and His Money

~

We very much enjoy reading history for pleasure, but relatively few history books are both well written enough and short enough to qualify as satisfactory one-night reads. Ann Wroe's colorful, incisive picture of life in a medieval town in the midst of the Hundred Years' War is one of the exceptions, and a thoroughly delightful book.

The Hundred Years' War, a long jumble of battles, bloody raids, and truces between England and France, unfolded from the late 1330s to 1453. It was a complex and deadly affair involving dynastic claims, desire for wealth and territory, and shifting alliances. This book shows us, however, a history that is not the traditional grand sweep of royal lineages, politics, and battles.

In 1369 or 1370—the records are not clear—Huc del Cayro, a master mason in the walled hill town of Rodez, in what is now southwestern France, was considering the case of a blocked drain. The foundations of the Segui family's cloth shop in the Bourg, the lower town, were flooded. Permission to open the drain that was causing the flood was obtained from Peyre Marques, an addle-brained old man in whose neighboring house the blockage was located. Del Cayro then left the dirty work to Johan Gasc, Marti Barbier, and Marot de Namaria. The workmen were stunned, after opening the drain, to find a pitcher of gold coins, which was immediately taken charge of by Gerald Canac, the son-in-law of Marques. The legal processes then undertaken to establish the ownership of the coins provide the story around which Wroe weaves this portrait of a medieval town.

Rodez was a town that regarded both England and France as foreign countries. The language of the town was not French but Occitan, a language similar to the Catalan of northeastern Spain, and the town records were kept in Latin and Occitan. On the infrequent occasions when it became necessary to send an embassy to Paris to plead for privileges, interpreters were probably necessary, and the outlay was devilish: Paris, then as now, was an expensive city. (One such journey happened at the time of this story, a bone-wrenching round trip of eight hundred miles.) Those who the people of Rodez regarded as "English" were equally distant. The Treaty of Brétigny, in 1360, had included Rodez in the area of southwestern France under English control, but the representatives of England (who rarely came within a few miles of Rodez during this narrative) were a miscellany of soldiers, rogues, and bullies from every nation, and indeed the people began to think of almost any foreigner as "English," including Bretons with names such as Alaric and Fulk, which they had never heard before.

Rodez was a divided town, a peculiarity that interested Wroe when she started her research. The upper part, the City, with its unfinished cathedral, owed allegiance to the Bishop, and the lower part, the larger commercial Bourg, owed allegiance to the Count of Armagnac. Perhaps the most striking fact that comes to us from the records is the high degree of government, business, and legal organization in Rodez. Rodez was not a disorganized frontier settlement. It had a long history as a settled place; residents frequently turned up tiles, for example, that they regarded as Saracen (Moorish). The government under the Count consisted of men of wealth serving as consuls, meeting regularly to discuss the business of the town; larger meetings were also held, and records were kept. Regulations for business were very detailed. Both Bourg and City had standardized weights and measures, and in the Count's building in the Bourg there was a cloth table on which cloth was measured and the Count's seal put on if it was of the proper standard. There were orderly court procedures, with witnesses deposed, financial records examined, and records kept. (The cumbrousness of these processes could, however, be discouraging: A riot in 1315 was still under litigation in 1370.)

There was a high degree of religious organization as well, but this takes a form that is somewhat distant from us. There were a vast number of relics, many of doubtful provenance, and the life of the clergy was tumultuous: Several priests in training visit a brothel, and a priest is punched in church by a disgruntled tenant (the church was also a landlord). The church played various official roles, for example, regularly excommunicating people for their debts, the sentence being read out in the parish church after the sermon. But there is also an entirely modern pleading: In order to raise desperately needed funds to advance the construction of the cathedral in the City, citizens are offered the opportunity to become "Friends of the Cathedral" in return for donations.

Perhaps most foreign to us in this account is the constant threat of death and violence faced by the citizens of Rodez, from disease (the plague was no stranger to the town), from soldiers and bandits on the road, and from violence in the town itself. Vicious punishments are meted out, and explosive fights materialize. There are murders in the market, and people are beaten for real or imagined trespasses. Assaults on women are common: Petronilla, who is selling pears brought in from the country, claims that Adhemar de Terralh pretended to be a customer and took advantage of her.

The townspeople's biggest problem, however, seeming to hover over every personal and business transaction, is the exactions of the overlords. There are taxes on everything, both in cash and in kind. The Segui family, for example, owed the Count twenty-five sous per year for one house, and a hen for a smaller one. The townspeople are engaged in constant efforts to avoid taxes, to delay payment of them, or simply to forget them: People move themselves and their goods back and forth between the City and the Bourg to confuse the two sets of tax collectors. It is in this area of life that the war impinges most strongly on the people of the Bourg: Their Count, having gone over to the French side, places extortionate demands on them. If the people of the town cared to forecast their future for the next decades, they would have expected nearly unending financial misery.

Wroe weaves all of this nicely around the story of the pot of gold. The available records tell of Peyre Marques' long history of claiming that he had hidden his wealth away and couldn't remember where; of his wife, Alumbars, from the powerful Rostanh family in the City, and her concerns with their financial distress; and Canac, the son-in-law who had rescued the family fortune after old Marques' increasing inability to manage his affairs, and his claim to the right to manage the gold as well. As it happens, the final disposition of the case is lost in the records, but we see Canac later as a prosperous merchant, selling clothes from Paris. The masons who fixed the drain that led to the discovery got a few coins each.

Wroe, a journalist and editor, does a fine job of bringing the town and its people to life, and in introductory and concluding remarks she sets out the framework within which she found Rodez's story and how she worked there. Through the story of Rodez, she shows us the richness and complexity of history everywhere, beyond the sweep of dynastic narratives, and we think, too, how many more such books remain to be written.

Ann Wroe (1951–), *A Fool and His Money* (New York: Hill and Wang, 1995).

About the Authors

DAVID C. MAJOR and JOHN S. MAJOR are brothers. Each is the author of numerous books: David mainly in natural resources and the environment, John mainly on East Asian history and culture. John is also coeditor of two poetry anthologies and coauthor of *The New Lifetime Reading Plan*.

The Majors are currently collaborating on works of history and biography, and on a guide to creating a satisfying lifestyle in New York City. They both live in Manhattan with their families.